PEANUTS®

Titan Facsimile Editions by Charles M. Schulz

On sale now:
Peanuts
More Peanuts

Coming soon:
Good Grief, More Peanuts!
Good Ol' Charlie Brown
Snoopy
You're Out of Your Mind, Charlie Brown!
But We Love You, Charlie Brown
Peanuts Revisited
Go Fly a Kite, Charlie Brown
Peanuts Every Sunday

PEANUTS

ISBN: 978-1-78276-155-6

PUBLISHED BY TITAN COMICS, A DIVISION OF TITAN PUBLISHING GROUP LTD,

144 SOUTHWARK ST, LONDON SE1 0UP. COPYRIGHT © 2015 BY PEANUTS WORLDWIDE LLC.

PRINTED IN INDIA.

10 9 8 7 6 5

WWW.TITAN-COMICS.COM

ORIGINALLY PUBLISHED IN 1952 BY

RHINEHART & CO. INCORPORATED

NEW YORK & TORONTO

A CIP CATALOGUE RECORD FOR THIS TITLE

IS AVAILABLE FROM THE BRITISH LIBRARY.

THIS EDITION FIRST PUBLISHED: AUGUST 2015

Charles Schulz's PEANUTS is the visual proof that kids are more grown up than adults. PEANUTS is, as strips go, very young indeed — a little over two years old. So Charlie Brown and Patty and Violet and Schroeder and Snoopy and the rest haven't had much time to settle the problems that confuse their elders, but they're trying, hilariously.

They operate logically, and their logic is the wonderful straight thinking of the very young. Yet they are just as puzzled as if they were grown up, and just as cockeyed. Few of their problems (if that's what they are) take more than one strip to settle, because Charlie Brown and his friends keep in the neighborhood, and ignore space ships, jungles, wild beasts and such like. Strip at a time, this little book would keep a good taste in the reader's mouth for the best part of a year. You'll probably take it in one or two doses, however, and be the better for it.

PEANUTS is just about the most original strip to appear since George Herriman's KRAZY KAT in its prime. And every bit as much fun.

By CHARLES M. SCHULZ

TITAN COMICS

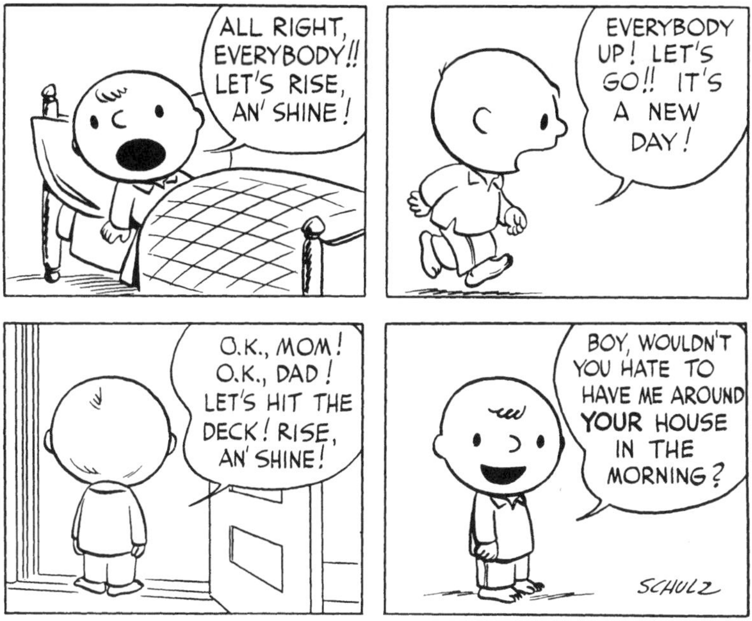
ALL RIGHT, EVERYBODY!! LET'S RISE, AN' SHINE!
EVERYBODY UP! LET'S GO!! IT'S A NEW DAY!
O.K., MOM! O.K., DAD! LET'S HIT THE DECK! RISE, AN' SHINE!
BOY, WOULDN'T YOU HATE TO HAVE ME AROUND YOUR HOUSE IN THE MORNING?
SCHULZ

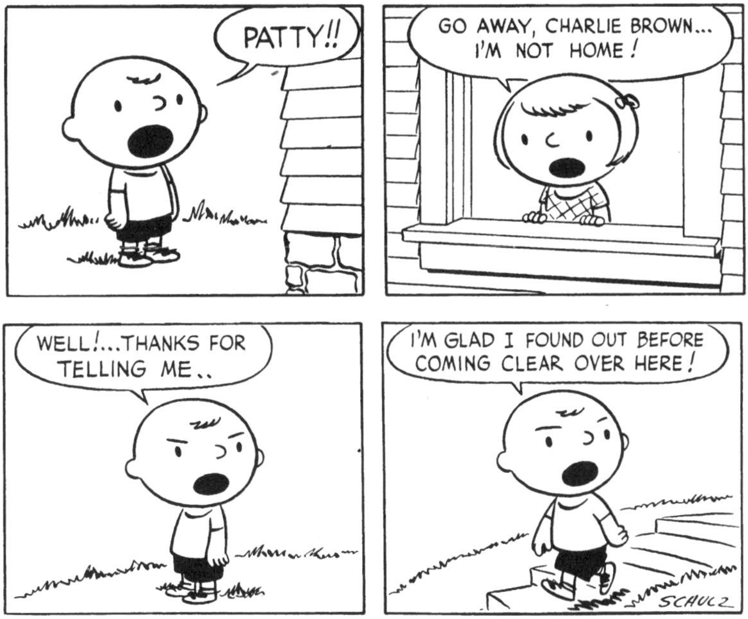
PATTY!!
GO AWAY, CHARLIE BROWN... I'M NOT HOME!
WELL!...THANKS FOR TELLING ME..
I'M GLAD I FOUND OUT BEFORE COMING CLEAR OVER HERE!
SCHULZ

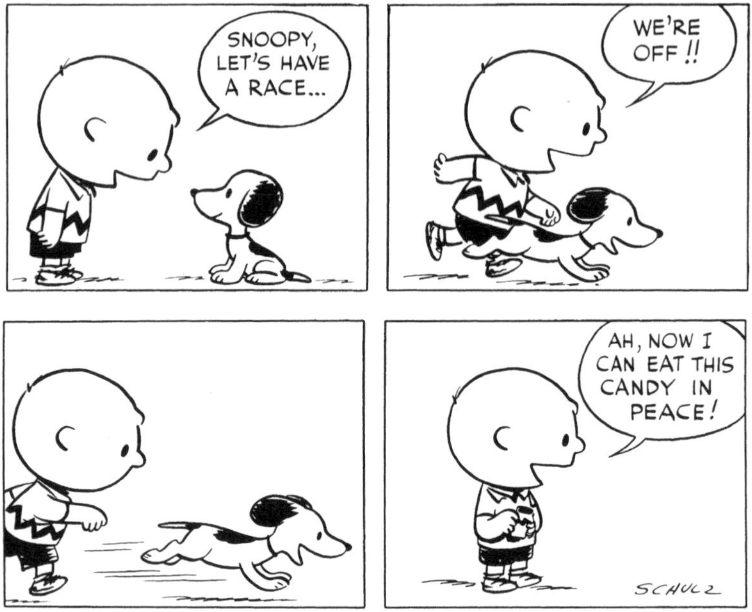
SNOOPY, LET'S HAVE A RACE...
WE'RE OFF !!
AH, NOW I CAN EAT THIS CANDY IN PEACE!
SCHULZ

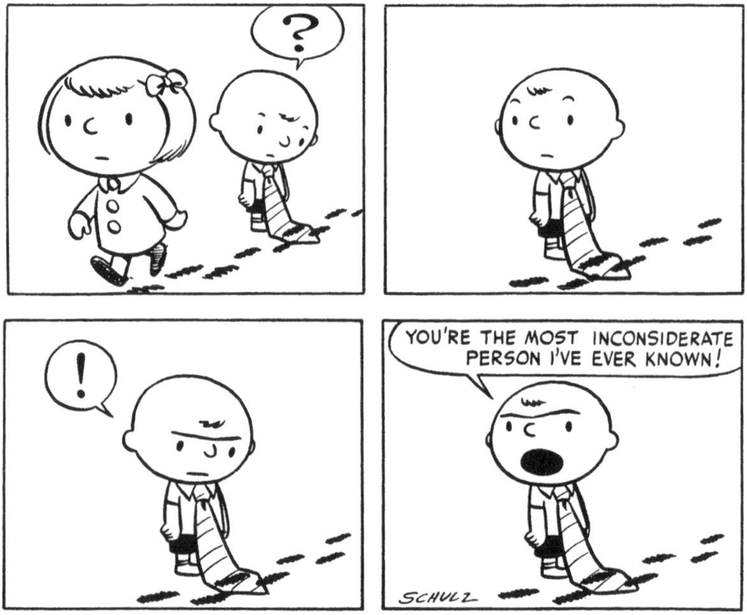
?
!
YOU'RE THE MOST INCONSIDERATE PERSON I'VE EVER KNOWN!
SCHULZ

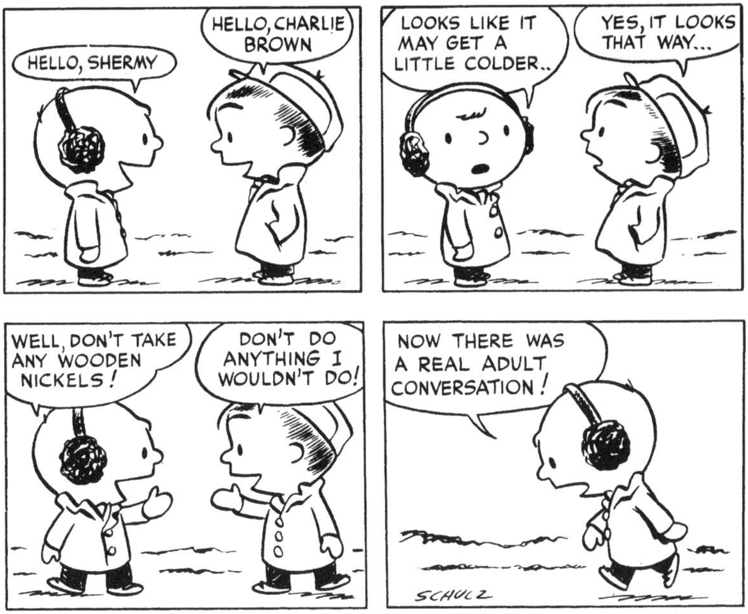
HELLO, SHERMY
HELLO, CHARLIE BROWN
LOOKS LIKE IT MAY GET A LITTLE COLDER..
YES, IT LOOKS THAT WAY...
WELL, DON'T TAKE ANY WOODEN NICKELS!
DON'T DO ANYTHING I WOULDN'T DO!
NOW THERE WAS A REAL ADULT CONVERSATION!
SCHULZ

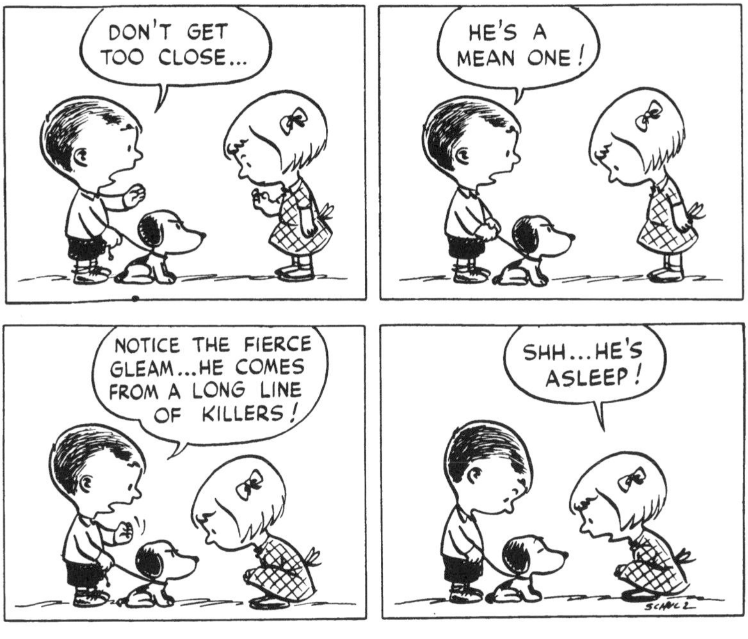
DON'T GET TOO CLOSE...
HE'S A MEAN ONE!
NOTICE THE FIERCE GLEAM...HE COMES FROM A LONG LINE OF KILLERS!
SHH...HE'S ASLEEP!
SCHULZ

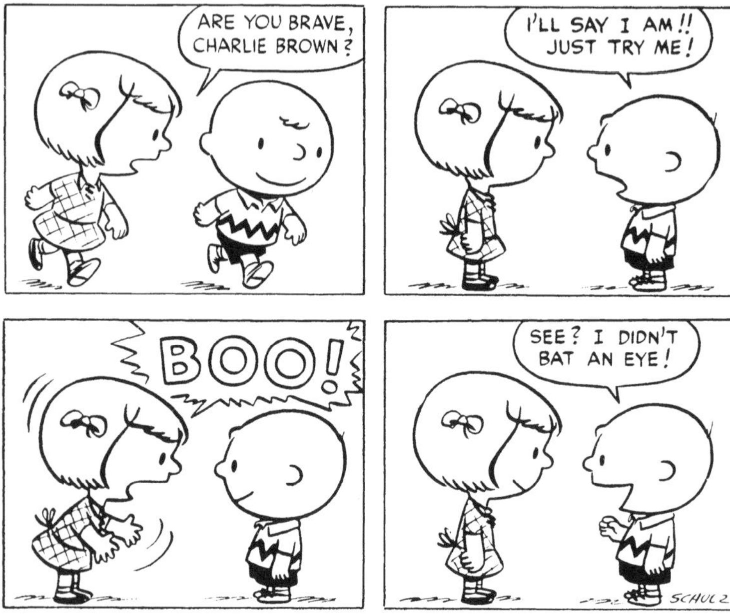
ARE YOU BRAVE, CHARLIE BROWN?
I'LL SAY I AM!! JUST TRY ME!
BOO!
SEE? I DIDN'T BAT AN EYE!
SCHULZ

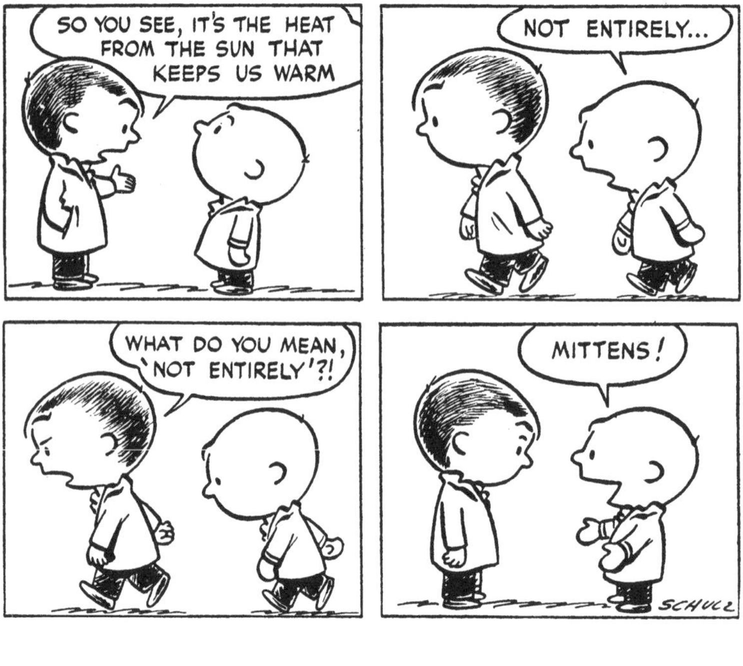
SO YOU SEE, IT'S THE HEAT FROM THE SUN THAT KEEPS US WARM
NOT ENTIRELY...
WHAT DO YOU MEAN, 'NOT ENTIRELY'?!
MITTENS!
SCHULZ

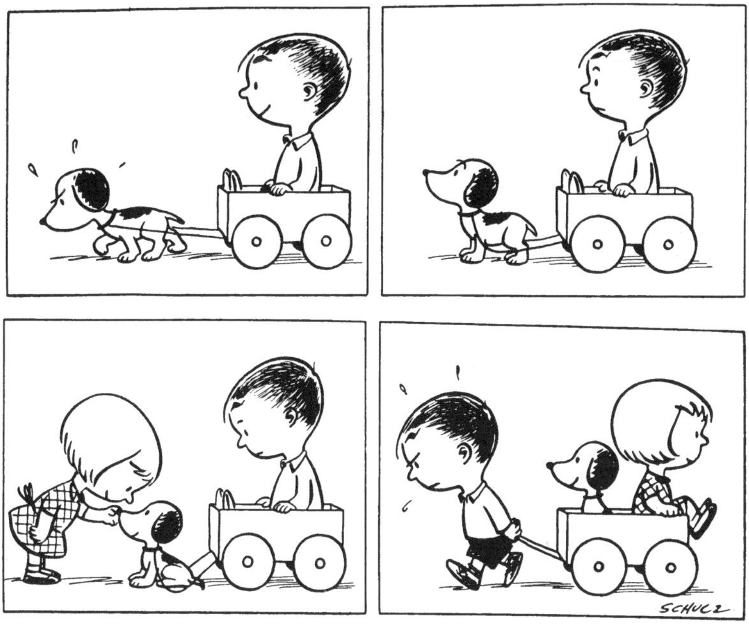
SCHULZ

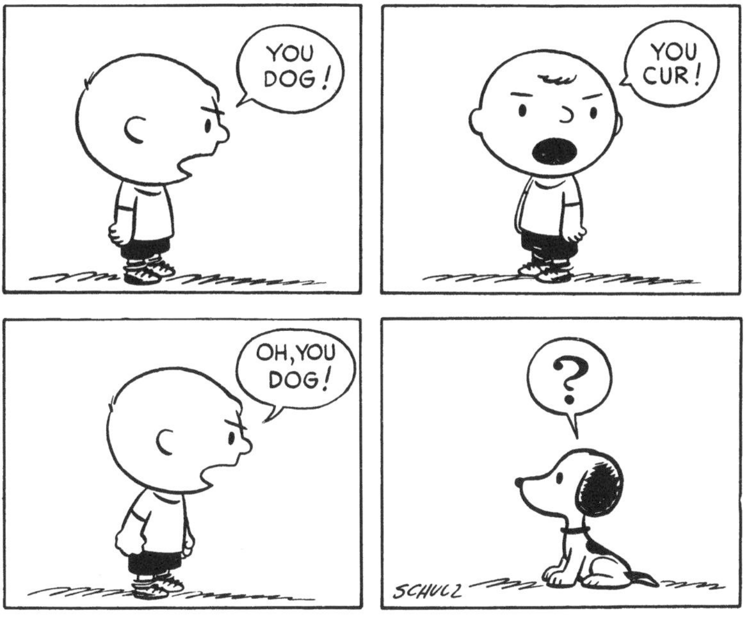
YOU DOG!
YOU CUR!
OH, YOU DOG!
?
SCHULZ

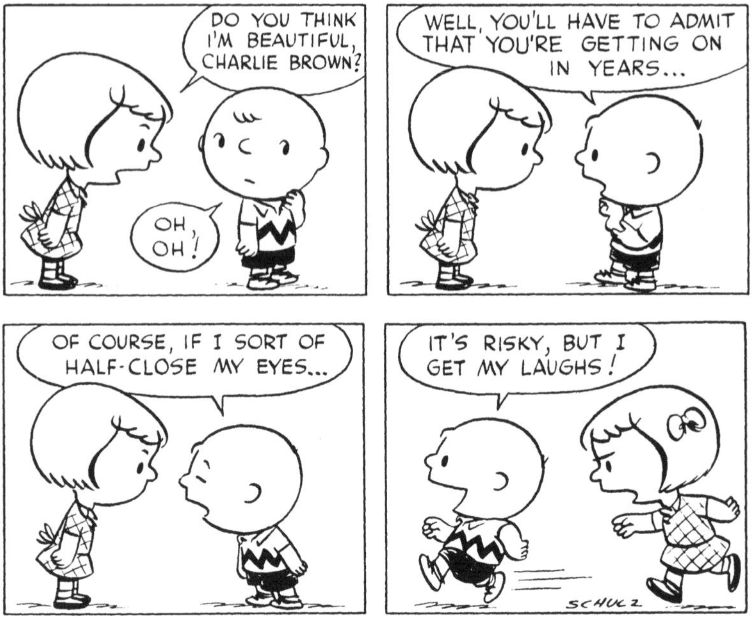
DO YOU THINK I'M BEAUTIFUL, CHARLIE BROWN?
OH, OH!
WELL, YOU'LL HAVE TO ADMIT THAT YOU'RE GETTING ON IN YEARS...
OF COURSE, IF I SORT OF HALF-CLOSE MY EYES...
IT'S RISKY, BUT I GET MY LAUGHS!
SCHULZ

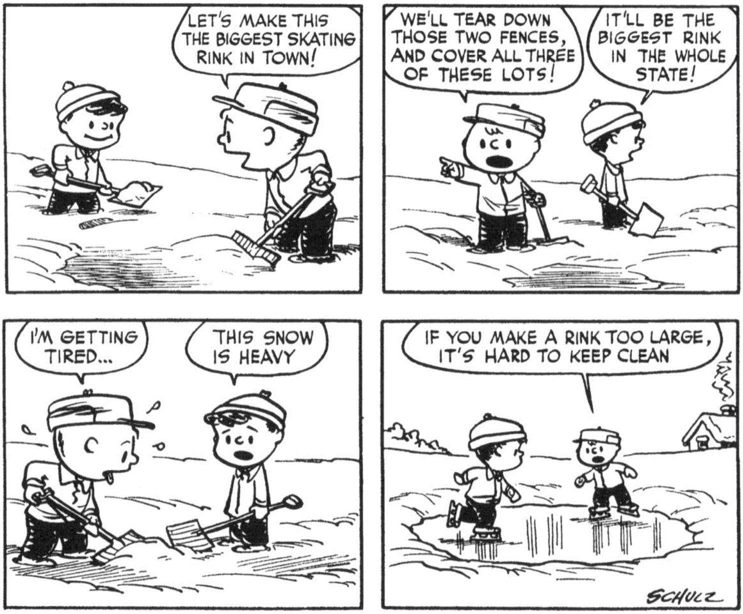
LET'S MAKE THIS THE BIGGEST SKATING RINK IN TOWN!
WE'LL TEAR DOWN THOSE TWO FENCES, AND COVER ALL THREE OF THESE LOTS!
IT'LL BE THE BIGGEST RINK IN THE WHOLE STATE!
I'M GETTING TIRED...
THIS SNOW IS HEAVY
IF YOU MAKE A RINK TOO LARGE, IT'S HARD TO KEEP CLEAN
SCHULZ

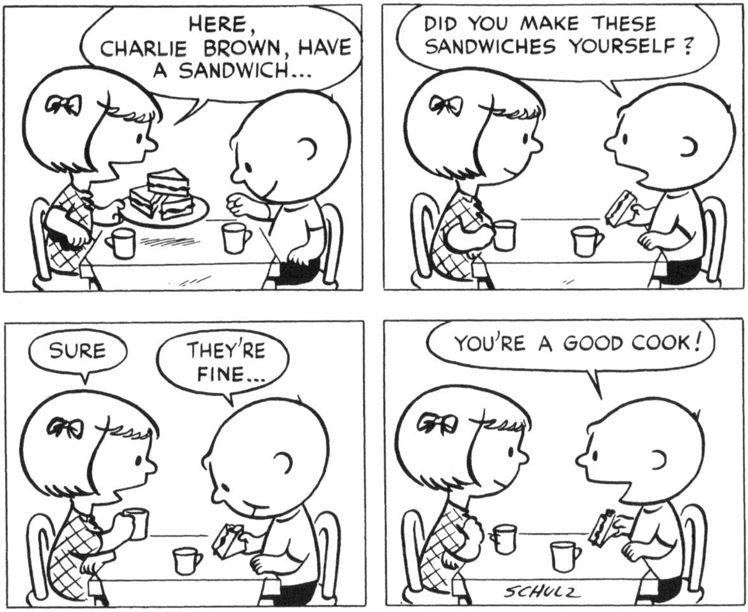
HERE, CHARLIE BROWN, HAVE A SANDWICH...
DID YOU MAKE THESE SANDWICHES YOURSELF?
SURE
THEY'RE FINE...
YOU'RE A GOOD COOK!
SCHULZ

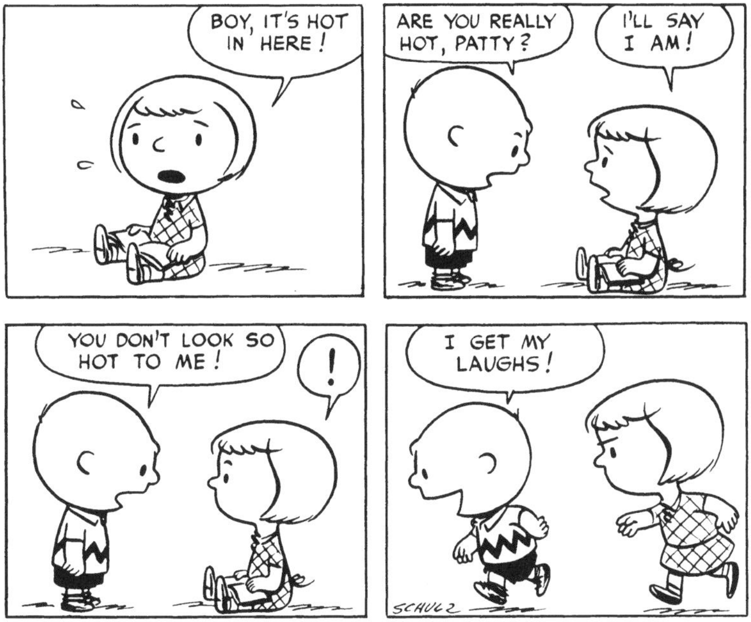
BOY, IT'S HOT IN HERE!
ARE YOU REALLY HOT, PATTY?
I'LL SAY I AM!
YOU DON'T LOOK SO HOT TO ME!
!
I GET MY LAUGHS!
SCHULZ

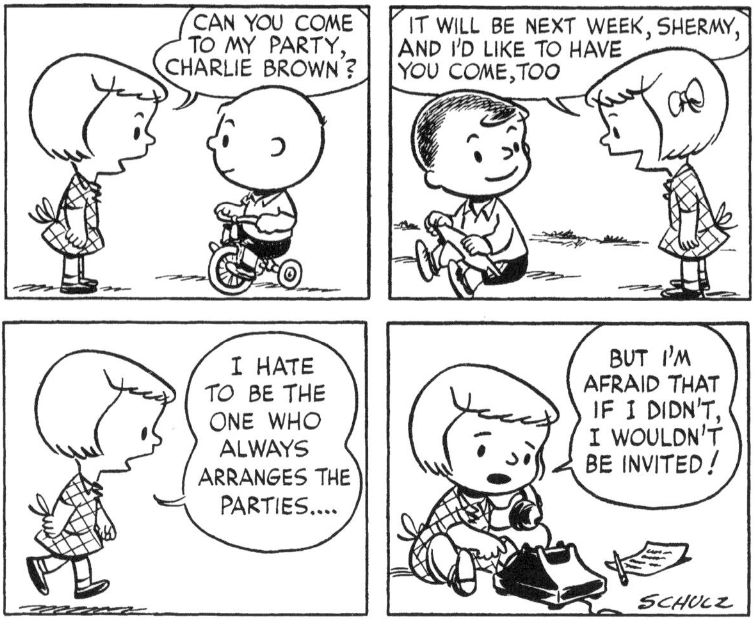
CAN YOU COME TO MY PARTY, CHARLIE BROWN?
IT WILL BE NEXT WEEK, SHERMY, AND I'D LIKE TO HAVE YOU COME, TOO
I HATE TO BE THE ONE WHO ALWAYS ARRANGES THE PARTIES....
BUT I'M AFRAID THAT IF I DIDN'T, I WOULDN'T BE INVITED!
SCHULZ

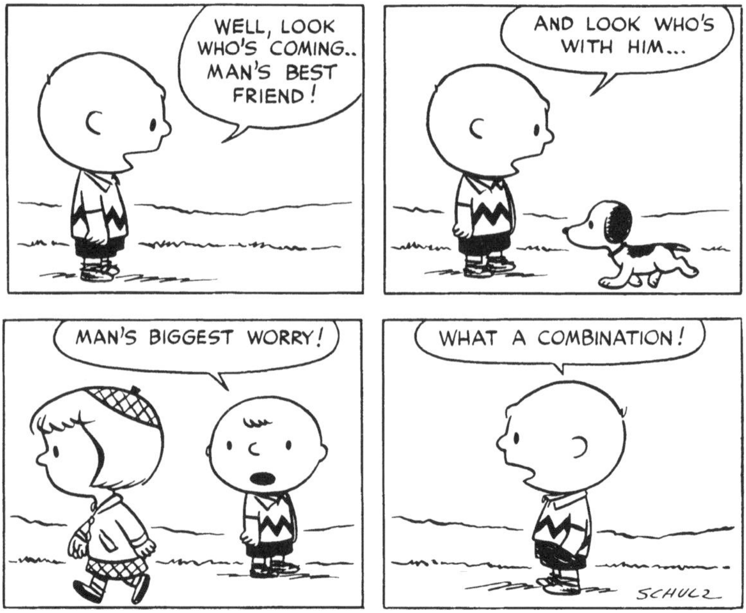
WELL, LOOK WHO'S COMING.. MAN'S BEST FRIEND!
AND LOOK WHO'S WITH HIM...
MAN'S BIGGEST WORRY!
WHAT A COMBINATION!
SCHULZ

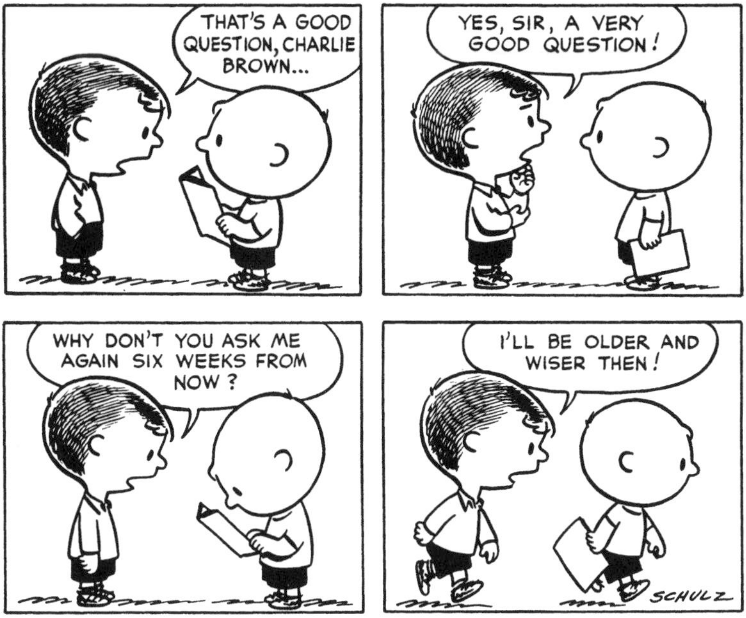
THAT'S A GOOD QUESTION, CHARLIE BROWN...
YES, SIR, A VERY GOOD QUESTION!
WHY DON'T YOU ASK ME AGAIN SIX WEEKS FROM NOW?
I'LL BE OLDER AND WISER THEN!
SCHULZ

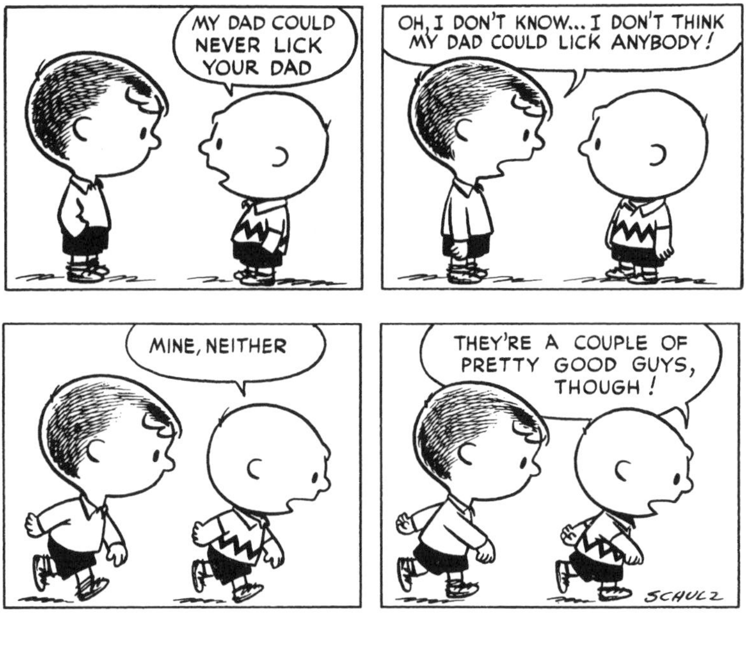
MY DAD COULD NEVER LICK YOUR DAD
OH, I DON'T KNOW... I DON'T THINK MY DAD COULD LICK ANYBODY!
MINE, NEITHER
THEY'RE A COUPLE OF PRETTY GOOD GUYS, THOUGH!
SCHULZ

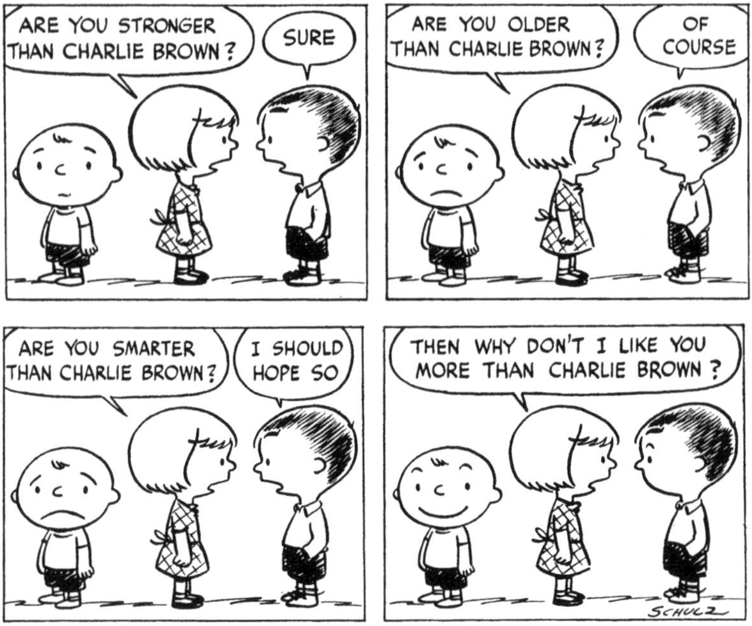
ARE YOU STRONGER THAN CHARLIE BROWN ?
SURE
ARE YOU OLDER THAN CHARLIE BROWN ?
OF COURSE
ARE YOU SMARTER THAN CHARLIE BROWN ?
I SHOULD HOPE SO
THEN WHY DON'T I LIKE YOU MORE THAN CHARLIE BROWN ?
SCHULZ

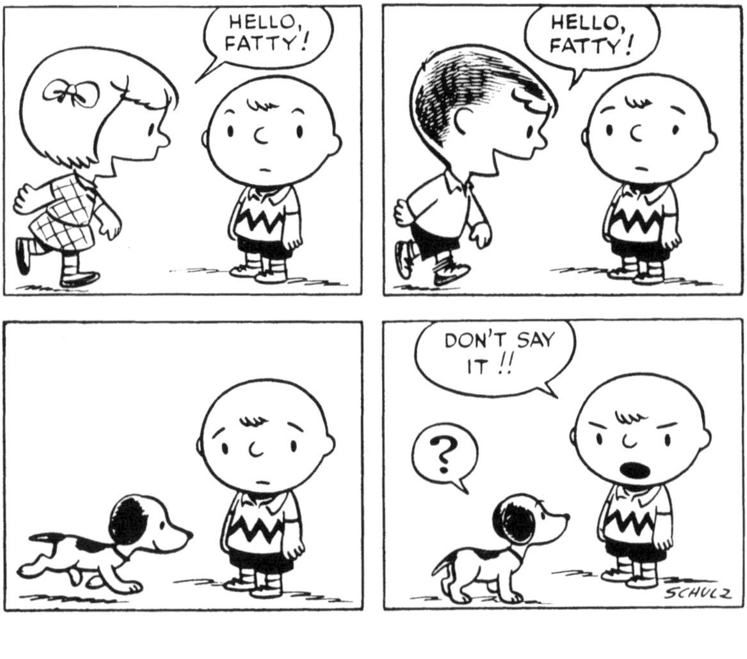
HELLO, FATTY !
HELLO, FATTY !
?
DON'T SAY IT !!
SCHULZ

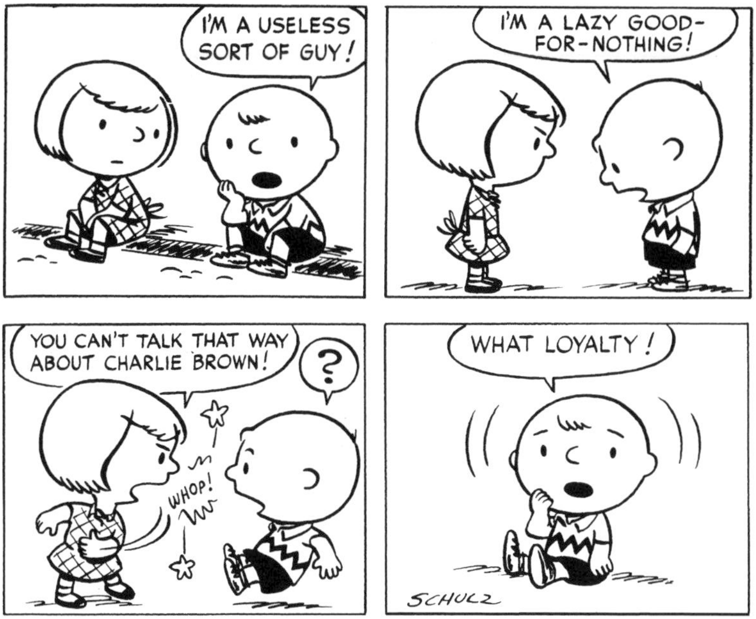
I'M A USELESS SORT OF GUY!
I'M A LAZY GOOD-FOR-NOTHING!
YOU CAN'T TALK THAT WAY ABOUT CHARLIE BROWN!
?
WHOP!
WHAT LOYALTY!
SCHULZ

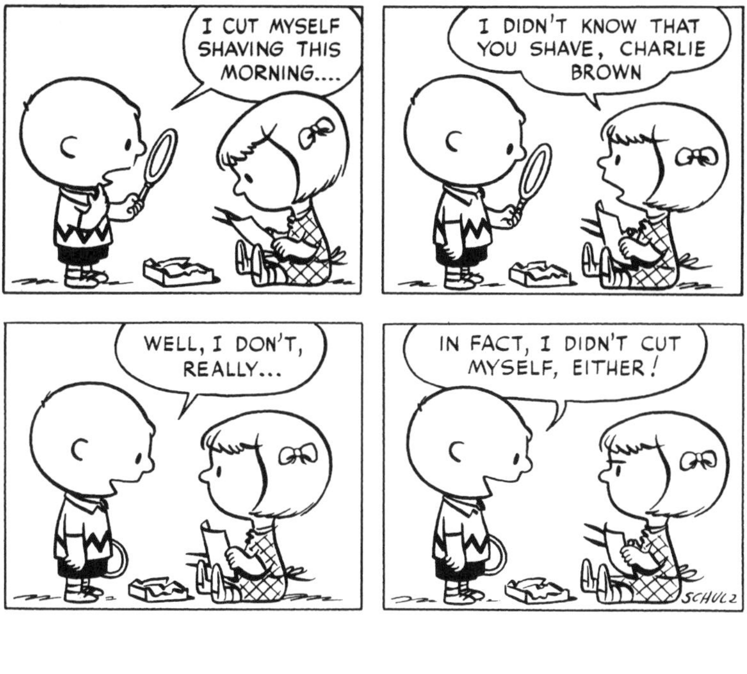
I CUT MYSELF SHAVING THIS MORNING....
I DIDN'T KNOW THAT YOU SHAVE, CHARLIE BROWN
WELL, I DON'T, REALLY...
IN FACT, I DIDN'T CUT MYSELF, EITHER!
SCHULZ

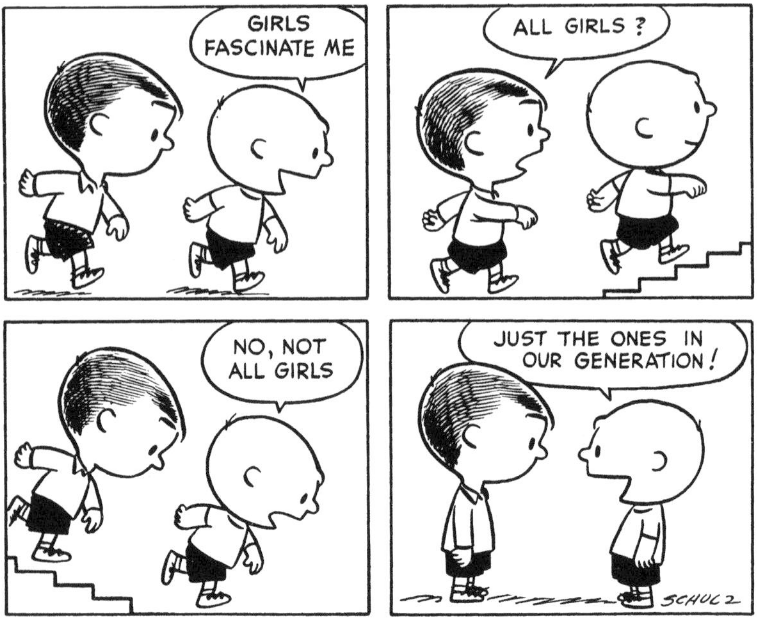
GIRLS FASCINATE ME
ALL GIRLS ?
NO, NOT ALL GIRLS
JUST THE ONES IN OUR GENERATION !
SCHULZ

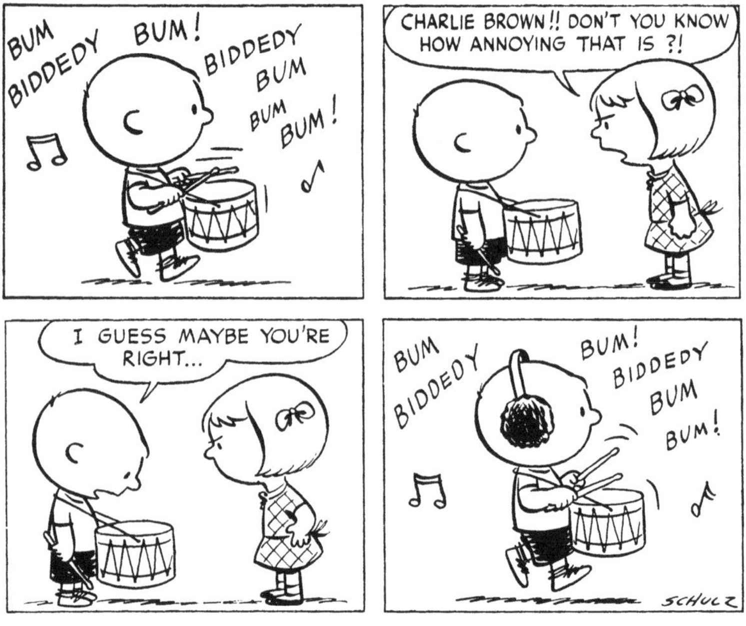
BUM BIDDEDY BUM! BIDDEDY BUM BUM BUM!
CHARLIE BROWN!! DON'T YOU KNOW HOW ANNOYING THAT IS ?!
I GUESS MAYBE YOU'RE RIGHT...
BUM BIDDEDY BUM! BIDDEDY BUM BUM!
SCHULZ

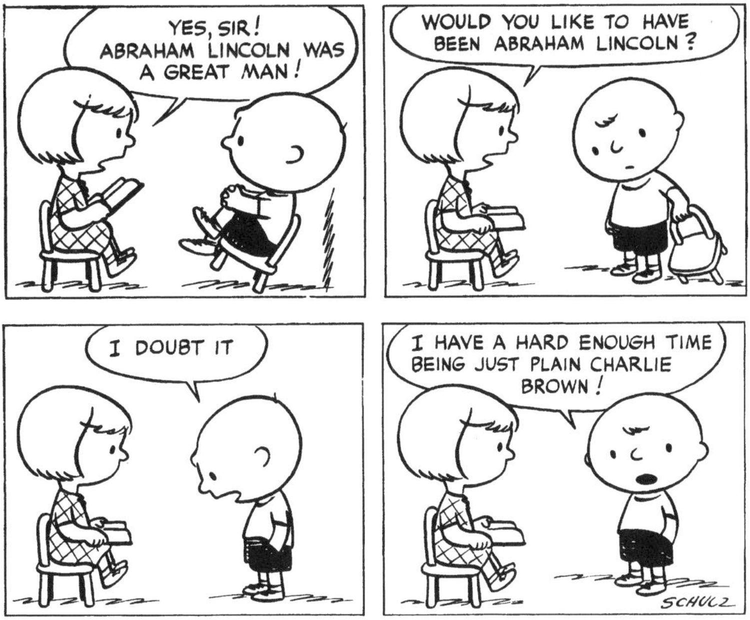
YES, SIR! ABRAHAM LINCOLN WAS A GREAT MAN!
WOULD YOU LIKE TO HAVE BEEN ABRAHAM LINCOLN?
I DOUBT IT
I HAVE A HARD ENOUGH TIME BEING JUST PLAIN CHARLIE BROWN!
SCHULZ

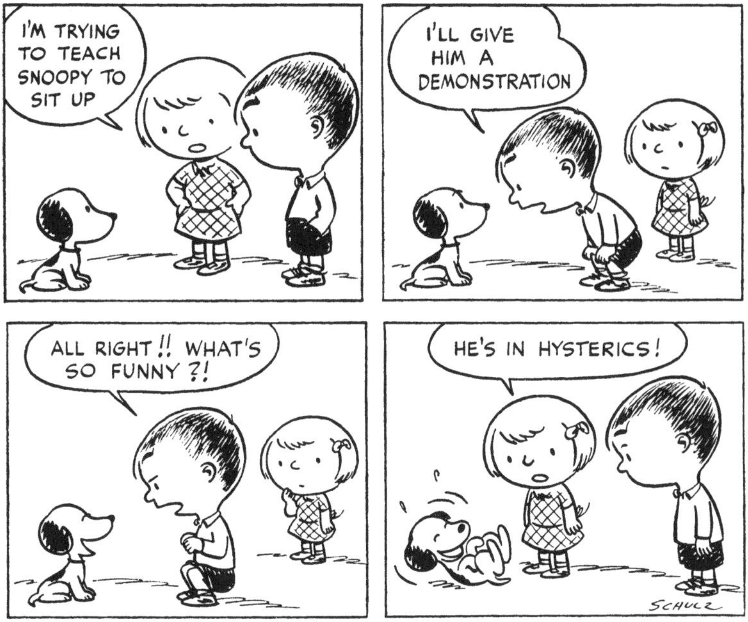
I'M TRYING TO TEACH SNOOPY TO SIT UP
I'LL GIVE HIM A DEMONSTRATION
ALL RIGHT!! WHAT'S SO FUNNY?!
HE'S IN HYSTERICS!
SCHULZ

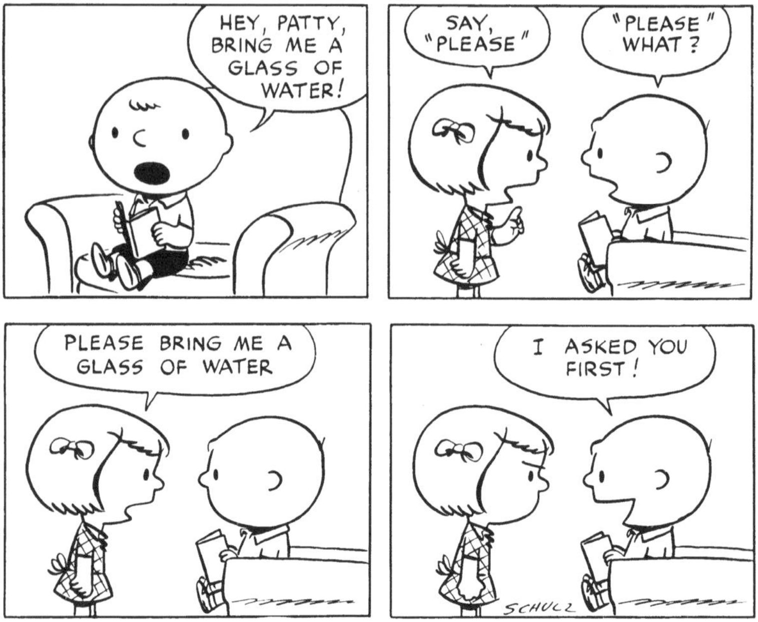
HEY, PATTY, BRING ME A GLASS OF WATER!
SAY, "PLEASE"
"PLEASE" WHAT?
PLEASE BRING ME A GLASS OF WATER
I ASKED YOU FIRST!
SCHULZ

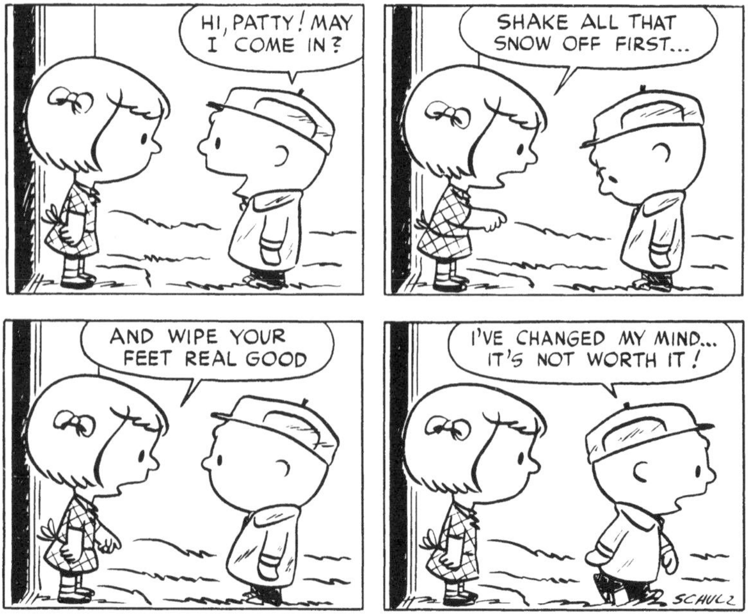
HI, PATTY! MAY I COME IN?
SHAKE ALL THAT SNOW OFF FIRST...
AND WIPE YOUR FEET REAL GOOD
I'VE CHANGED MY MIND... IT'S NOT WORTH IT!
SCHULZ

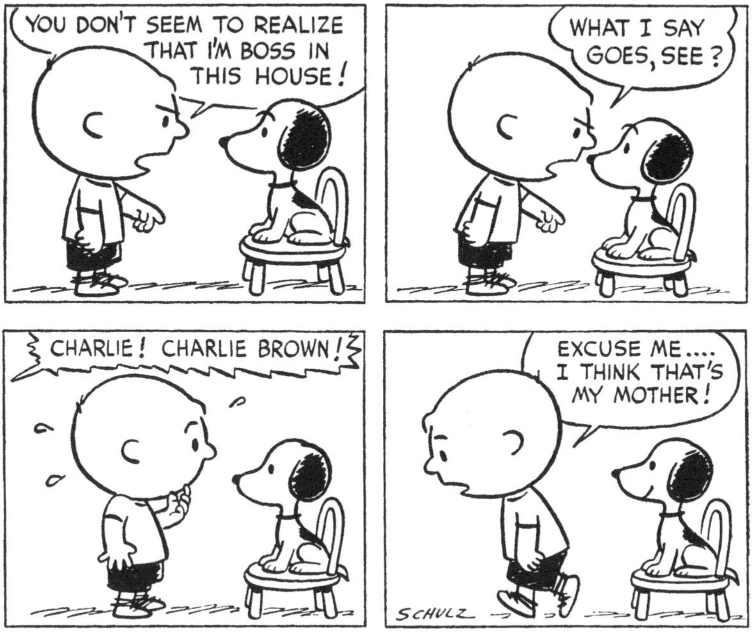
YOU DON'T SEEM TO REALIZE THAT I'M BOSS IN THIS HOUSE!
WHAT I SAY GOES, SEE?
CHARLIE! CHARLIE BROWN!
EXCUSE ME.... I THINK THAT'S MY MOTHER!
SCHULZ

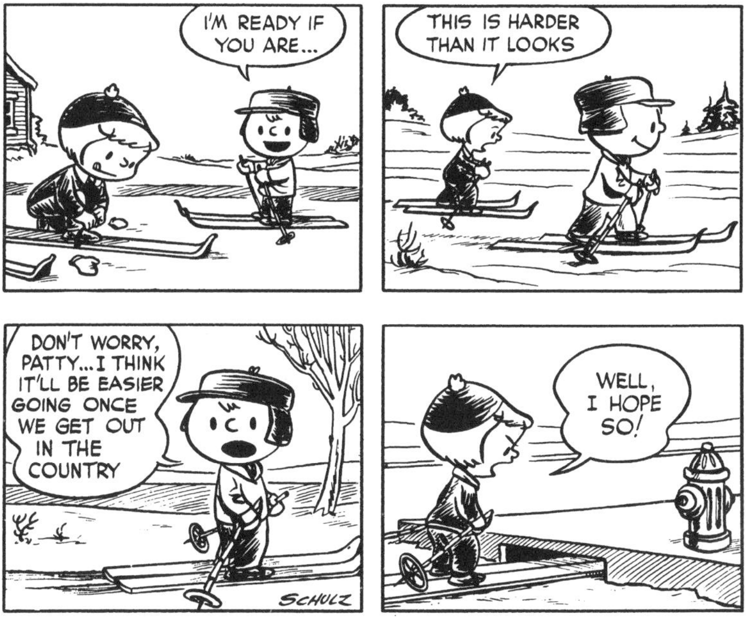
I'M READY IF YOU ARE...
THIS IS HARDER THAN IT LOOKS
DON'T WORRY, PATTY...I THINK IT'LL BE EASIER GOING ONCE WE GET OUT IN THE COUNTRY
SCHULZ
WELL, I HOPE SO!

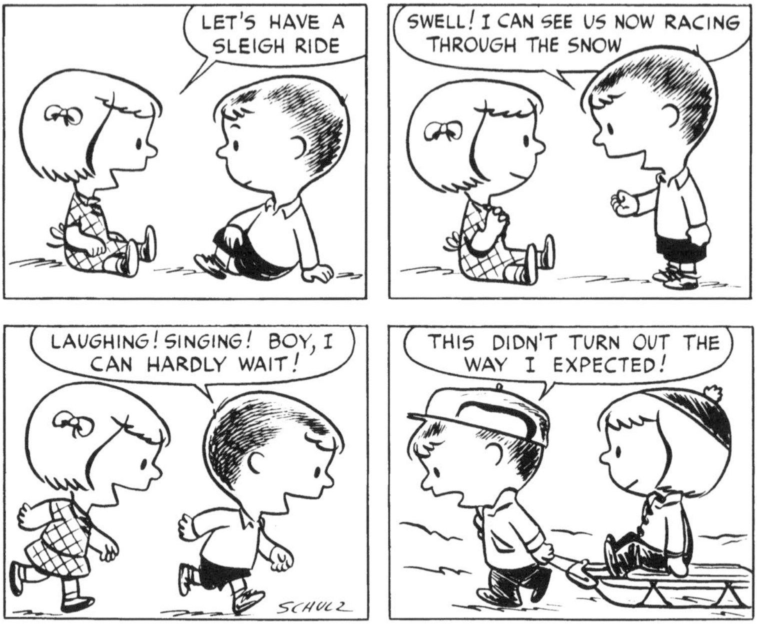
LET'S HAVE A SLEIGH RIDE
SWELL! I CAN SEE US NOW RACING THROUGH THE SNOW
LAUGHING! SINGING! BOY, I CAN HARDLY WAIT!
THIS DIDN'T TURN OUT THE WAY I EXPECTED!
SCHULZ

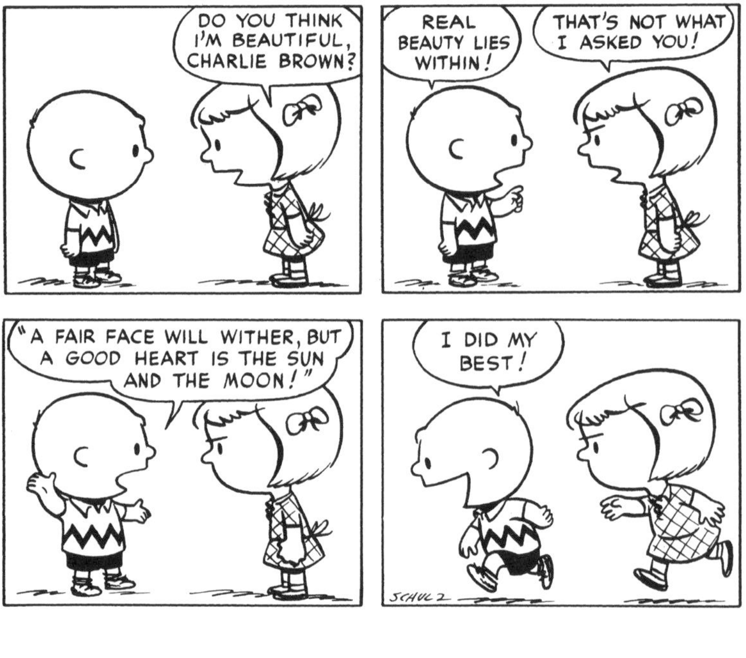
DO YOU THINK I'M BEAUTIFUL, CHARLIE BROWN?
REAL BEAUTY LIES WITHIN!
THAT'S NOT WHAT I ASKED YOU!
"A FAIR FACE WILL WITHER, BUT A GOOD HEART IS THE SUN AND THE MOON!"
I DID MY BEST!
SCHULZ

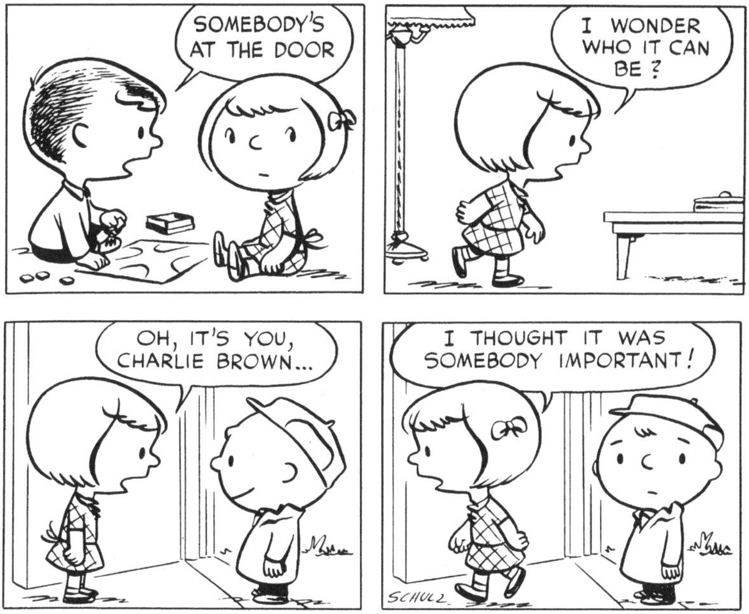
SOMEBODY'S AT THE DOOR
I WONDER WHO IT CAN BE ?
OH, IT'S YOU, CHARLIE BROWN...
I THOUGHT IT WAS SOMEBODY IMPORTANT!
SCHULZ

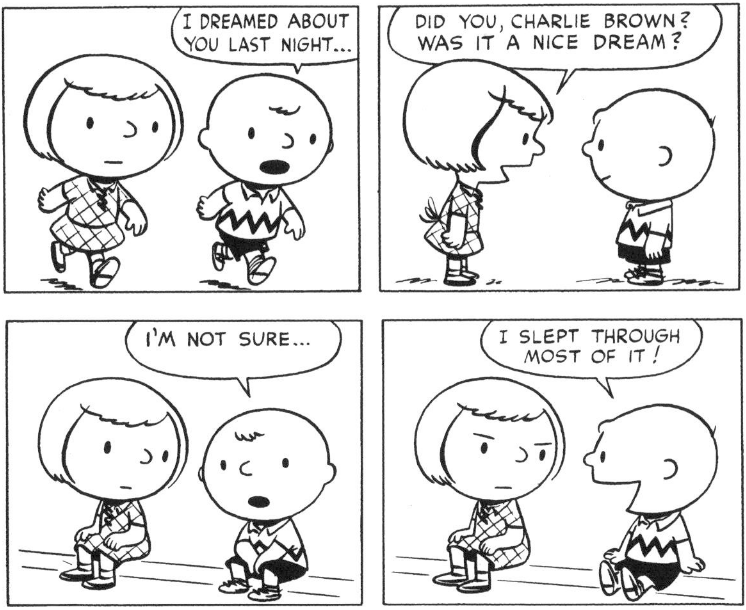
I DREAMED ABOUT YOU LAST NIGHT...
DID YOU, CHARLIE BROWN? WAS IT A NICE DREAM?
I'M NOT SURE...
I SLEPT THROUGH MOST OF IT!

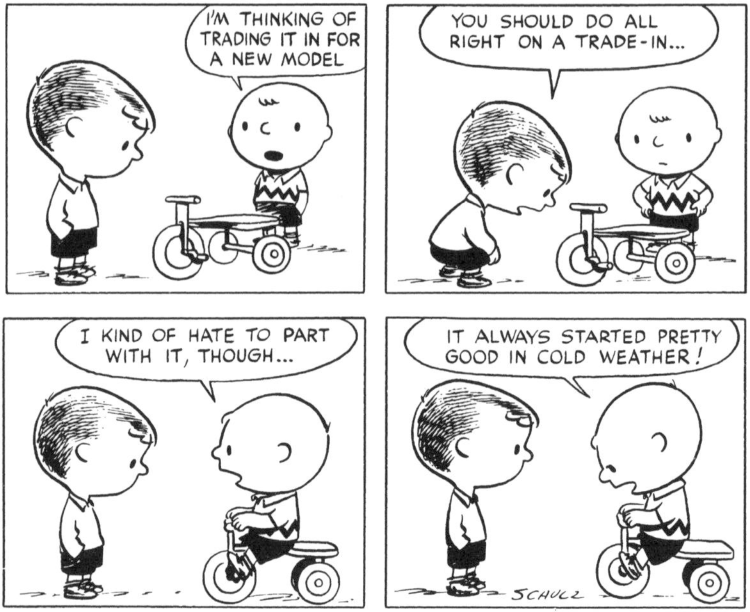
I'M THINKING OF TRADING IT IN FOR A NEW MODEL
YOU SHOULD DO ALL RIGHT ON A TRADE-IN...
I KIND OF HATE TO PART WITH IT, THOUGH...
IT ALWAYS STARTED PRETTY GOOD IN COLD WEATHER!
SCHULZ

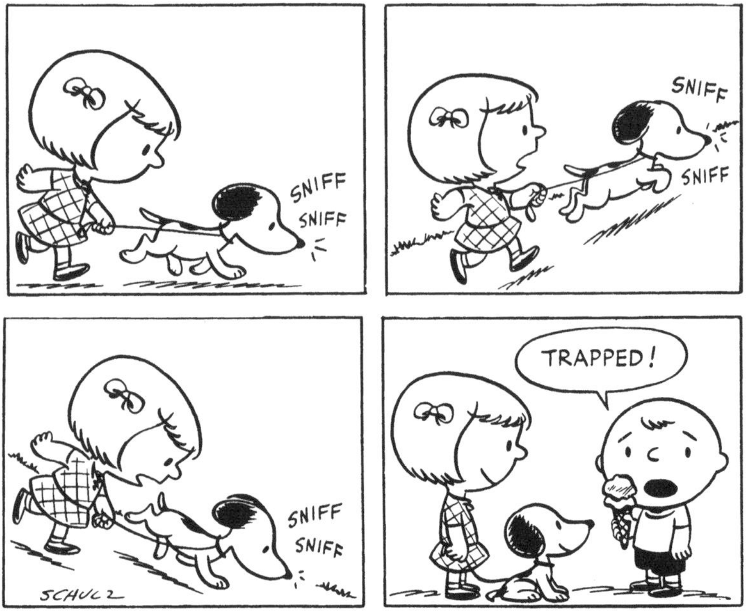
SNIFF
SNIFF
SNIFF
SNIFF
SNIFF
SNIFF
SCHULZ
TRAPPED!

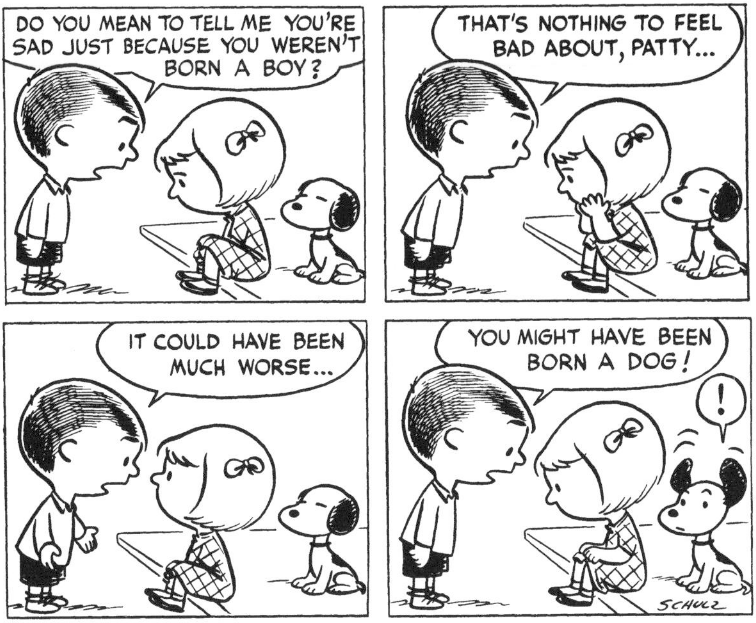
DO YOU MEAN TO TELL ME YOU'RE SAD JUST BECAUSE YOU WEREN'T BORN A BOY?
THAT'S NOTHING TO FEEL BAD ABOUT, PATTY...
IT COULD HAVE BEEN MUCH WORSE...
YOU MIGHT HAVE BEEN BORN A DOG!
!
SCHULZ

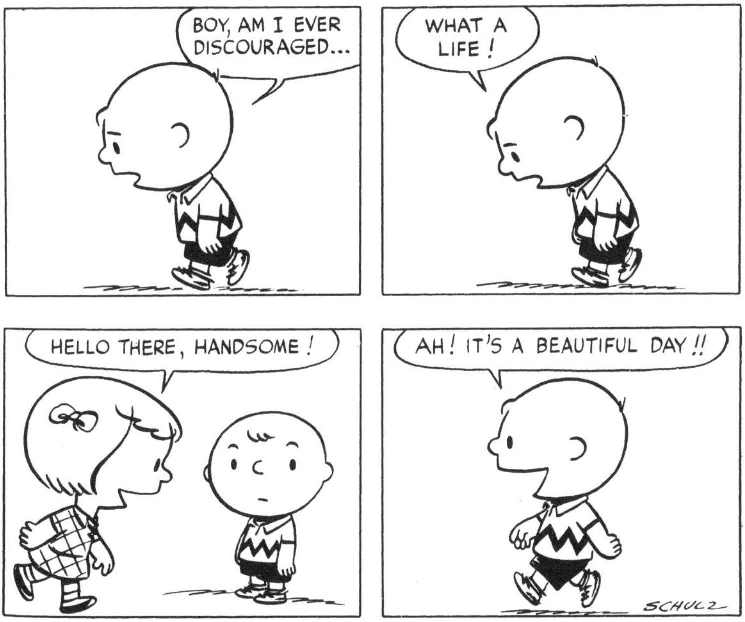
BOY, AM I EVER DISCOURAGED...
WHAT A LIFE!
HELLO THERE, HANDSOME!
AH! IT'S A BEAUTIFUL DAY!!
SCHULZ

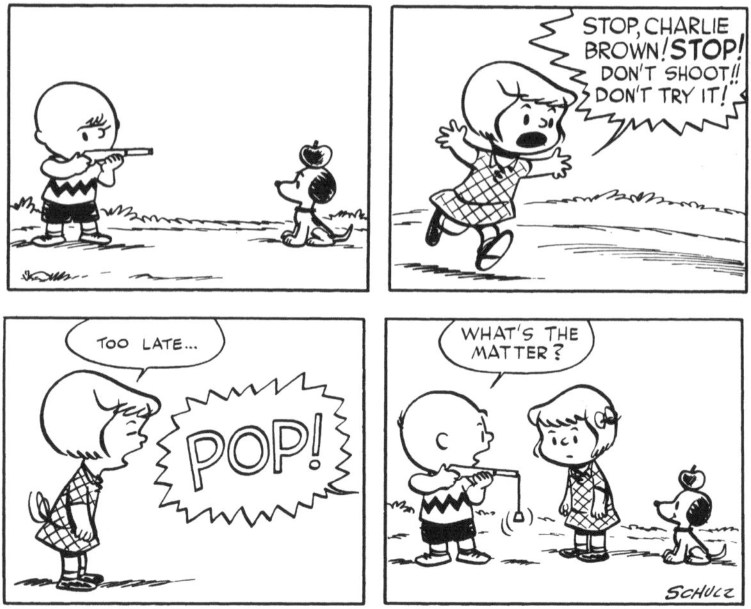
STOP, CHARLIE BROWN! STOP! DON'T SHOOT!! DON'T TRY IT!
TOO LATE...
POP!
WHAT'S THE MATTER?
SCHULZ

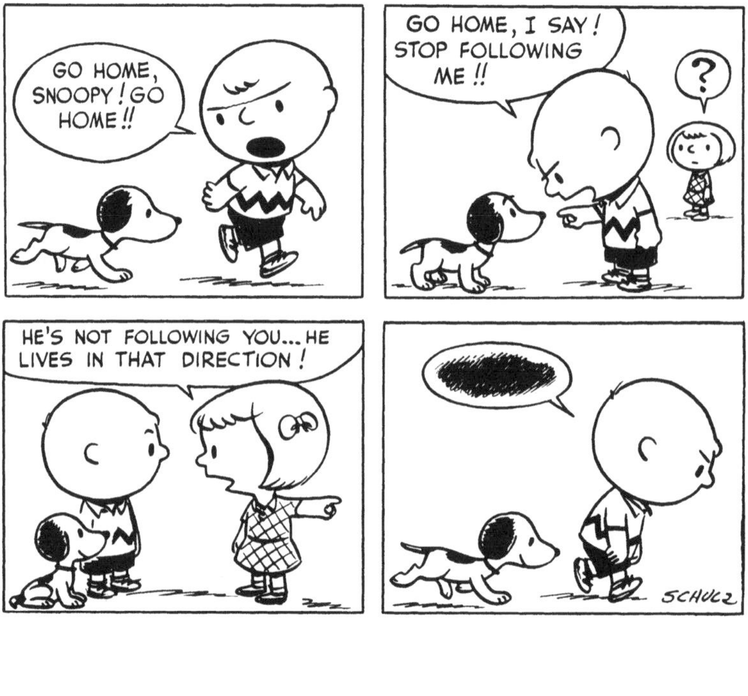
GO HOME, SNOOPY! GO HOME!!
GO HOME, I SAY! STOP FOLLOWING ME!!
?
HE'S NOT FOLLOWING YOU... HE LIVES IN THAT DIRECTION!
SCHULZ

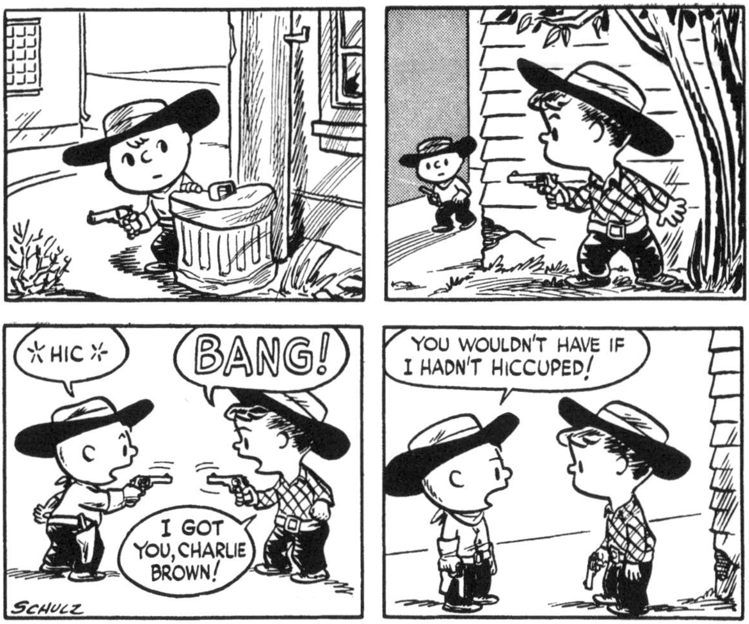
HIC
BANG!
I GOT YOU, CHARLIE BROWN!
SCHULZ
YOU WOULDN'T HAVE IF I HADN'T HICCUPED!

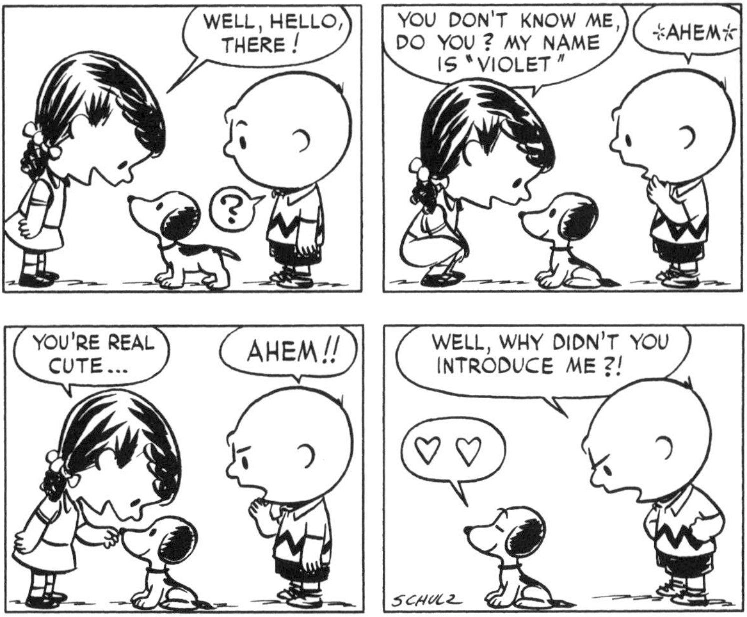
WELL, HELLO, THERE!
?
YOU DON'T KNOW ME, DO YOU? MY NAME IS "VIOLET"
AHEM
YOU'RE REAL CUTE...
AHEM!!
WELL, WHY DIDN'T YOU INTRODUCE ME?!
SCHULZ

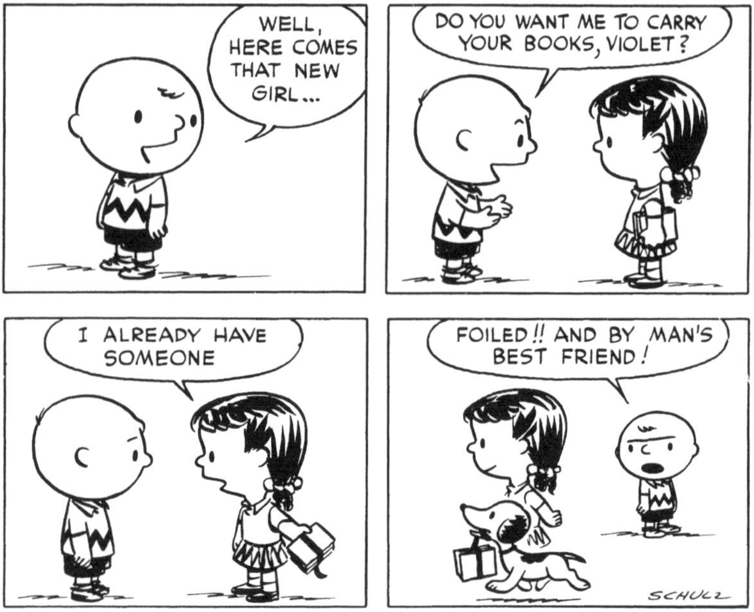
WELL, HERE COMES THAT NEW GIRL...
DO YOU WANT ME TO CARRY YOUR BOOKS, VIOLET?
I ALREADY HAVE SOMEONE
FOILED!! AND BY MAN'S BEST FRIEND!
SCHULZ

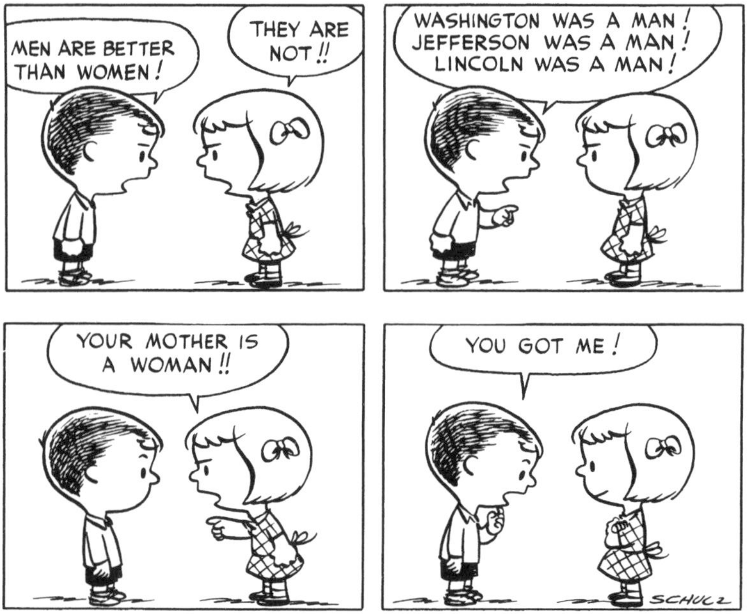
MEN ARE BETTER THAN WOMEN!
THEY ARE NOT!!
WASHINGTON WAS A MAN! JEFFERSON WAS A MAN! LINCOLN WAS A MAN!
YOUR MOTHER IS A WOMAN!!
YOU GOT ME!
SCHULZ

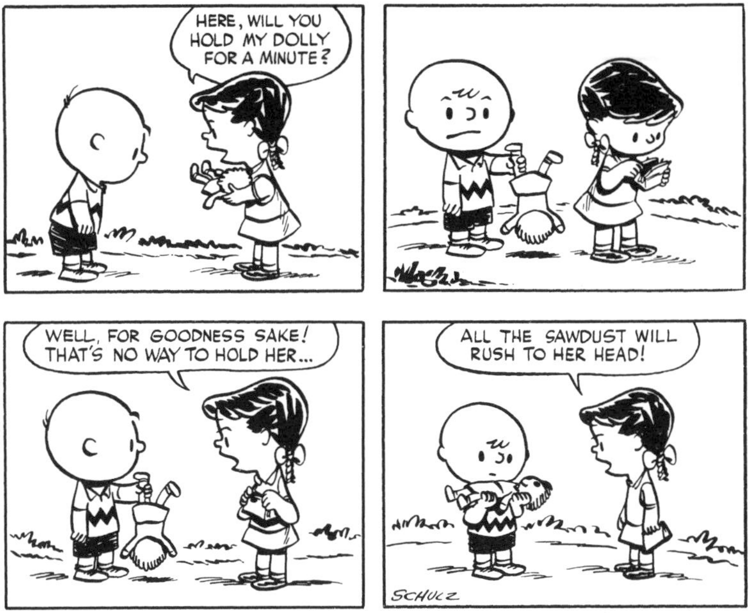
HERE, WILL YOU HOLD MY DOLLY FOR A MINUTE?
WELL, FOR GOODNESS SAKE! THAT'S NO WAY TO HOLD HER...
ALL THE SAWDUST WILL RUSH TO HER HEAD!
SCHULZ

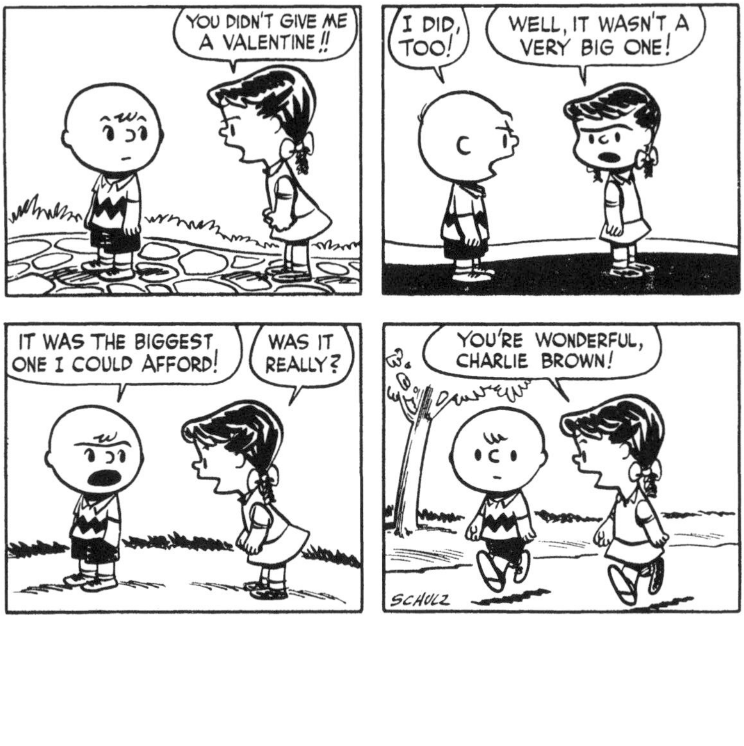
YOU DIDN'T GIVE ME A VALENTINE!!
I DID, TOO!
WELL, IT WASN'T A VERY BIG ONE!
IT WAS THE BIGGEST ONE I COULD AFFORD!
WAS IT REALLY?
YOU'RE WONDERFUL, CHARLIE BROWN!
SCHULZ

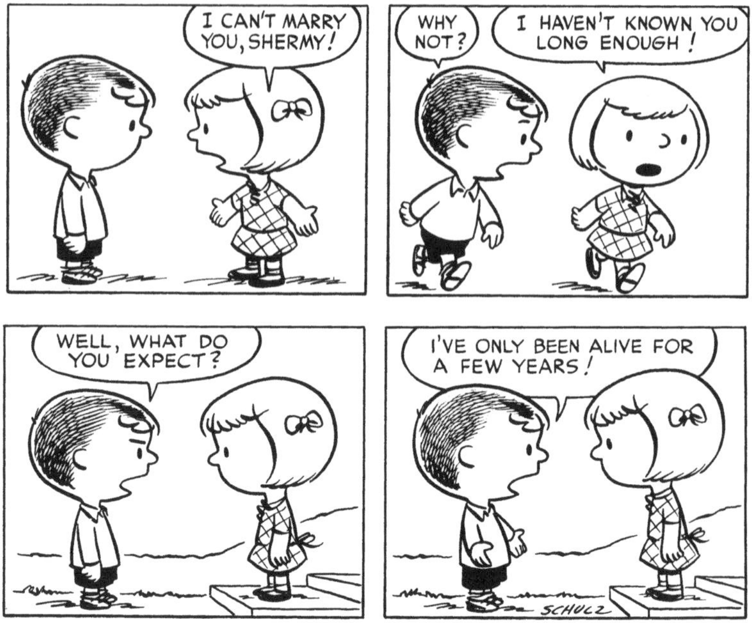
I CAN'T MARRY YOU, SHERMY!
WHY NOT?
I HAVEN'T KNOWN YOU LONG ENOUGH!
WELL, WHAT DO YOU EXPECT?
I'VE ONLY BEEN ALIVE FOR A FEW YEARS!
SCHULZ

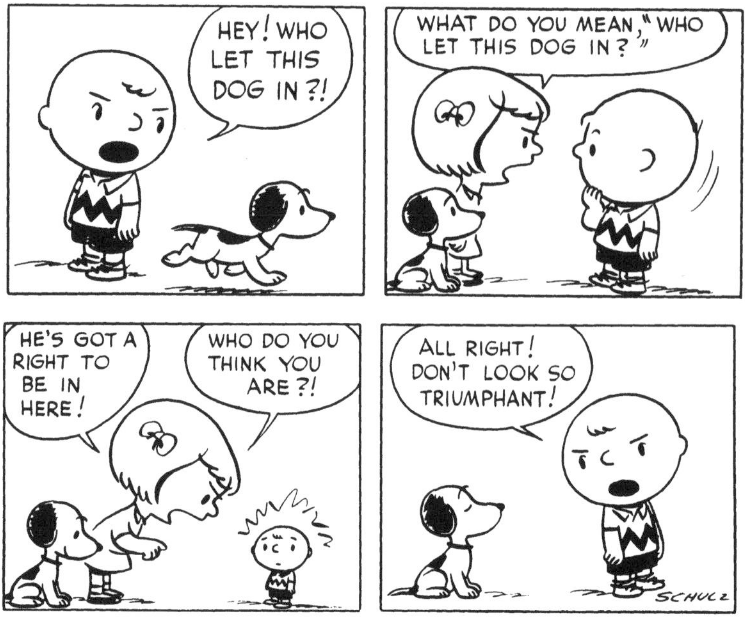
HEY! WHO LET THIS DOG IN?!
WHAT DO YOU MEAN, "WHO LET THIS DOG IN?"
HE'S GOT A RIGHT TO BE IN HERE!
WHO DO YOU THINK YOU ARE?!
ALL RIGHT! DON'T LOOK SO TRIUMPHANT!
SCHULZ

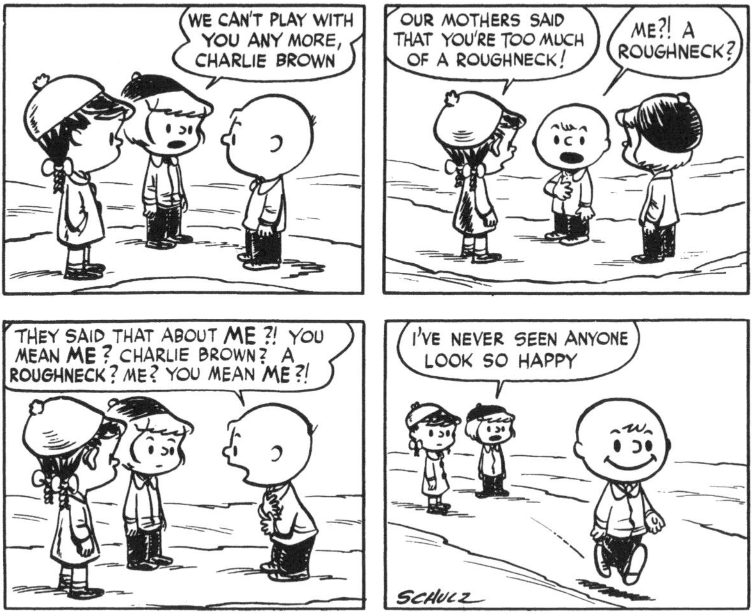
WE CAN'T PLAY WITH YOU ANY MORE, CHARLIE BROWN
OUR MOTHERS SAID THAT YOU'RE TOO MUCH OF A ROUGHNECK!
ME?! A ROUGHNECK?
THEY SAID THAT ABOUT ME?! YOU MEAN ME? CHARLIE BROWN? A ROUGHNECK? ME? YOU MEAN ME?!
I'VE NEVER SEEN ANYONE LOOK SO HAPPY
SCHULZ

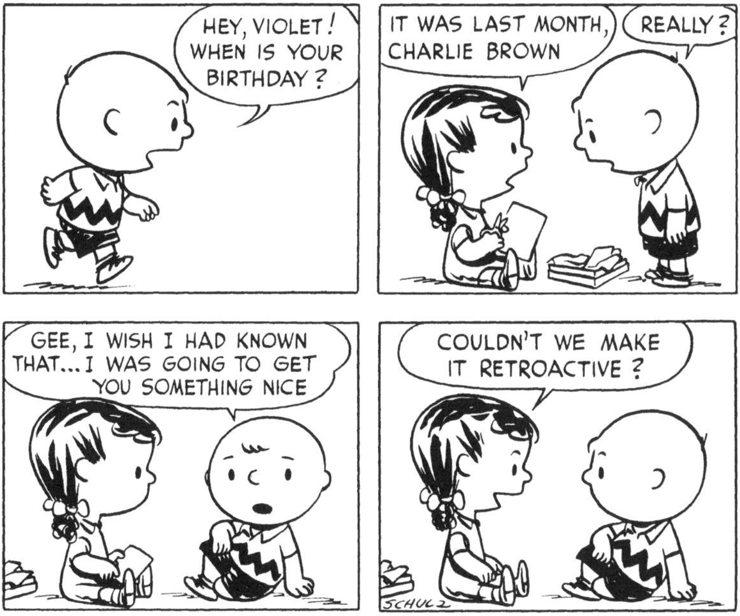
HEY, VIOLET! WHEN IS YOUR BIRTHDAY?
IT WAS LAST MONTH, CHARLIE BROWN
REALLY?
GEE, I WISH I HAD KNOWN THAT...I WAS GOING TO GET YOU SOMETHING NICE
COULDN'T WE MAKE IT RETROACTIVE?
SCHULZ

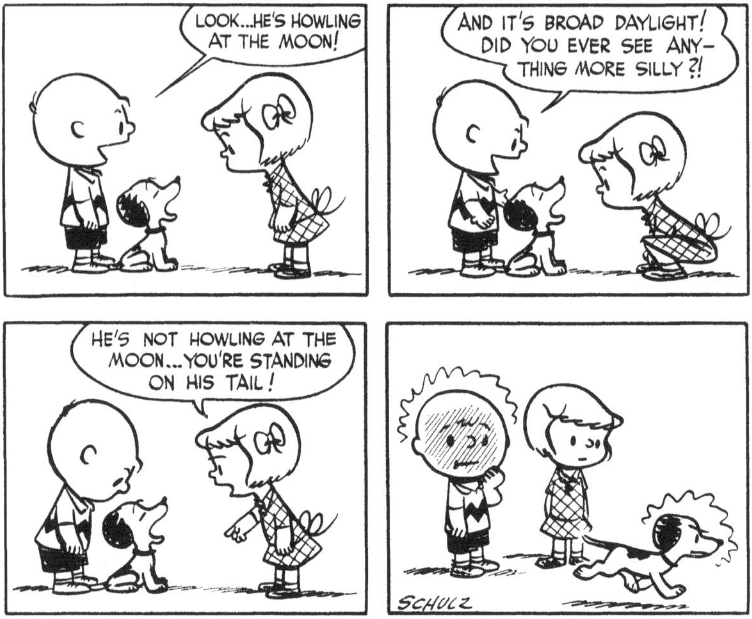
LOOK...HE'S HOWLING AT THE MOON!
AND IT'S BROAD DAYLIGHT! DID YOU EVER SEE ANY-THING MORE SILLY ?!
HE'S NOT HOWLING AT THE MOON...YOU'RE STANDING ON HIS TAIL!
SCHULZ

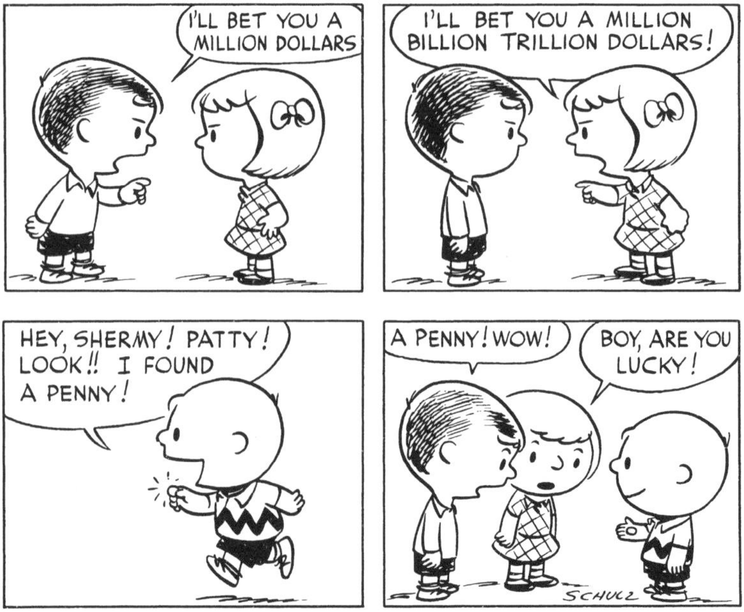
I'LL BET YOU A MILLION DOLLARS
I'LL BET YOU A MILLION BILLION TRILLION DOLLARS!
HEY, SHERMY! PATTY! LOOK!! I FOUND A PENNY!
A PENNY! WOW!
BOY, ARE YOU LUCKY!
SCHULZ

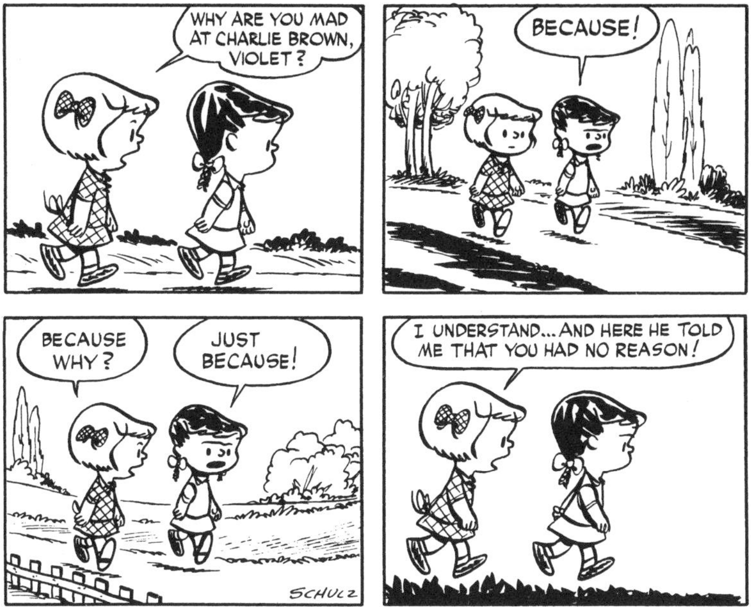
WHY ARE YOU MAD AT CHARLIE BROWN, VIOLET?
BECAUSE!
BECAUSE WHY?
JUST BECAUSE!
I UNDERSTAND... AND HERE HE TOLD ME THAT YOU HAD NO REASON!
SCHULZ

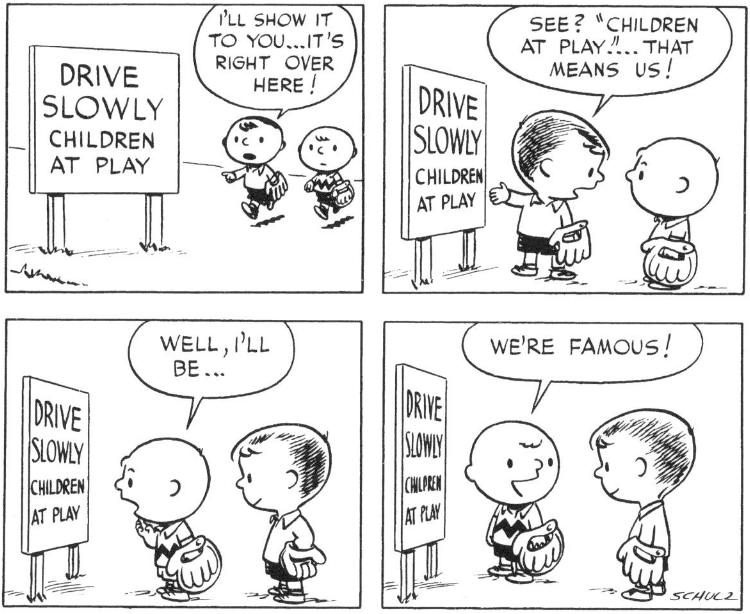
I'LL SHOW IT TO YOU...IT'S RIGHT OVER HERE!
DRIVE SLOWLY CHILDREN AT PLAY
SEE? "CHILDREN AT PLAY!"... THAT MEANS US!
DRIVE SLOWLY CHILDREN AT PLAY
WELL, I'LL BE...
DRIVE SLOWLY CHILDREN AT PLAY
WE'RE FAMOUS!
DRIVE SLOWLY CHILDREN AT PLAY
SCHULZ

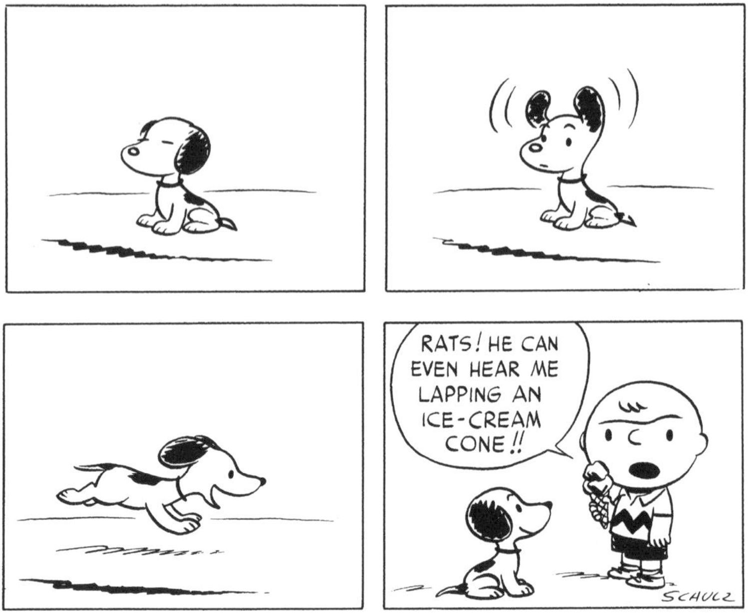
RATS! HE CAN EVEN HEAR ME LAPPING AN ICE-CREAM CONE!!
SCHULZ

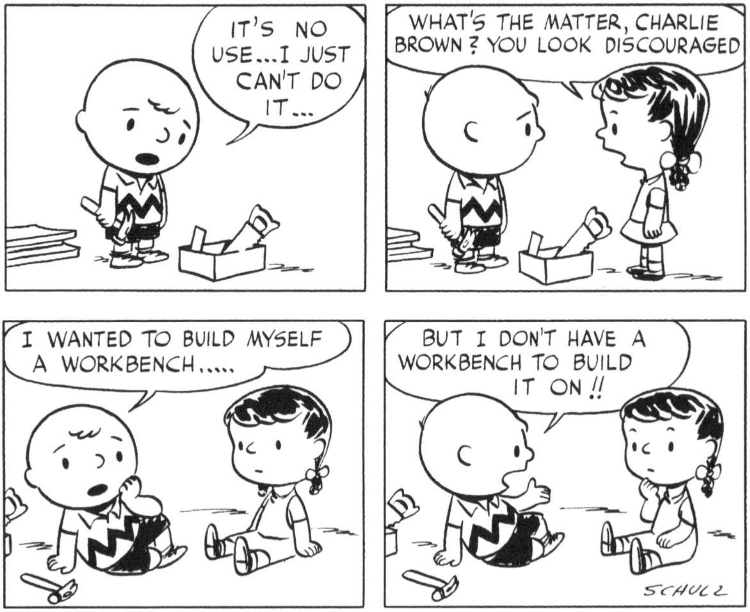
IT'S NO USE...I JUST CAN'T DO IT...
WHAT'S THE MATTER, CHARLIE BROWN? YOU LOOK DISCOURAGED
I WANTED TO BUILD MYSELF A WORKBENCH.....
BUT I DON'T HAVE A WORKBENCH TO BUILD IT ON!!
SCHULZ

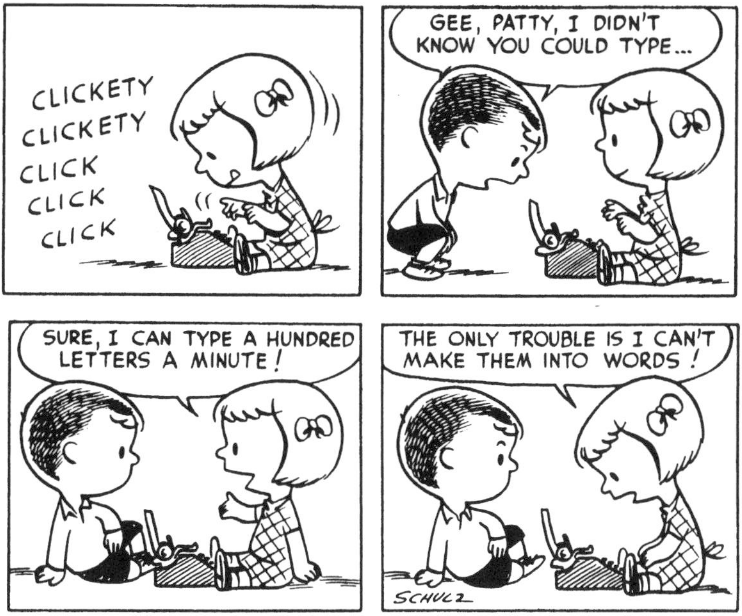
CLICKETY
CLICKETY
CLICK
CLICK
CLICK
GEE, PATTY, I DIDN'T KNOW YOU COULD TYPE...
SURE, I CAN TYPE A HUNDRED LETTERS A MINUTE!
THE ONLY TROUBLE IS I CAN'T MAKE THEM INTO WORDS!
SCHULZ

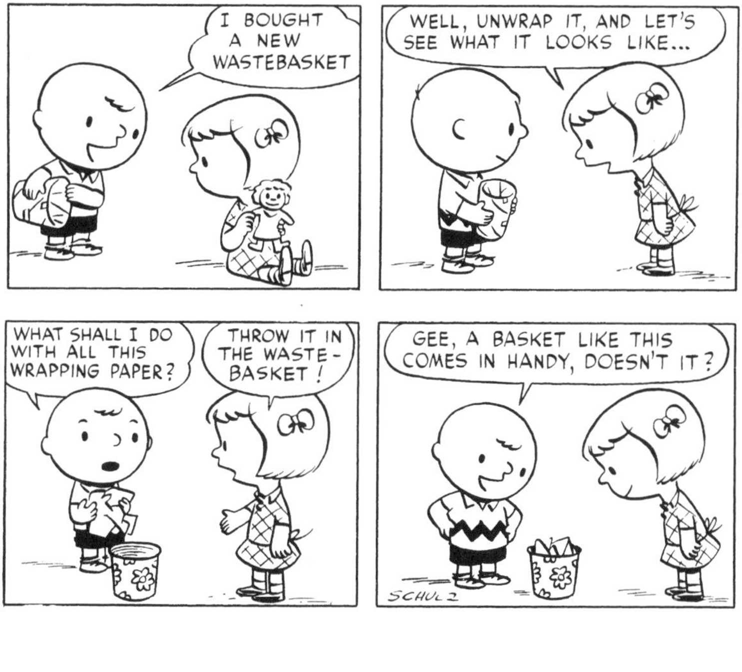
I BOUGHT A NEW WASTEBASKET
WELL, UNWRAP IT, AND LET'S SEE WHAT IT LOOKS LIKE...
WHAT SHALL I DO WITH ALL THIS WRAPPING PAPER?
THROW IT IN THE WASTE-BASKET!
GEE, A BASKET LIKE THIS COMES IN HANDY, DOESN'T IT?
SCHULZ

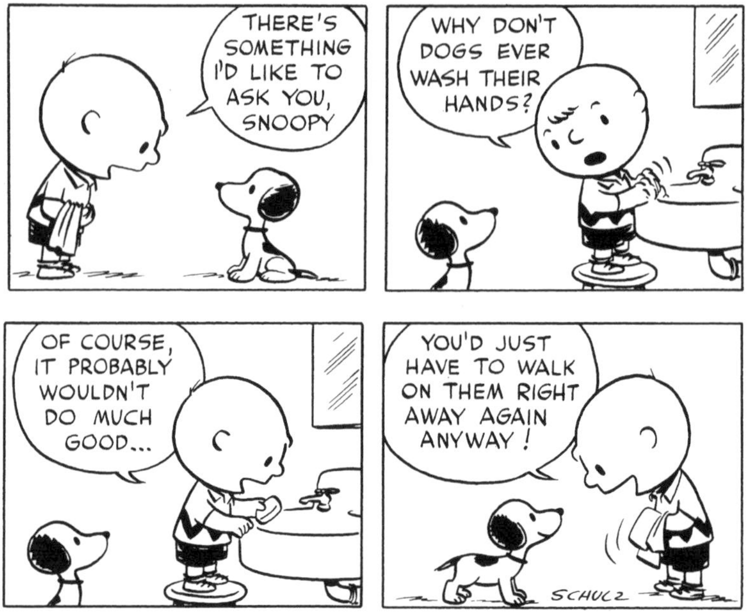
THERE'S SOMETHING I'D LIKE TO ASK YOU, SNOOPY
WHY DON'T DOGS EVER WASH THEIR HANDS?
OF COURSE, IT PROBABLY WOULDN'T DO MUCH GOOD...
YOU'D JUST HAVE TO WALK ON THEM RIGHT AWAY AGAIN ANYWAY!
SCHULZ

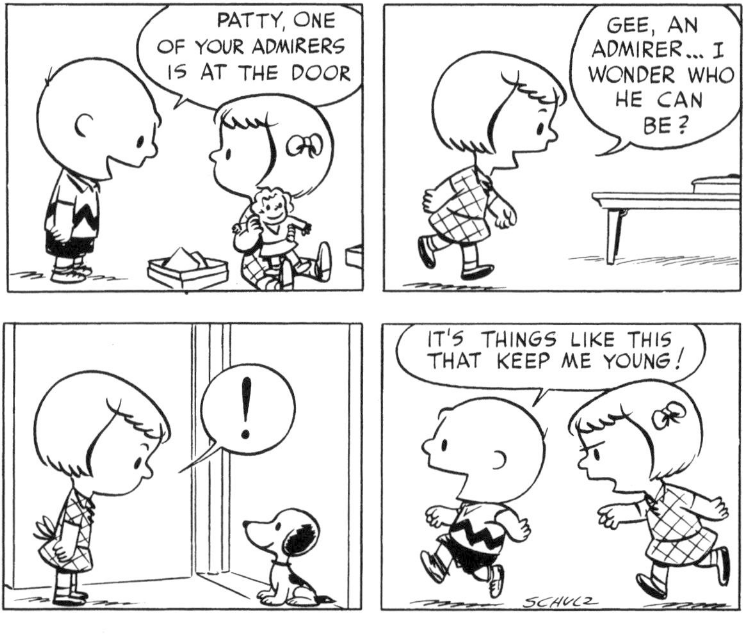
PATTY, ONE OF YOUR ADMIRERS IS AT THE DOOR
GEE, AN ADMIRER... I WONDER WHO HE CAN BE?
!
IT'S THINGS LIKE THIS THAT KEEP ME YOUNG!
SCHULZ

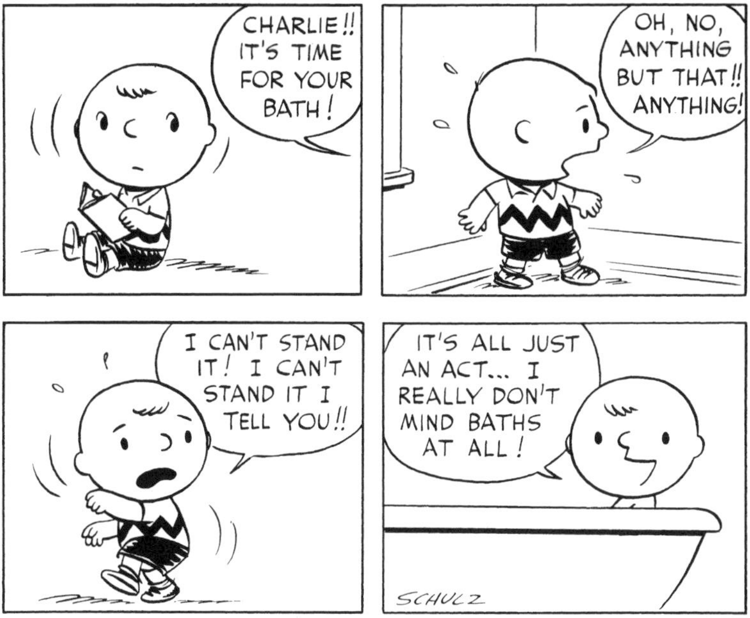
CHARLIE!! IT'S TIME FOR YOUR BATH!
OH, NO, ANYTHING BUT THAT!! ANYTHING!
I CAN'T STAND IT! I CAN'T STAND IT I TELL YOU!!
IT'S ALL JUST AN ACT... I REALLY DON'T MIND BATHS AT ALL!
SCHULZ

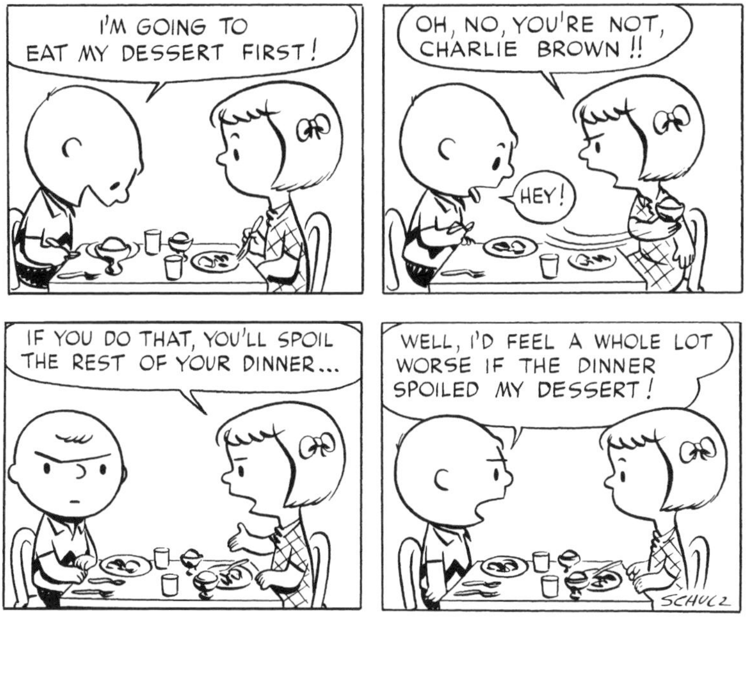
I'M GOING TO EAT MY DESSERT FIRST!
OH, NO, YOU'RE NOT, CHARLIE BROWN!!
HEY!
IF YOU DO THAT, YOU'LL SPOIL THE REST OF YOUR DINNER...
WELL, I'D FEEL A WHOLE LOT WORSE IF THE DINNER SPOILED MY DESSERT!
SCHULZ

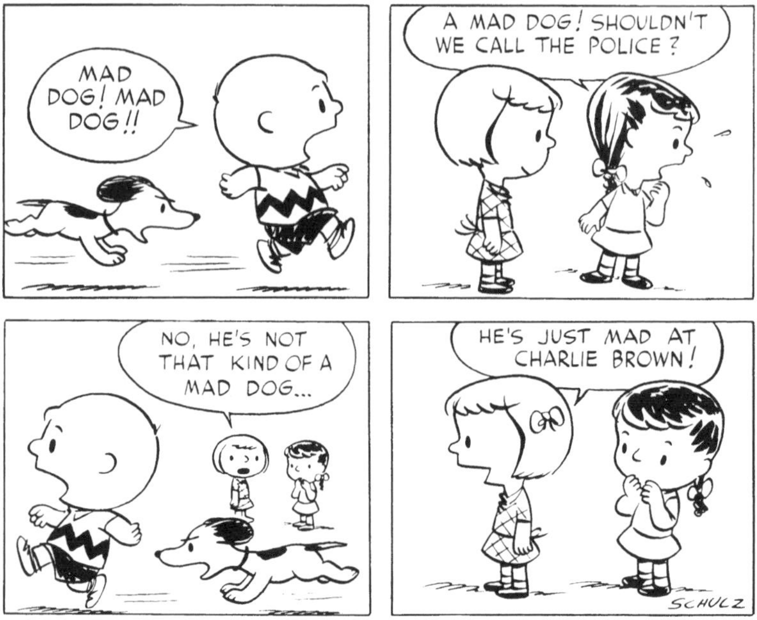
MAD DOG! MAD DOG!!
A MAD DOG! SHOULDN'T WE CALL THE POLICE?
NO, HE'S NOT THAT KIND OF A MAD DOG...
HE'S JUST MAD AT CHARLIE BROWN!
SCHULZ

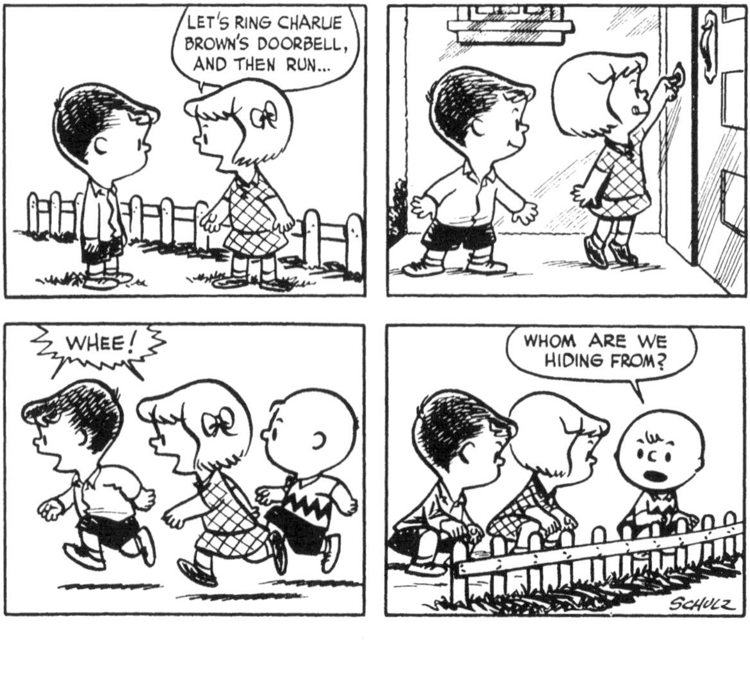
LET'S RING CHARLIE BROWN'S DOORBELL, AND THEN RUN...
WHEE!
WHOM ARE WE HIDING FROM?
SCHULZ

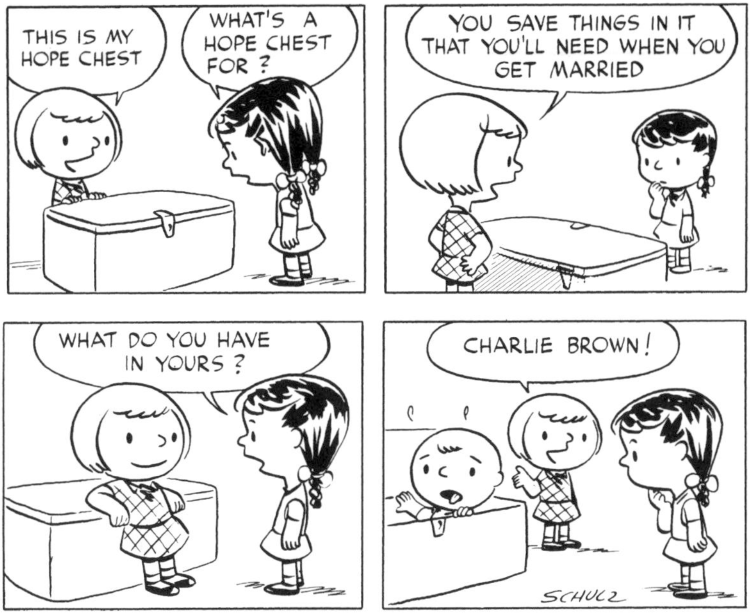
THIS IS MY HOPE CHEST
WHAT'S A HOPE CHEST FOR ?
YOU SAVE THINGS IN IT THAT YOU'LL NEED WHEN YOU GET MARRIED
WHAT DO YOU HAVE IN YOURS ?
CHARLIE BROWN !
SCHULZ

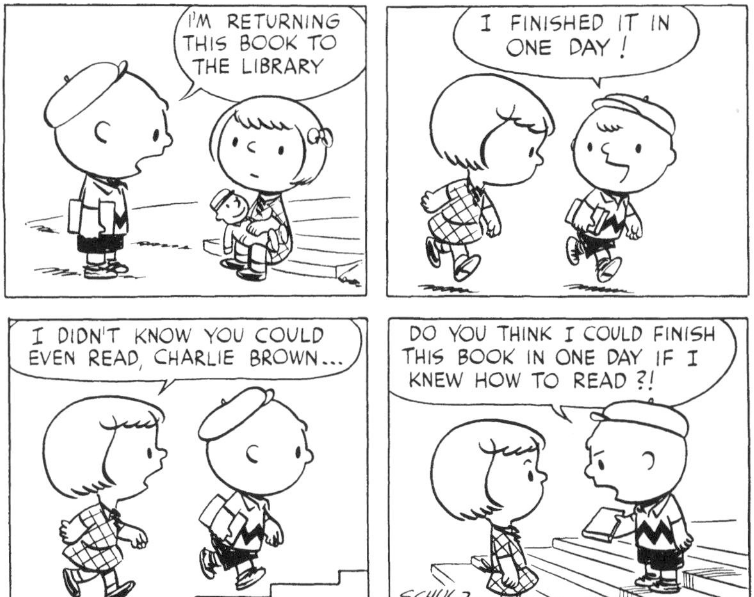
I'M RETURNING THIS BOOK TO THE LIBRARY
I FINISHED IT IN ONE DAY !
I DIDN'T KNOW YOU COULD EVEN READ, CHARLIE BROWN...
DO YOU THINK I COULD FINISH THIS BOOK IN ONE DAY IF I KNEW HOW TO READ ?!
SCHULZ

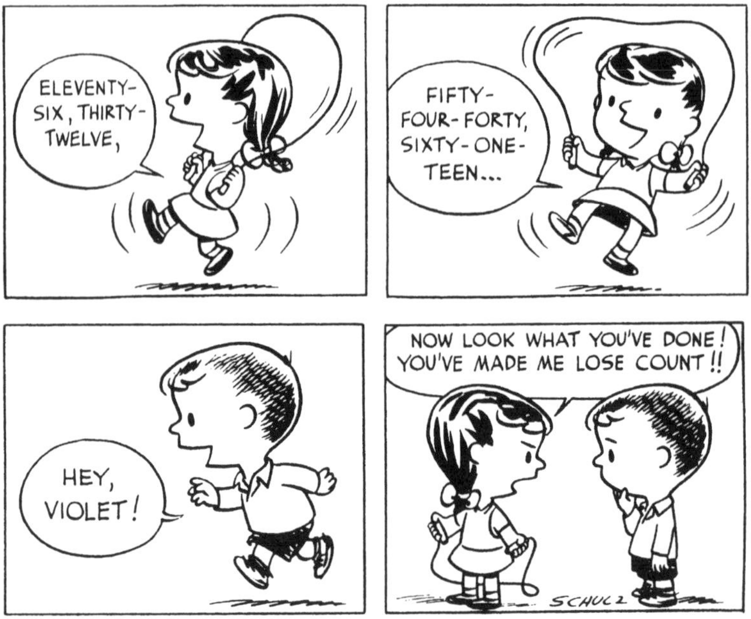
ELEVENTY-SIX, THIRTY-TWELVE,
FIFTY-FOUR-FORTY, SIXTY-ONE-TEEN...
HEY, VIOLET!
NOW LOOK WHAT YOU'VE DONE! YOU'VE MADE ME LOSE COUNT!!
SCHULZ

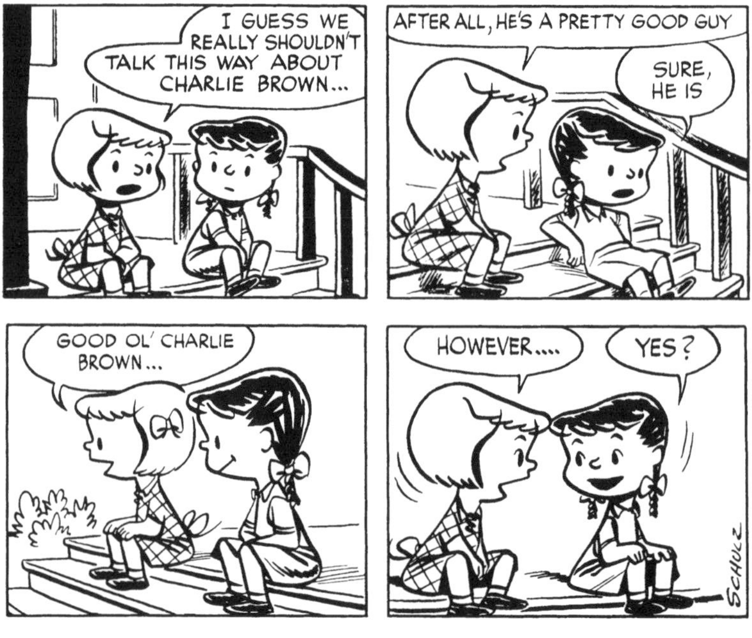
I GUESS WE REALLY SHOULDN'T TALK THIS WAY ABOUT CHARLIE BROWN...
AFTER ALL, HE'S A PRETTY GOOD GUY
SURE, HE IS
GOOD OL' CHARLIE BROWN...
HOWEVER....
YES?
SCHULZ

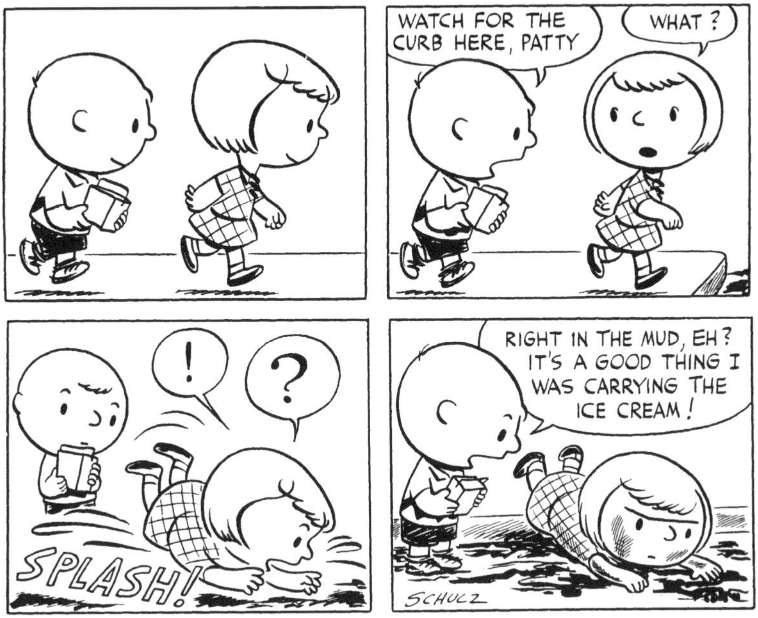
WATCH FOR THE CURB HERE, PATTY
WHAT ?
!
?
SPLASH!
RIGHT IN THE MUD, EH? IT'S A GOOD THING I WAS CARRYING THE ICE CREAM!
SCHULZ

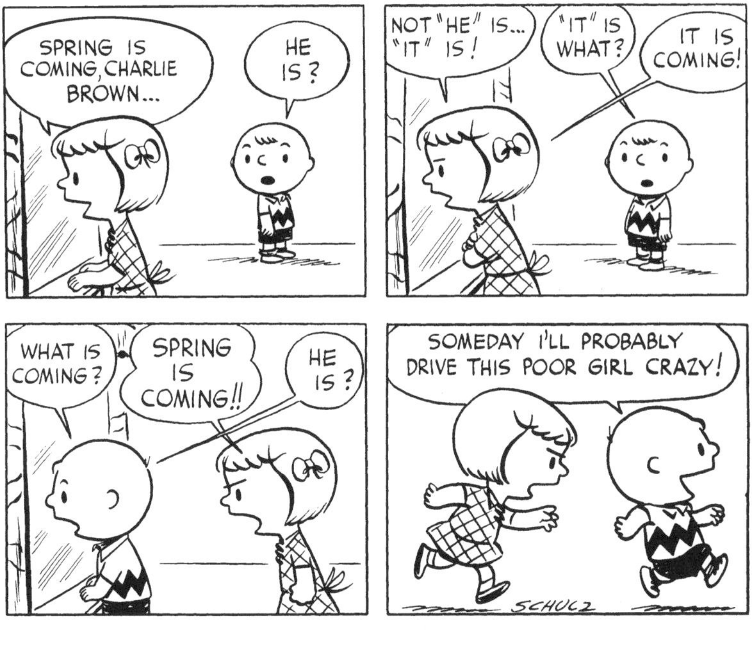
SPRING IS COMING, CHARLIE BROWN...
HE IS?
NOT "HE" IS... "IT" IS!
"IT" IS WHAT?
IT IS COMING!
WHAT IS COMING?
SPRING IS COMING!!
HE IS?
SOMEDAY I'LL PROBABLY DRIVE THIS POOR GIRL CRAZY!
SCHULZ

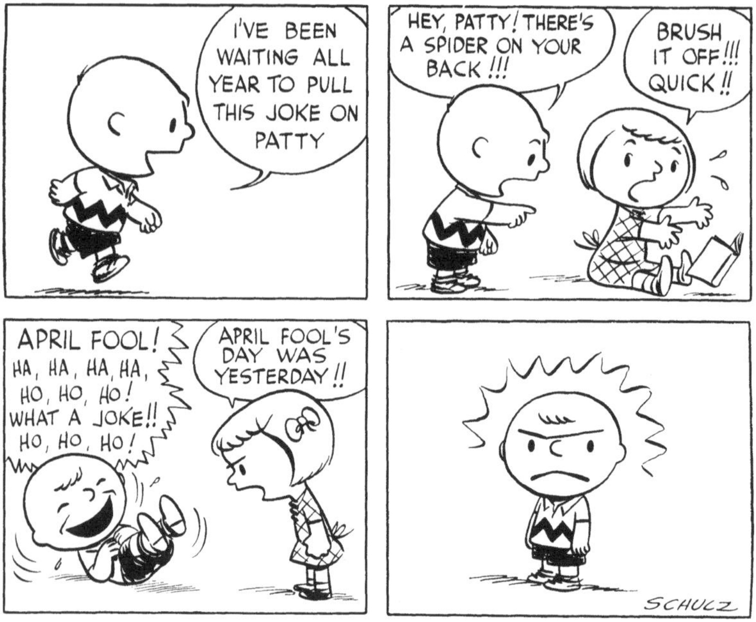
I'VE BEEN WAITING ALL YEAR TO PULL THIS JOKE ON PATTY
HEY, PATTY! THERE'S A SPIDER ON YOUR BACK!!!
BRUSH IT OFF!!! QUICK!!
APRIL FOOL! HA, HA, HA, HA, HO, HO, HO! WHAT A JOKE!! HO, HO, HO!
APRIL FOOL'S DAY WAS YESTERDAY!!
SCHULZ

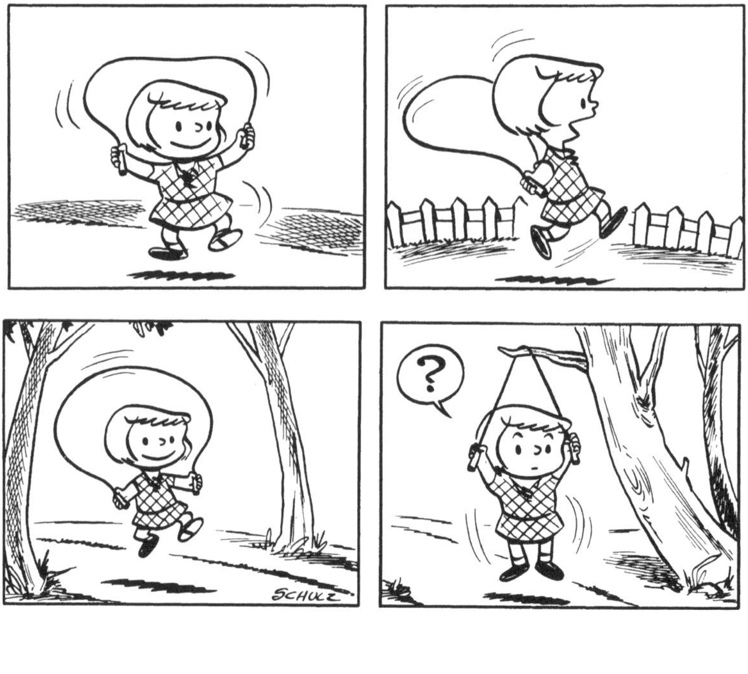
SCHULZ
?

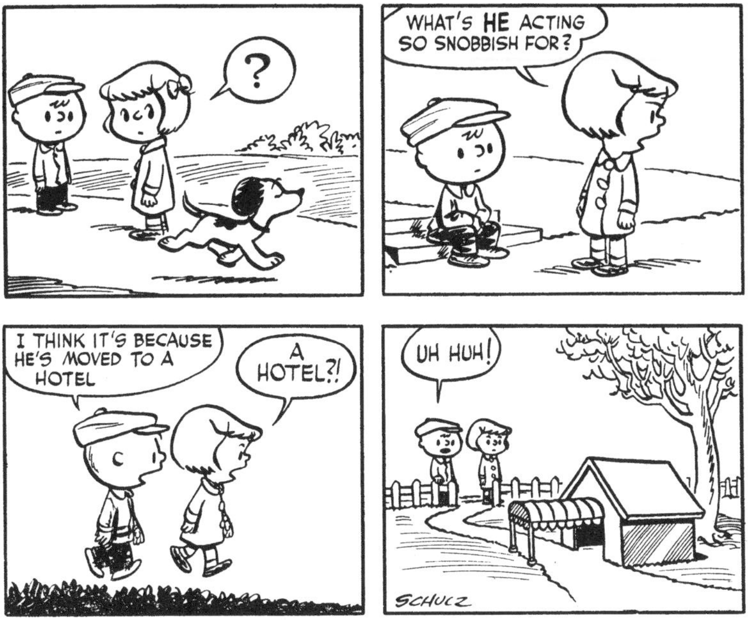
?
WHAT'S HE ACTING SO SNOBBISH FOR?
I THINK IT'S BECAUSE HE'S MOVED TO A HOTEL
A HOTEL?!
UH HUH!
SCHULZ

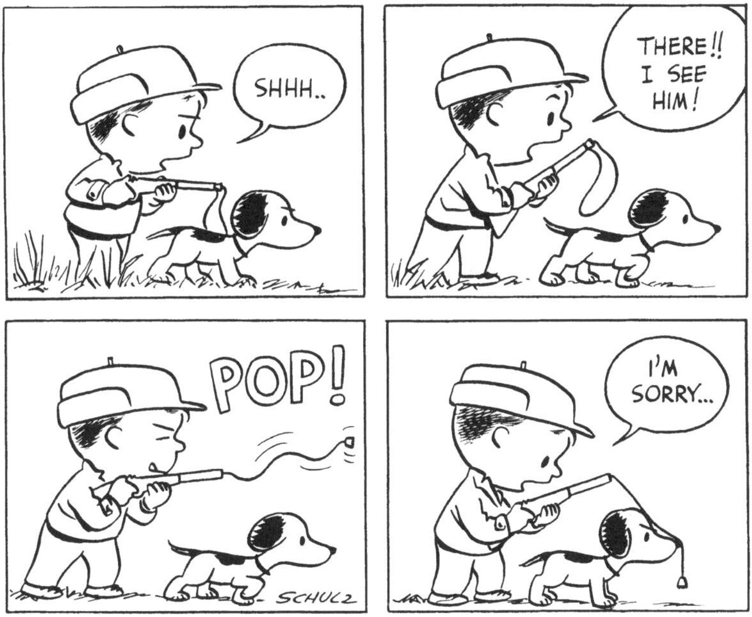
SHHH..
THERE!! I SEE HIM!
POP!
SCHULZ
I'M SORRY...

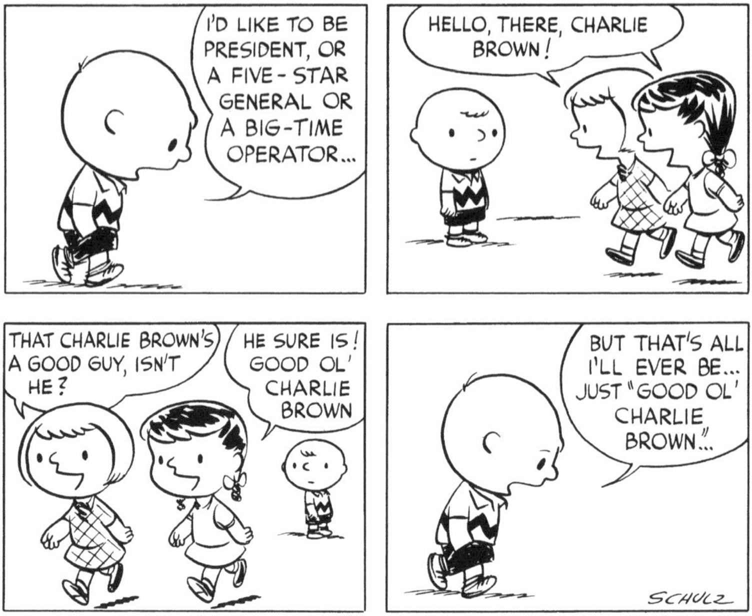
I'D LIKE TO BE PRESIDENT, OR A FIVE-STAR GENERAL OR A BIG-TIME OPERATOR...
HELLO, THERE, CHARLIE BROWN!
THAT CHARLIE BROWN'S A GOOD GUY, ISN'T HE?
HE SURE IS! GOOD OL' CHARLIE BROWN
BUT THAT'S ALL I'LL EVER BE... JUST "GOOD OL' CHARLIE BROWN."...
SCHULZ

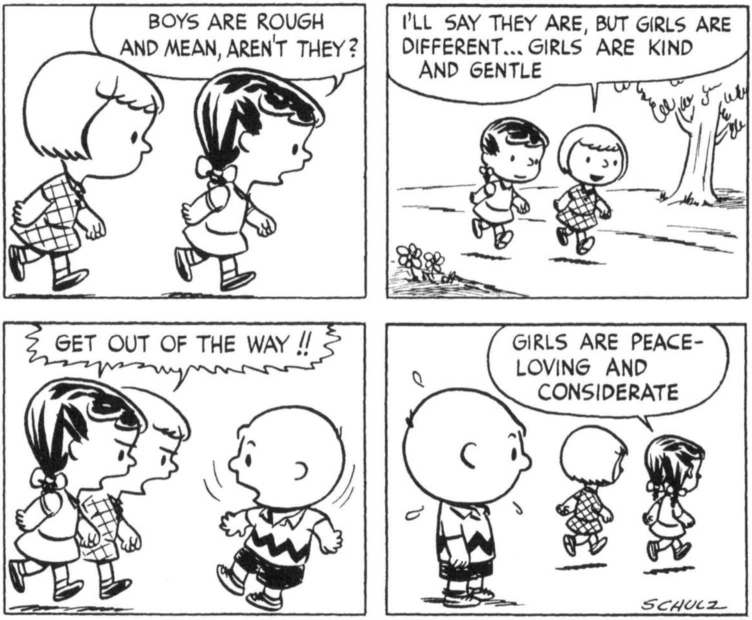
BOYS ARE ROUGH AND MEAN, AREN'T THEY?
I'LL SAY THEY ARE, BUT GIRLS ARE DIFFERENT... GIRLS ARE KIND AND GENTLE
GET OUT OF THE WAY!!
GIRLS ARE PEACE-LOVING AND CONSIDERATE
SCHULZ

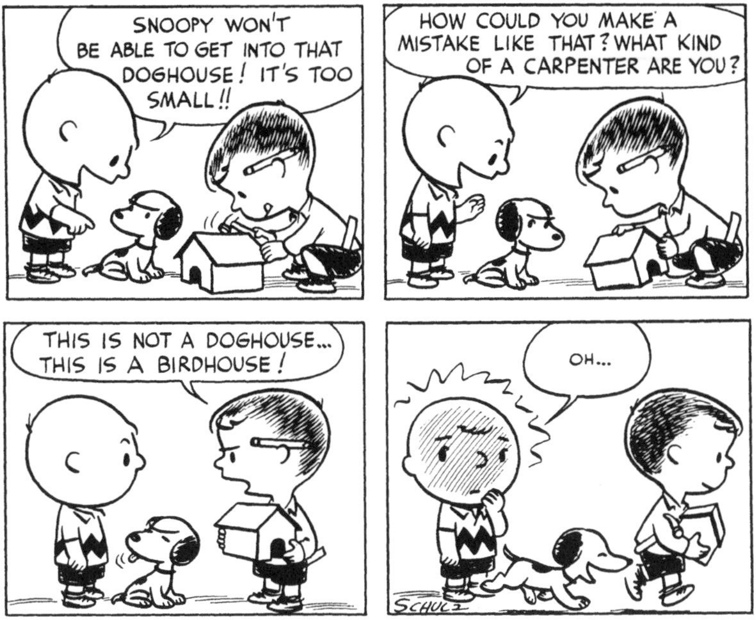
SNOOPY WON'T BE ABLE TO GET INTO THAT DOGHOUSE! IT'S TOO SMALL!!
HOW COULD YOU MAKE A MISTAKE LIKE THAT? WHAT KIND OF A CARPENTER ARE YOU?
THIS IS NOT A DOGHOUSE... THIS IS A BIRDHOUSE!
OH...
SCHULZ

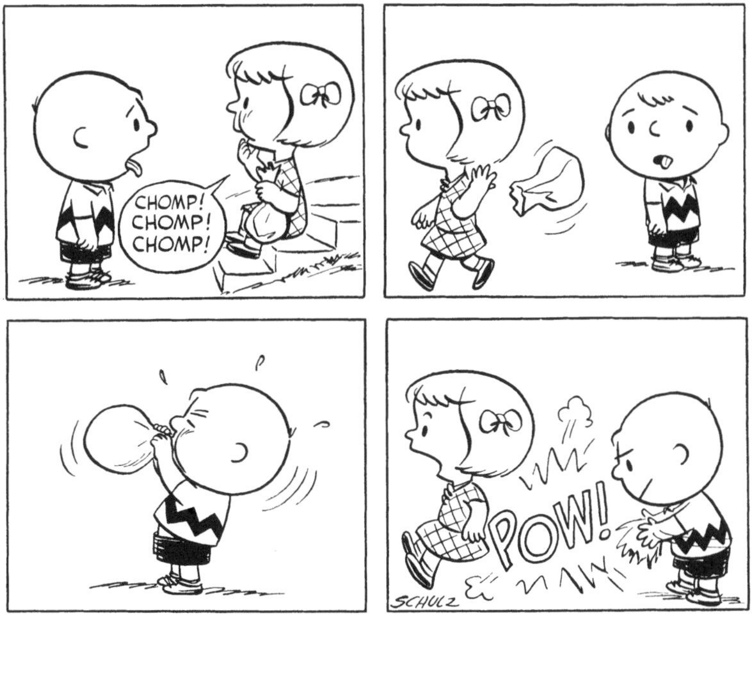
CHOMP! CHOMP! CHOMP!
POW!
SCHULZ

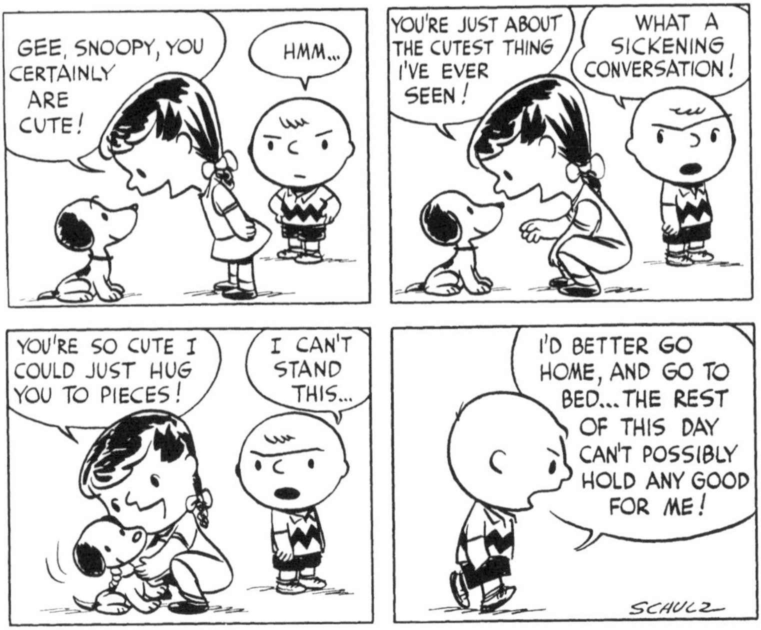
GEE, SNOOPY, YOU CERTAINLY ARE CUTE!
HMM...
YOU'RE JUST ABOUT THE CUTEST THING I'VE EVER SEEN!
WHAT A SICKENING CONVERSATION!
YOU'RE SO CUTE I COULD JUST HUG YOU TO PIECES!
I CAN'T STAND THIS...
I'D BETTER GO HOME, AND GO TO BED...THE REST OF THIS DAY CAN'T POSSIBLY HOLD ANY GOOD FOR ME!
SCHULZ

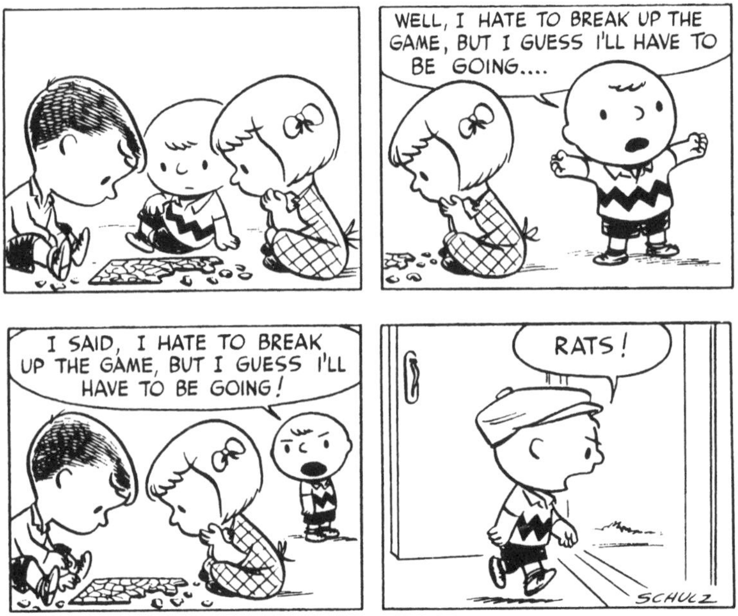
WELL, I HATE TO BREAK UP THE GAME, BUT I GUESS I'LL HAVE TO BE GOING....
I SAID, I HATE TO BREAK UP THE GAME, BUT I GUESS I'LL HAVE TO BE GOING!
RATS!
SCHULZ

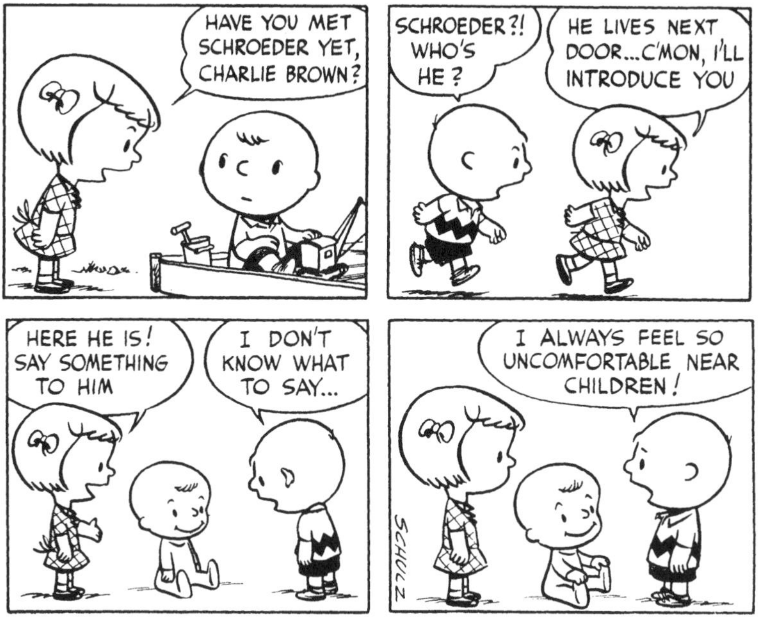
HAVE YOU MET SCHROEDER YET, CHARLIE BROWN?
SCHROEDER?! WHO'S HE?
HE LIVES NEXT DOOR...C'MON, I'LL INTRODUCE YOU
HERE HE IS! SAY SOMETHING TO HIM
I DON'T KNOW WHAT TO SAY...
I ALWAYS FEEL SO UNCOMFORTABLE NEAR CHILDREN!
SCHULZ

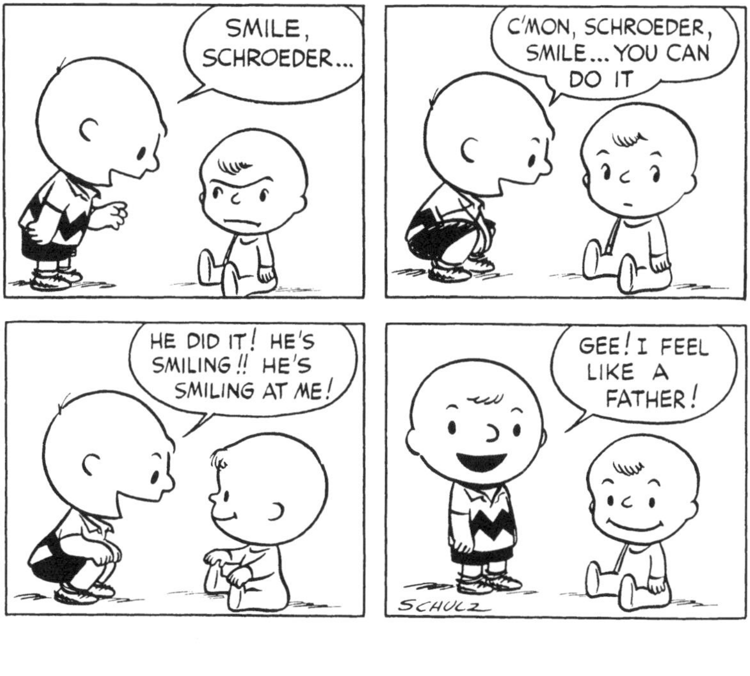
SMILE, SCHROEDER...
C'MON, SCHROEDER, SMILE...YOU CAN DO IT
HE DID IT! HE'S SMILING!! HE'S SMILING AT ME!
GEE! I FEEL LIKE A FATHER!
SCHULZ

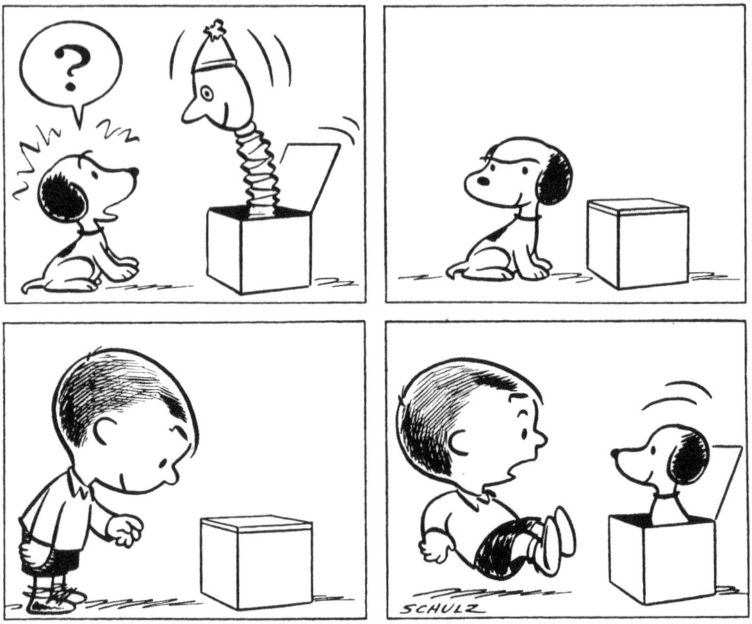
?
SCHULZ

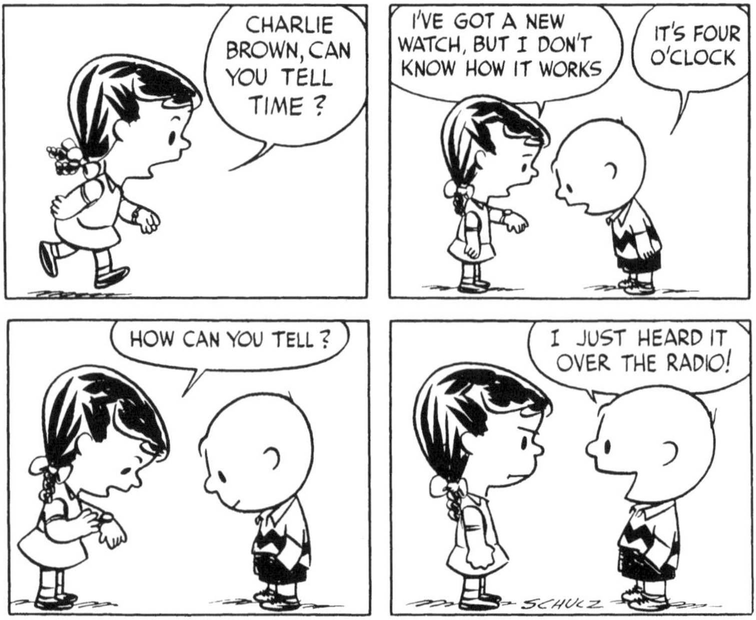
CHARLIE BROWN, CAN YOU TELL TIME ?
I'VE GOT A NEW WATCH, BUT I DON'T KNOW HOW IT WORKS
IT'S FOUR O'CLOCK
HOW CAN YOU TELL ?
I JUST HEARD IT OVER THE RADIO!
SCHULZ

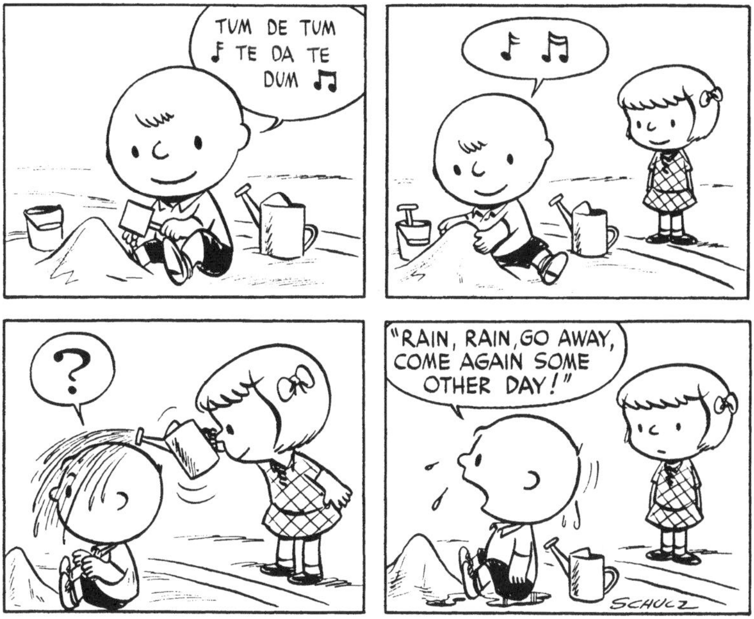
TUM DE TUM ♪ TE DA TE DUM ♫
?
"RAIN, RAIN, GO AWAY, COME AGAIN SOME OTHER DAY!"
SCHULZ

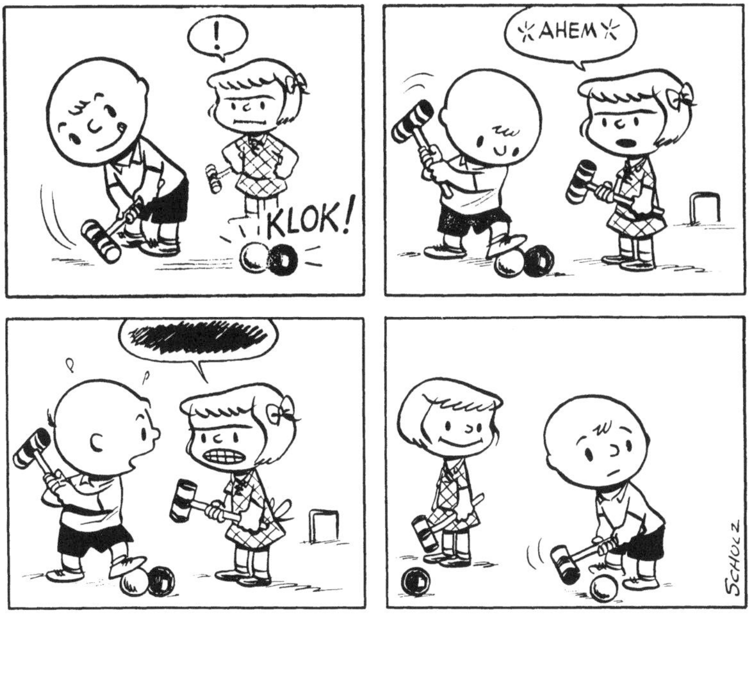
!
KLOK!
AHEM
SCHULZ

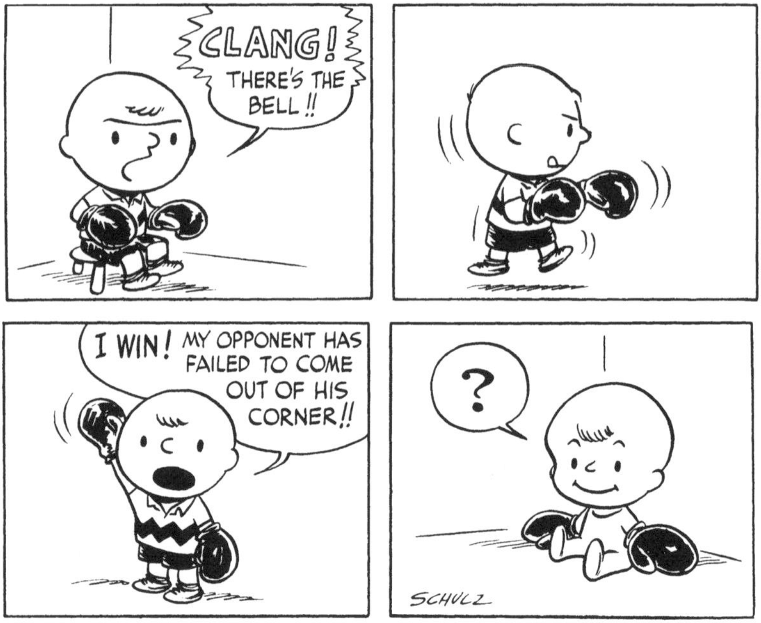
CLANG!
THERE'S THE BELL!!
I WIN! MY OPPONENT HAS FAILED TO COME OUT OF HIS CORNER!!
?
SCHULZ

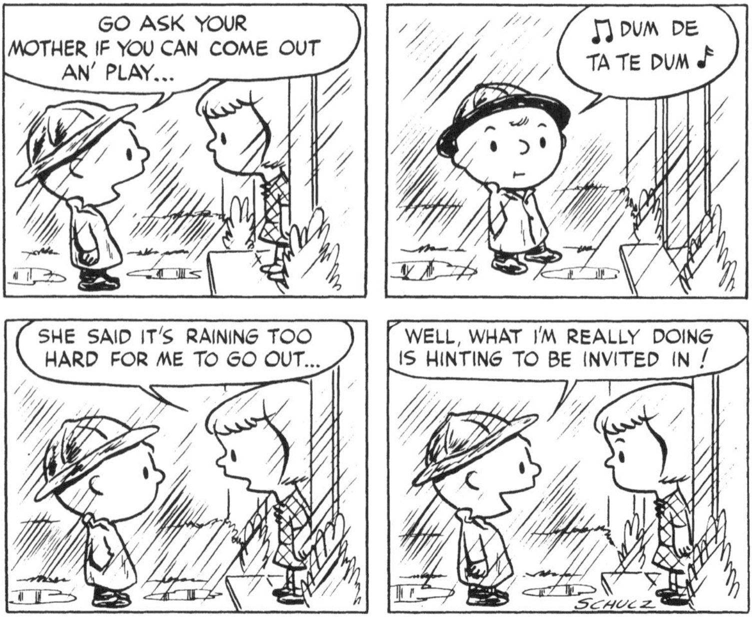
GO ASK YOUR MOTHER IF YOU CAN COME OUT AN' PLAY...
DUM DE TA TE DUM
SHE SAID IT'S RAINING TOO HARD FOR ME TO GO OUT...
WELL, WHAT I'M REALLY DOING IS HINTING TO BE INVITED IN!
SCHULZ

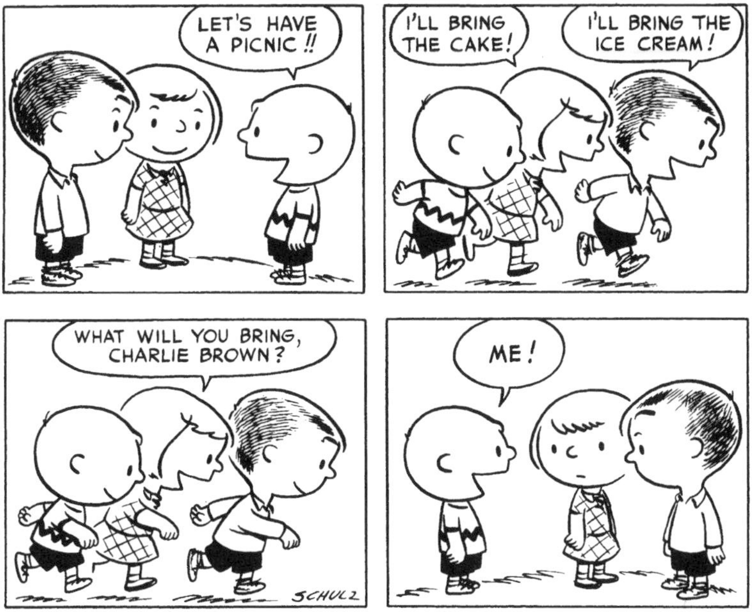
LET'S HAVE A PICNIC !!
I'LL BRING THE CAKE!
I'LL BRING THE ICE CREAM!
WHAT WILL YOU BRING, CHARLIE BROWN?
ME!
SCHULZ

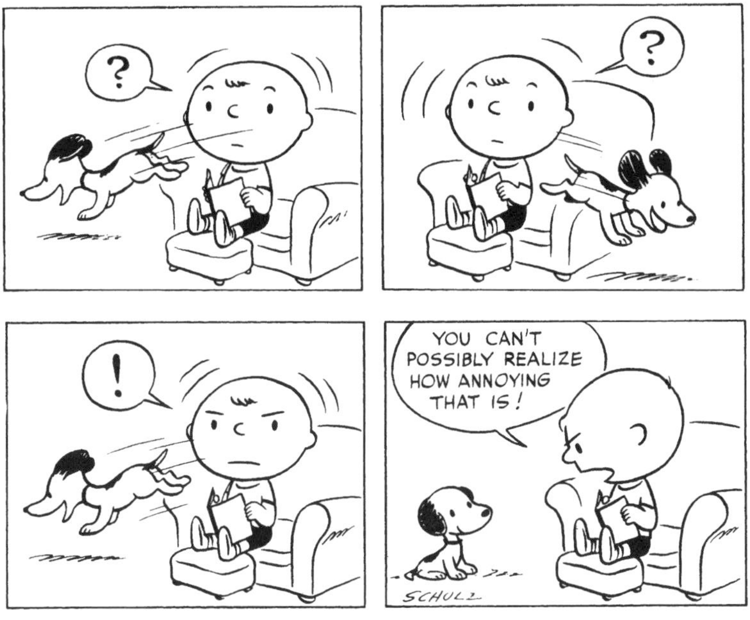
?
?
!
YOU CAN'T POSSIBLY REALIZE HOW ANNOYING THAT IS!
SCHULZ

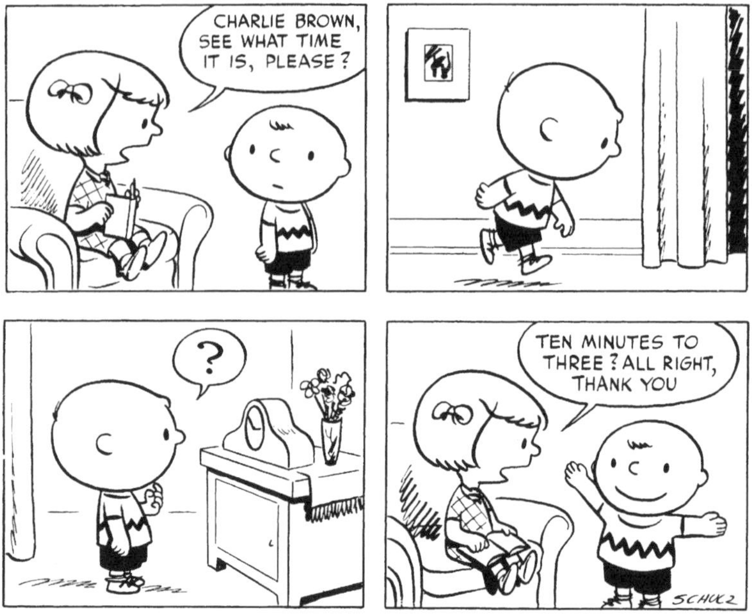
CHARLIE BROWN, SEE WHAT TIME IT IS, PLEASE?
?
TEN MINUTES TO THREE? ALL RIGHT, THANK YOU
SCHULZ

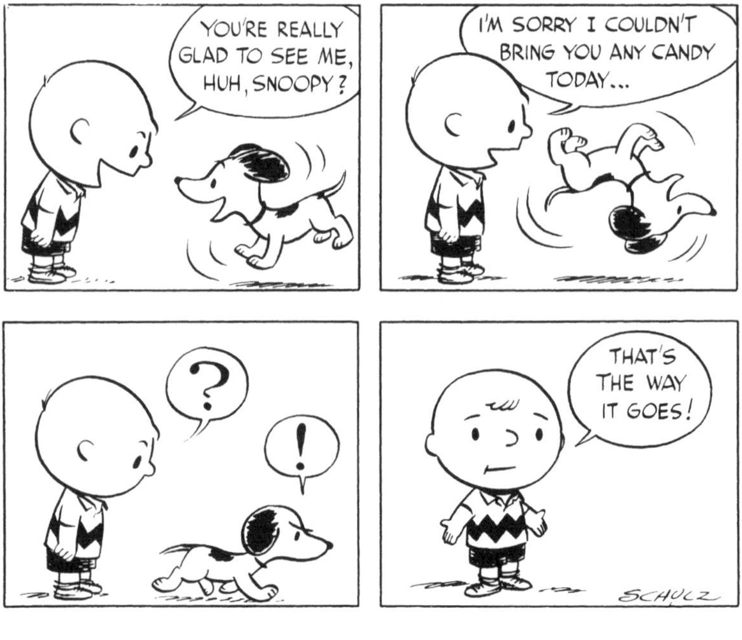
YOU'RE REALLY GLAD TO SEE ME, HUH, SNOOPY?
I'M SORRY I COULDN'T BRING YOU ANY CANDY TODAY...
?
!
THAT'S THE WAY IT GOES!
SCHULZ

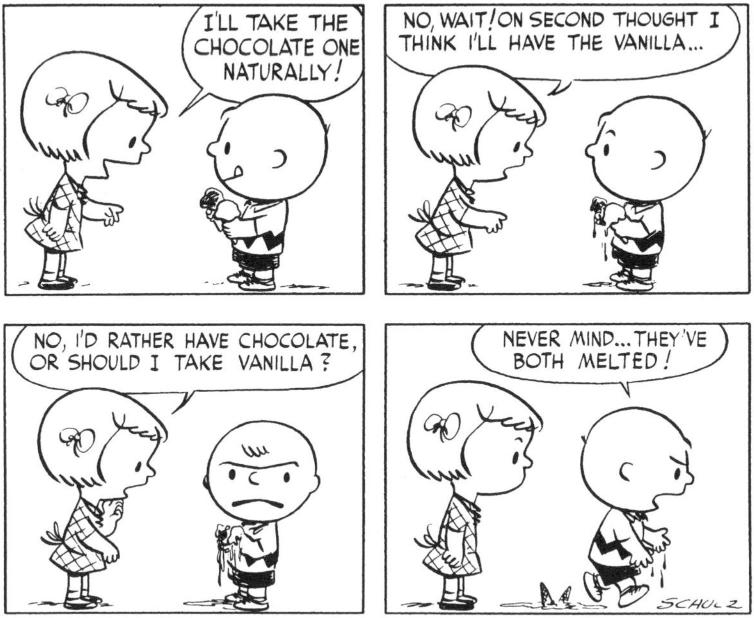
I'LL TAKE THE CHOCOLATE ONE NATURALLY!
NO, WAIT! ON SECOND THOUGHT I THINK I'LL HAVE THE VANILLA...
NO, I'D RATHER HAVE CHOCOLATE, OR SHOULD I TAKE VANILLA?
NEVER MIND...THEY'VE BOTH MELTED!
SCHULZ

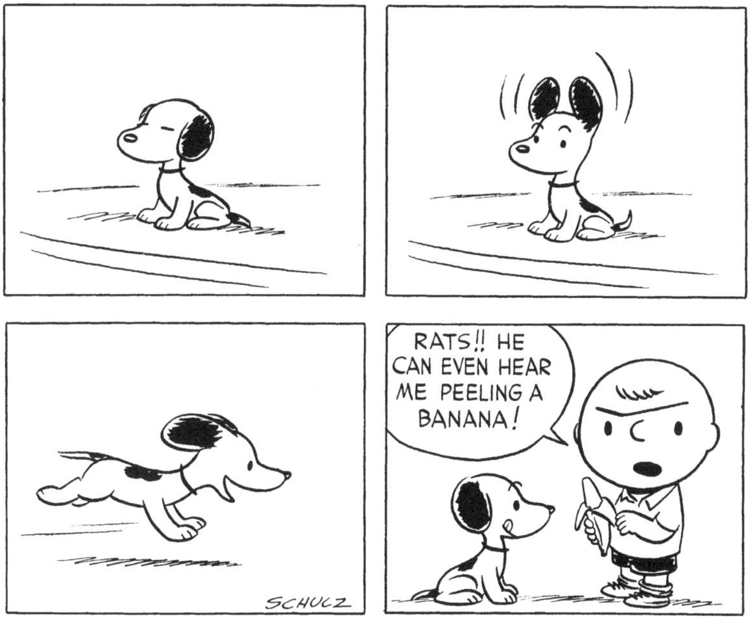
SCHULZ
RATS!! HE CAN EVEN HEAR ME PEELING A BANANA!

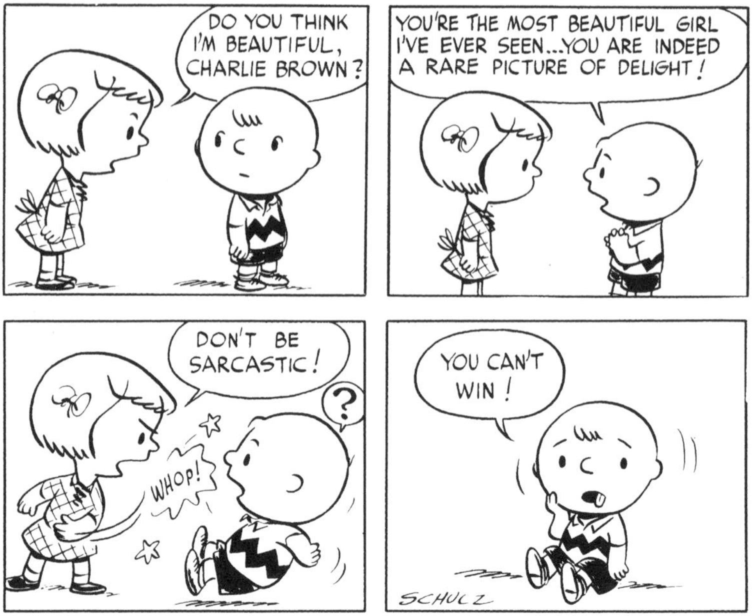
DO YOU THINK I'M BEAUTIFUL, CHARLIE BROWN?
YOU'RE THE MOST BEAUTIFUL GIRL I'VE EVER SEEN...YOU ARE INDEED A RARE PICTURE OF DELIGHT!
DON'T BE SARCASTIC!
?
WHOP!
YOU CAN'T WIN!
SCHULZ

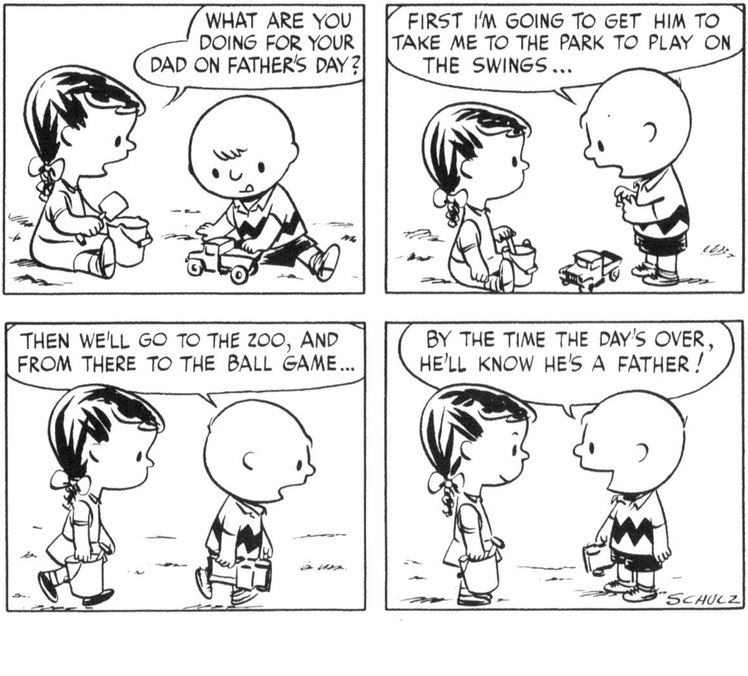
WHAT ARE YOU DOING FOR YOUR DAD ON FATHER'S DAY?
FIRST I'M GOING TO GET HIM TO TAKE ME TO THE PARK TO PLAY ON THE SWINGS...
THEN WE'LL GO TO THE ZOO, AND FROM THERE TO THE BALL GAME...
BY THE TIME THE DAY'S OVER, HE'LL KNOW HE'S A FATHER!
SCHULZ

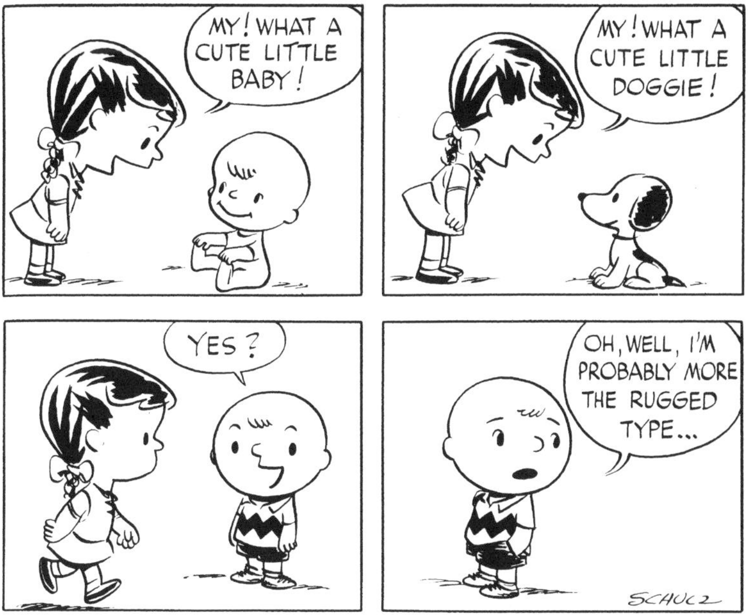
MY! WHAT A CUTE LITTLE BABY!
MY! WHAT A CUTE LITTLE DOGGIE!
YES?
OH, WELL, I'M PROBABLY MORE THE RUGGED TYPE...
SCHULZ

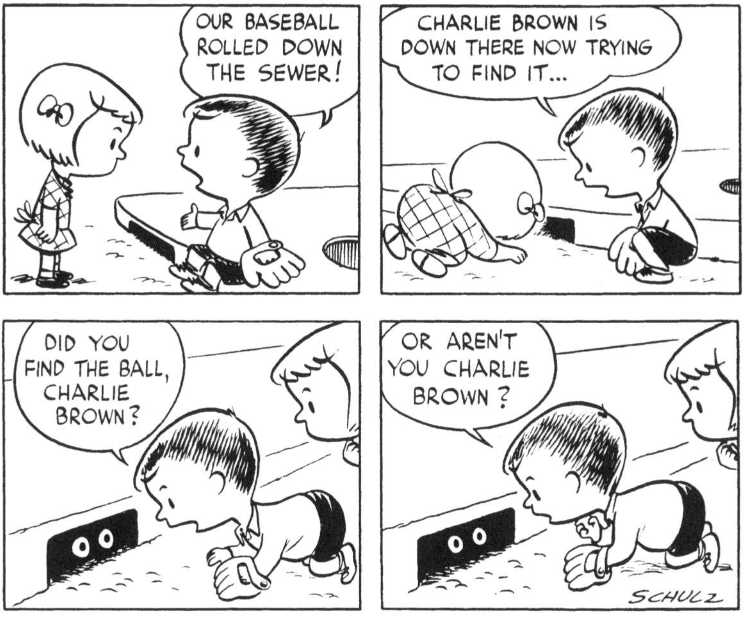
OUR BASEBALL ROLLED DOWN THE SEWER!
CHARLIE BROWN IS DOWN THERE NOW TRYING TO FIND IT...
DID YOU FIND THE BALL, CHARLIE BROWN?
OR AREN'T YOU CHARLIE BROWN?
SCHULZ

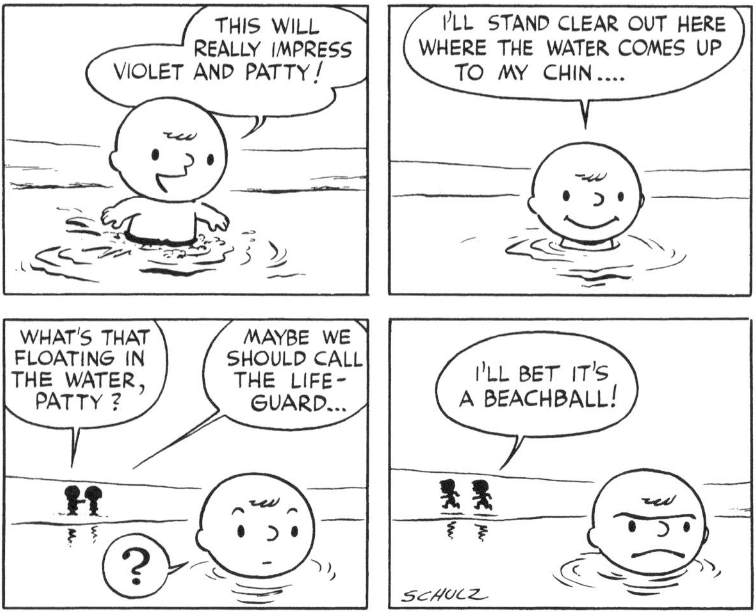
THIS WILL REALLY IMPRESS VIOLET AND PATTY!
I'LL STAND CLEAR OUT HERE WHERE THE WATER COMES UP TO MY CHIN....
WHAT'S THAT FLOATING IN THE WATER, PATTY?
MAYBE WE SHOULD CALL THE LIFE-GUARD...
?
I'LL BET IT'S A BEACHBALL!
SCHULZ

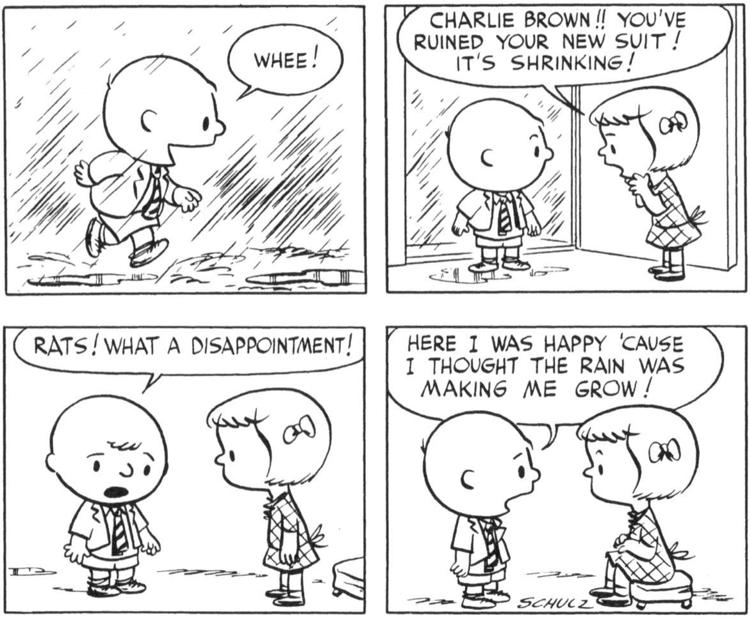
WHEE!
CHARLIE BROWN!! YOU'VE RUINED YOUR NEW SUIT! IT'S SHRINKING!
RATS! WHAT A DISAPPOINTMENT!
HERE I WAS HAPPY 'CAUSE I THOUGHT THE RAIN WAS MAKING ME GROW!
SCHULZ

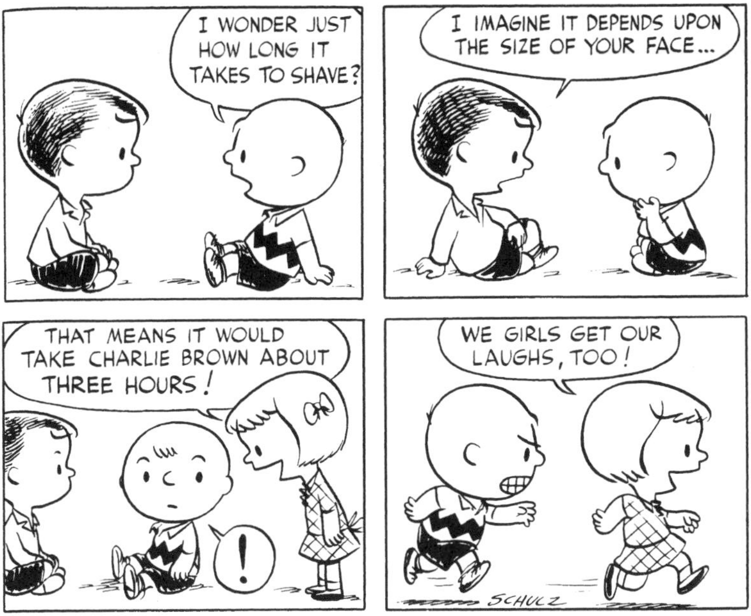
I WONDER JUST HOW LONG IT TAKES TO SHAVE?
I IMAGINE IT DEPENDS UPON THE SIZE OF YOUR FACE...
THAT MEANS IT WOULD TAKE CHARLIE BROWN ABOUT THREE HOURS!
!
WE GIRLS GET OUR LAUGHS, TOO!
SCHULZ

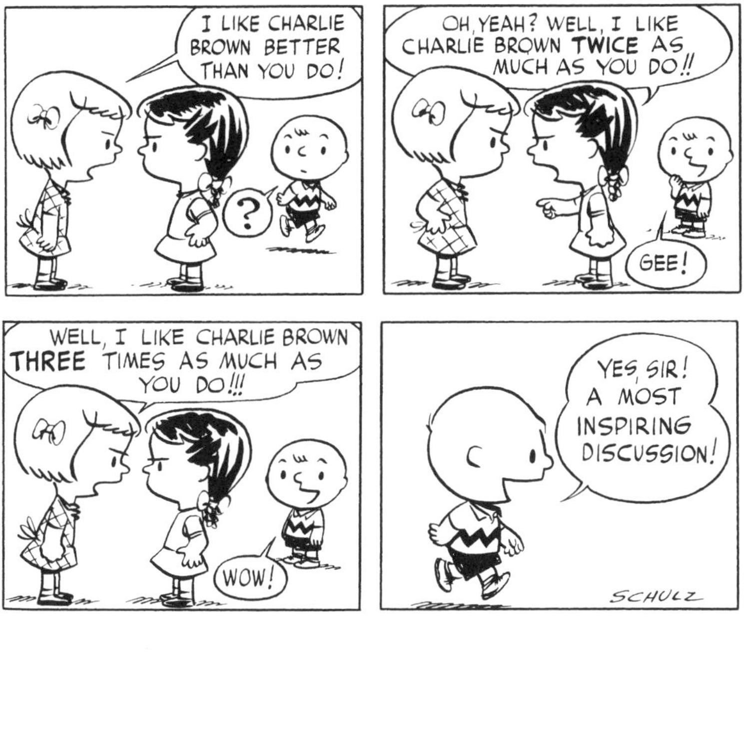
I LIKE CHARLIE BROWN BETTER THAN YOU DO!
?
OH, YEAH? WELL, I LIKE CHARLIE BROWN TWICE AS MUCH AS YOU DO!!
GEE!
WELL, I LIKE CHARLIE BROWN THREE TIMES AS MUCH AS YOU DO!!!
WOW!
YES, SIR! A MOST INSPIRING DISCUSSION!
SCHULZ

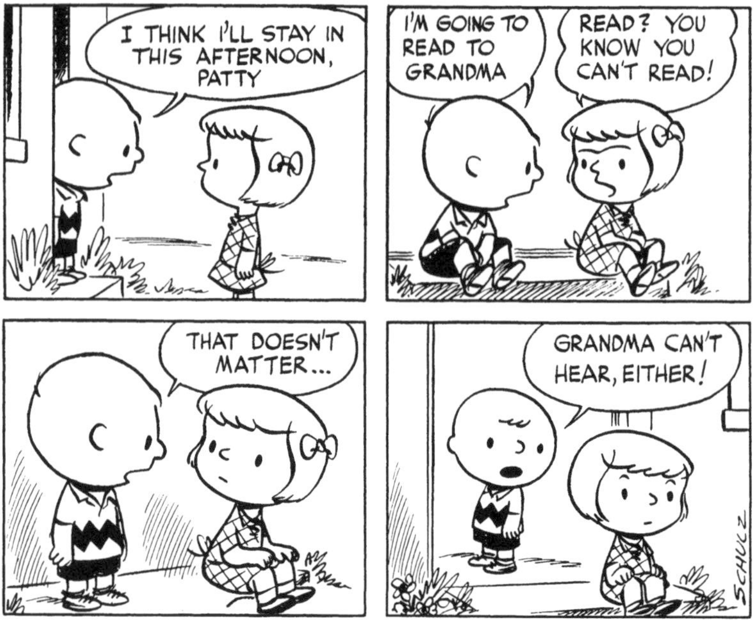
I THINK I'LL STAY IN THIS AFTERNOON, PATTY
I'M GOING TO READ TO GRANDMA
READ? YOU KNOW YOU CAN'T READ!
THAT DOESN'T MATTER...
GRANDMA CAN'T HEAR, EITHER!
SCHULZ

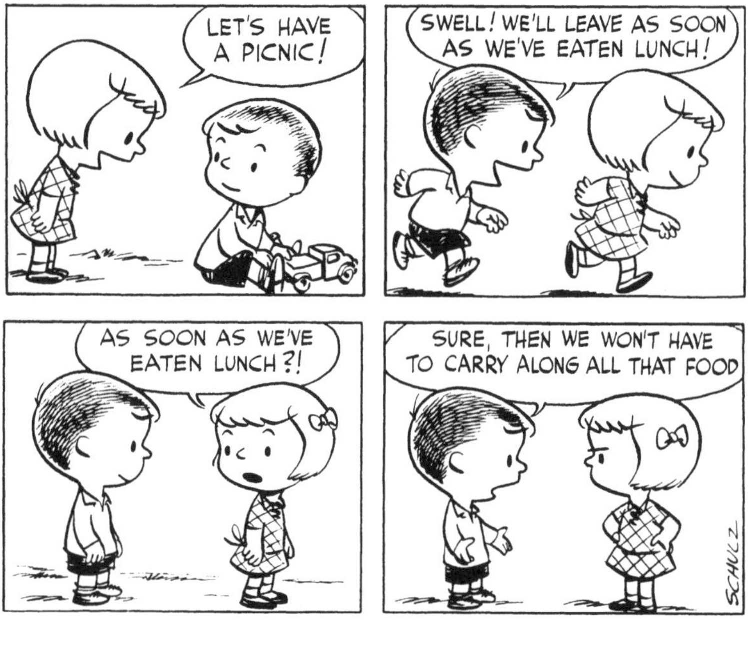
LET'S HAVE A PICNIC!
SWELL! WE'LL LEAVE AS SOON AS WE'VE EATEN LUNCH!
AS SOON AS WE'VE EATEN LUNCH?!
SURE, THEN WE WON'T HAVE TO CARRY ALONG ALL THAT FOOD
SCHULZ

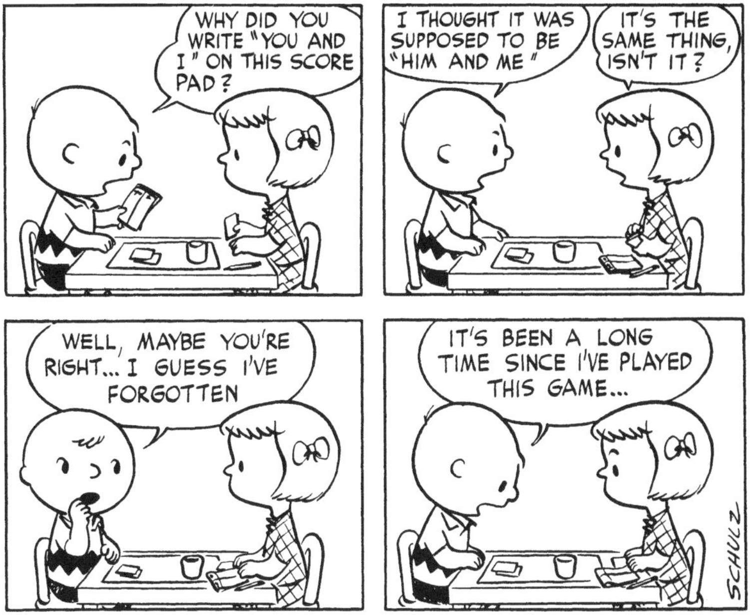
WHY DID YOU WRITE "YOU AND I" ON THIS SCORE PAD?
I THOUGHT IT WAS SUPPOSED TO BE "HIM AND ME"
IT'S THE SAME THING, ISN'T IT?
WELL, MAYBE YOU'RE RIGHT... I GUESS I'VE FORGOTTEN
IT'S BEEN A LONG TIME SINCE I'VE PLAYED THIS GAME...
SCHULZ

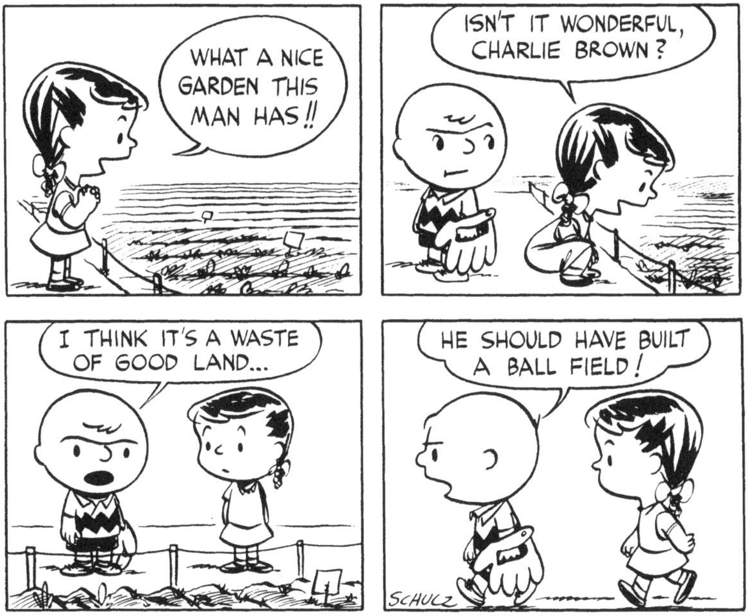
WHAT A NICE GARDEN THIS MAN HAS!!
ISN'T IT WONDERFUL, CHARLIE BROWN?
I THINK IT'S A WASTE OF GOOD LAND...
HE SHOULD HAVE BUILT A BALL FIELD!
SCHULZ

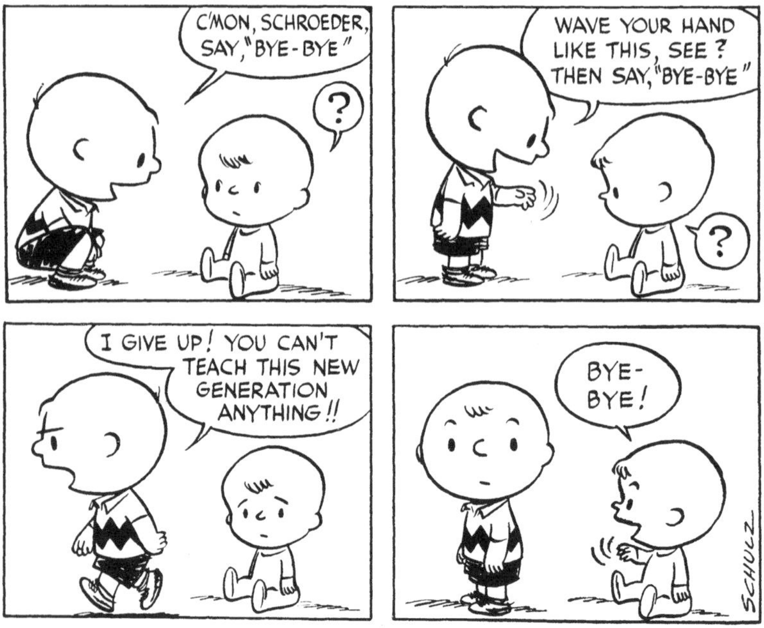
C'MON, SCHROEDER, SAY, "BYE-BYE"
?
WAVE YOUR HAND LIKE THIS, SEE? THEN SAY, "BYE-BYE"
?
I GIVE UP! YOU CAN'T TEACH THIS NEW GENERATION ANYTHING!!
BYE-BYE!
SCHULZ

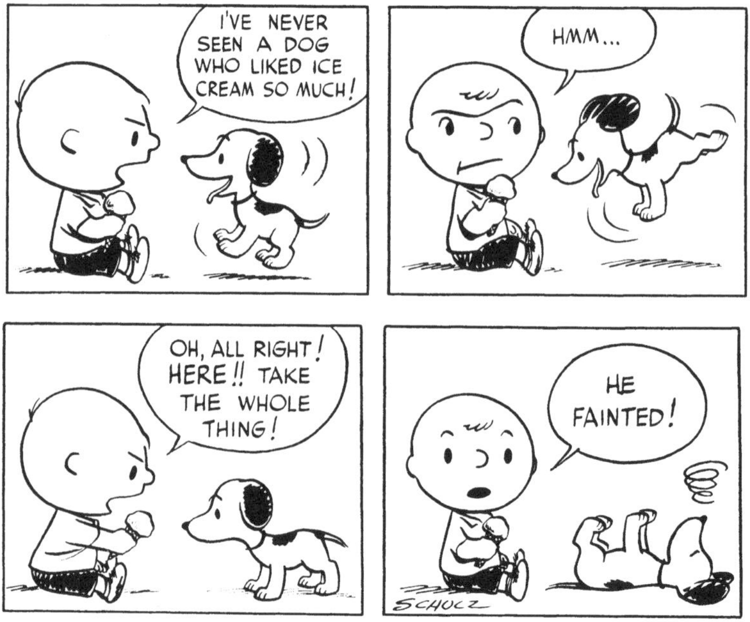
I'VE NEVER SEEN A DOG WHO LIKED ICE CREAM SO MUCH!
HMM...
OH, ALL RIGHT! HERE!! TAKE THE WHOLE THING!
HE FAINTED!
SCHULZ

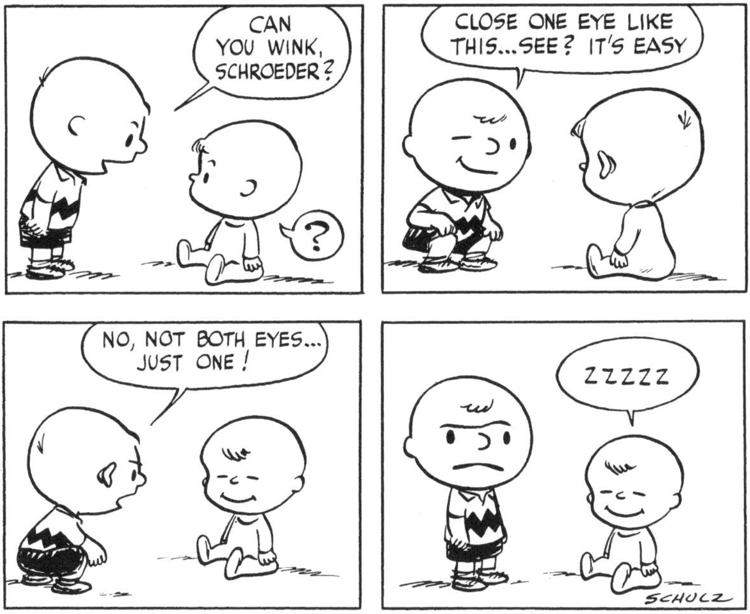
CAN YOU WINK, SCHROEDER?
?
CLOSE ONE EYE LIKE THIS...SEE? IT'S EASY
NO, NOT BOTH EYES... JUST ONE!
ZZZZZ
SCHULZ

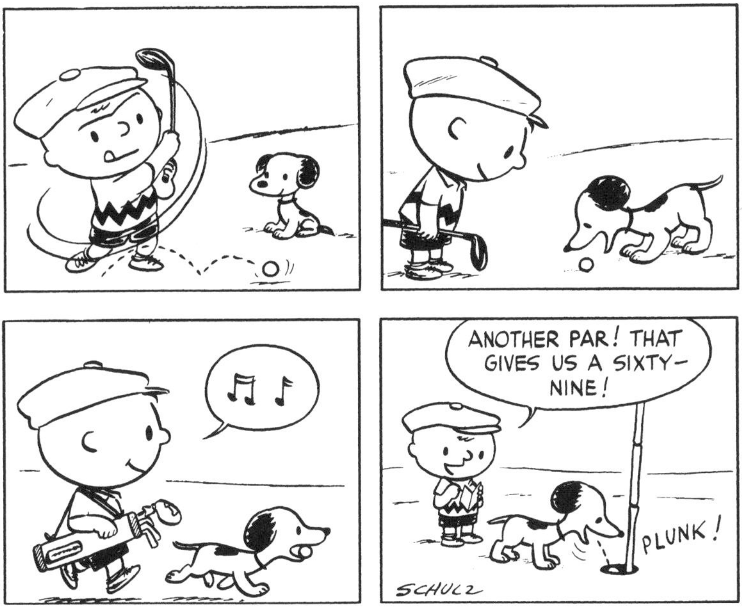
ANOTHER PAR! THAT GIVES US A SIXTY-NINE!
PLUNK!
SCHULZ

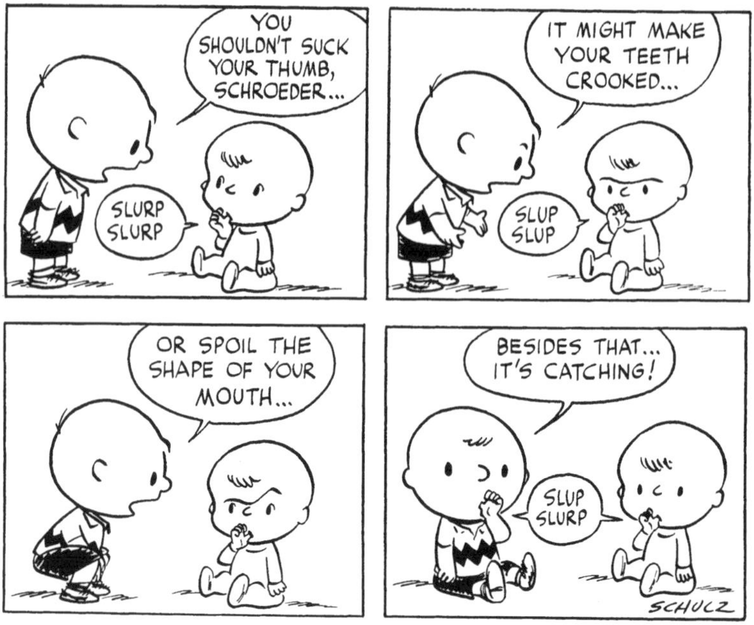
YOU SHOULDN'T SUCK YOUR THUMB, SCHROEDER...
SLURP SLURP
IT MIGHT MAKE YOUR TEETH CROOKED...
SLUP SLUP
OR SPOIL THE SHAPE OF YOUR MOUTH...
BESIDES THAT... IT'S CATCHING!
SLUP SLURP
SCHULZ

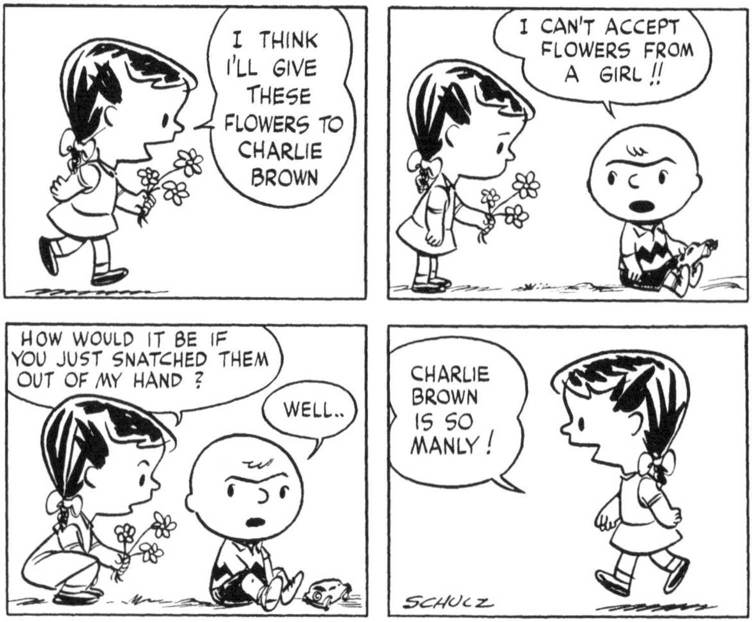
I THINK I'LL GIVE THESE FLOWERS TO CHARLIE BROWN
I CAN'T ACCEPT FLOWERS FROM A GIRL!!
HOW WOULD IT BE IF YOU JUST SNATCHED THEM OUT OF MY HAND ?
WELL..
CHARLIE BROWN IS SO MANLY!
SCHULZ

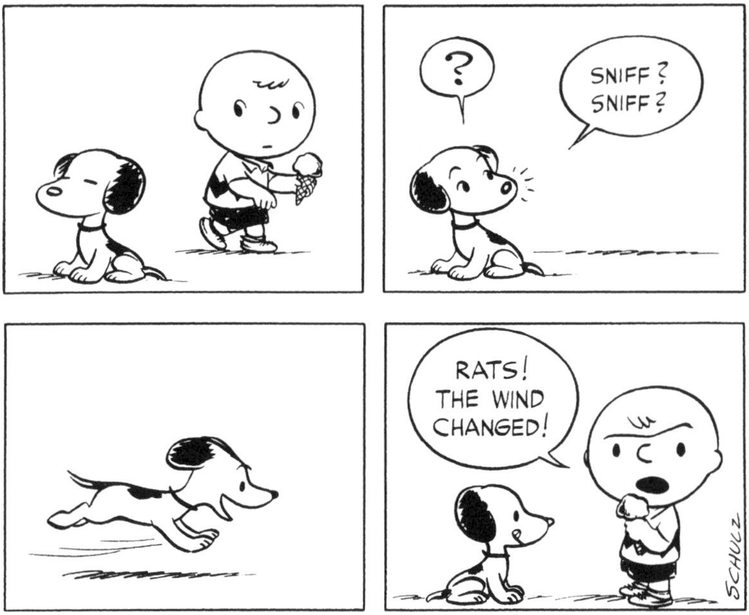
?
SNIFF? SNIFF?
RATS! THE WIND CHANGED!
SCHULZ

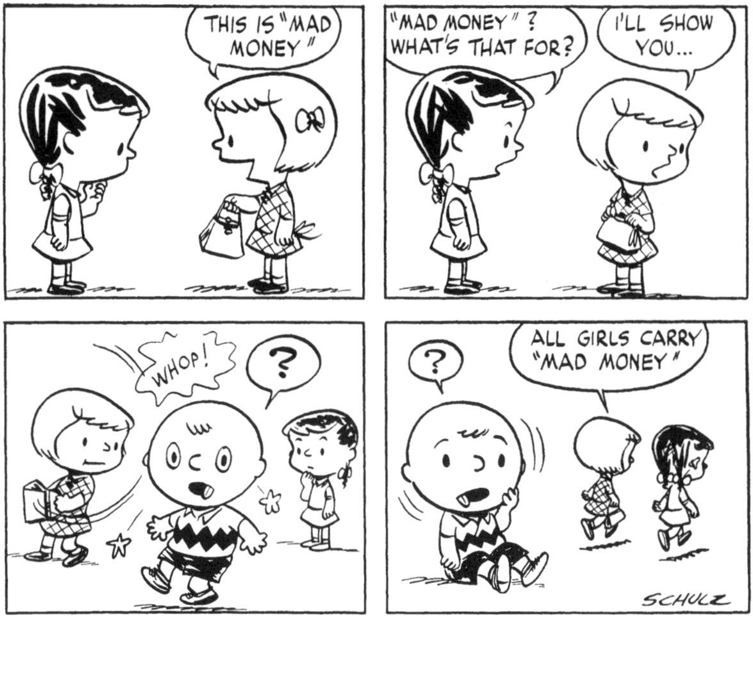
THIS IS "MAD MONEY"
"MAD MONEY"? WHAT'S THAT FOR?
I'LL SHOW YOU...
WHOP!
?
?
ALL GIRLS CARRY "MAD MONEY"
SCHULZ

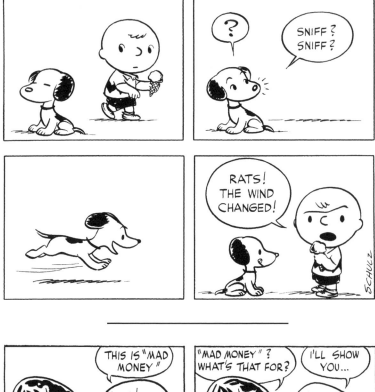

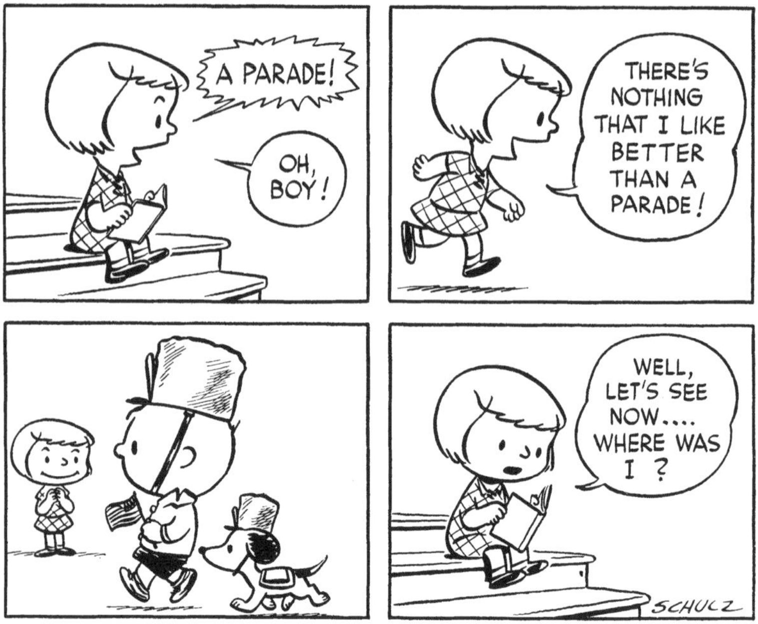
A PARADE!
OH, BOY!
THERE'S NOTHING THAT I LIKE BETTER THAN A PARADE!
WELL, LET'S SEE NOW.... WHERE WAS I ?
SCHULZ

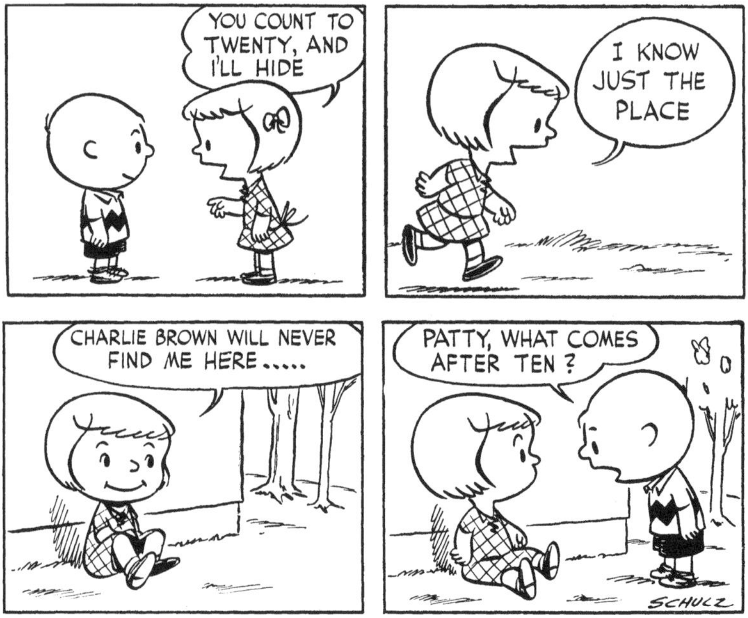
YOU COUNT TO TWENTY, AND I'LL HIDE
I KNOW JUST THE PLACE
CHARLIE BROWN WILL NEVER FIND ME HERE.....
PATTY, WHAT COMES AFTER TEN ?
SCHULZ

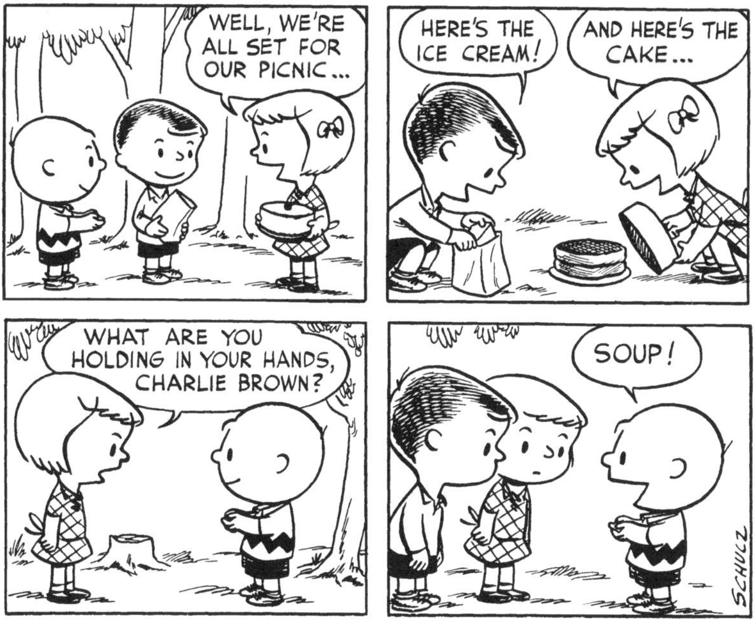
WELL, WE'RE ALL SET FOR OUR PICNIC...
HERE'S THE ICE CREAM!
AND HERE'S THE CAKE...
WHAT ARE YOU HOLDING IN YOUR HANDS, CHARLIE BROWN?
SOUP!
SCHULZ

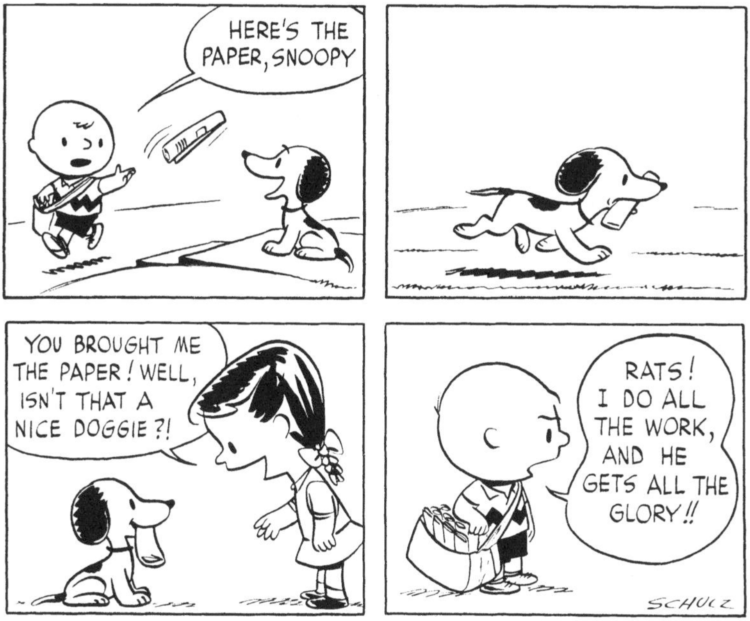
HERE'S THE PAPER, SNOOPY
YOU BROUGHT ME THE PAPER! WELL, ISN'T THAT A NICE DOGGIE?!
RATS! I DO ALL THE WORK, AND HE GETS ALL THE GLORY!!
SCHULZ

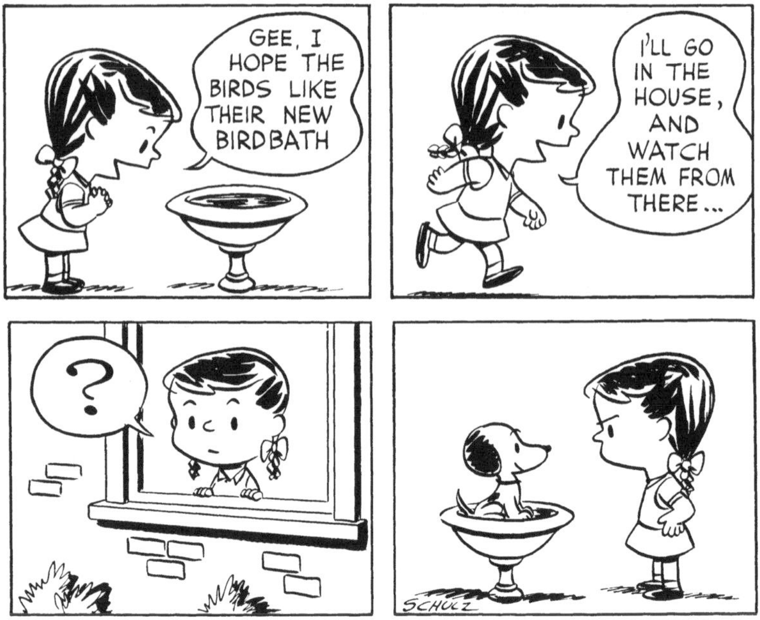
GEE, I HOPE THE BIRDS LIKE THEIR NEW BIRDBATH
I'LL GO IN THE HOUSE, AND WATCH THEM FROM THERE...
?
SCHULZ

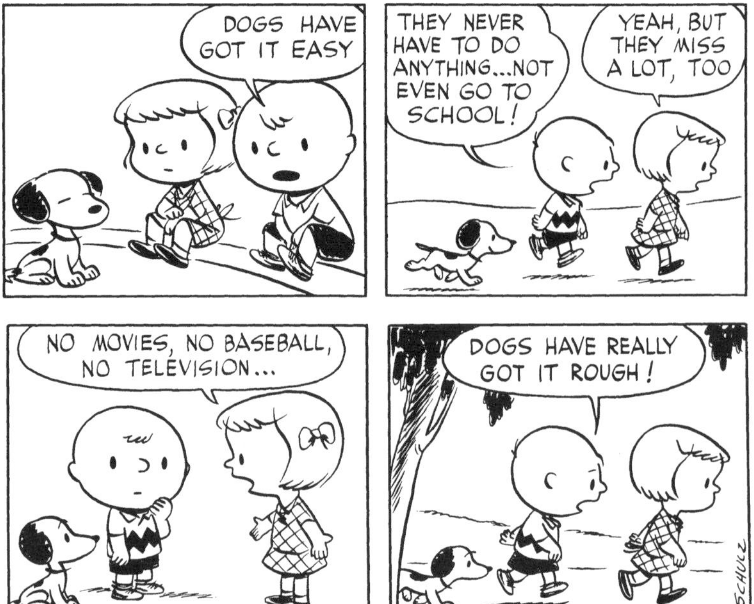
DOGS HAVE GOT IT EASY
THEY NEVER HAVE TO DO ANYTHING...NOT EVEN GO TO SCHOOL!
YEAH, BUT THEY MISS A LOT, TOO
NO MOVIES, NO BASEBALL, NO TELEVISION...
DOGS HAVE REALLY GOT IT ROUGH!
SCHULZ

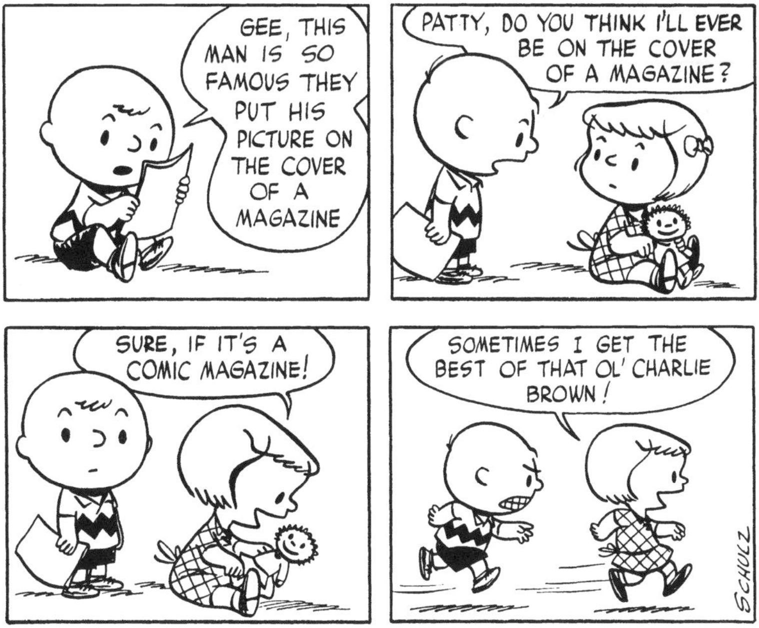
GEE, THIS MAN IS SO FAMOUS THEY PUT HIS PICTURE ON THE COVER OF A MAGAZINE
PATTY, DO YOU THINK I'LL EVER BE ON THE COVER OF A MAGAZINE?
SURE, IF IT'S A COMIC MAGAZINE!
SOMETIMES I GET THE BEST OF THAT OL' CHARLIE BROWN!
SCHULZ

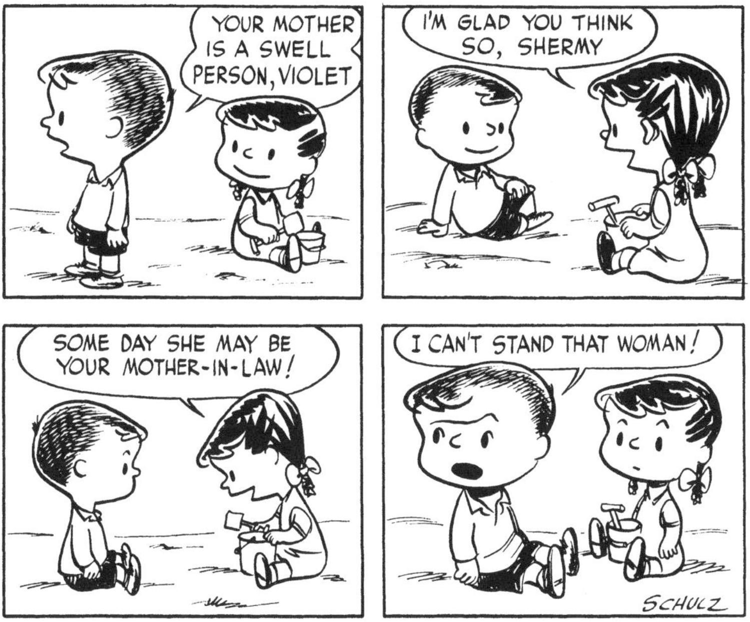
YOUR MOTHER IS A SWELL PERSON, VIOLET
I'M GLAD YOU THINK SO, SHERMY
SOME DAY SHE MAY BE YOUR MOTHER-IN-LAW!
I CAN'T STAND THAT WOMAN!
SCHULZ

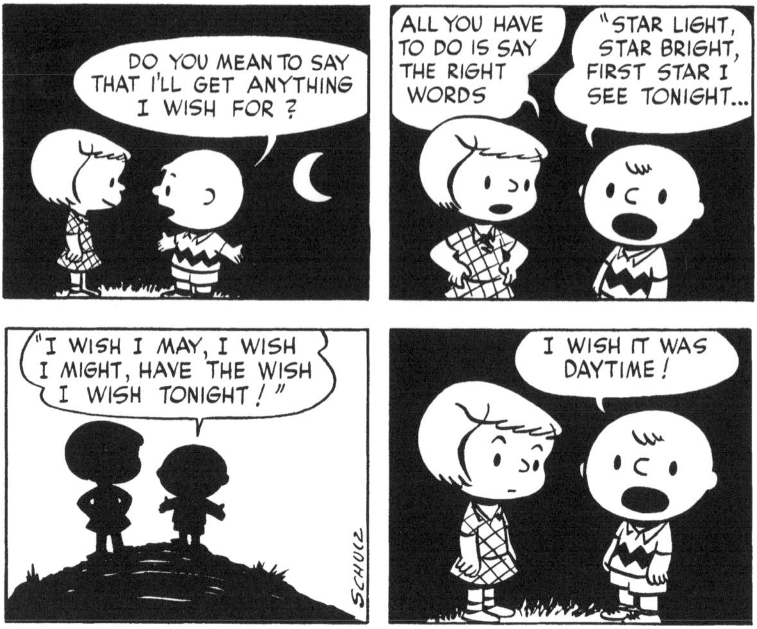
DO YOU MEAN TO SAY THAT I'LL GET ANYTHING I WISH FOR ?
ALL YOU HAVE TO DO IS SAY THE RIGHT WORDS
"STAR LIGHT, STAR BRIGHT, FIRST STAR I SEE TONIGHT...
"I WISH I MAY, I WISH I MIGHT, HAVE THE WISH I WISH TONIGHT!"
SCHULZ
I WISH IT WAS DAYTIME!

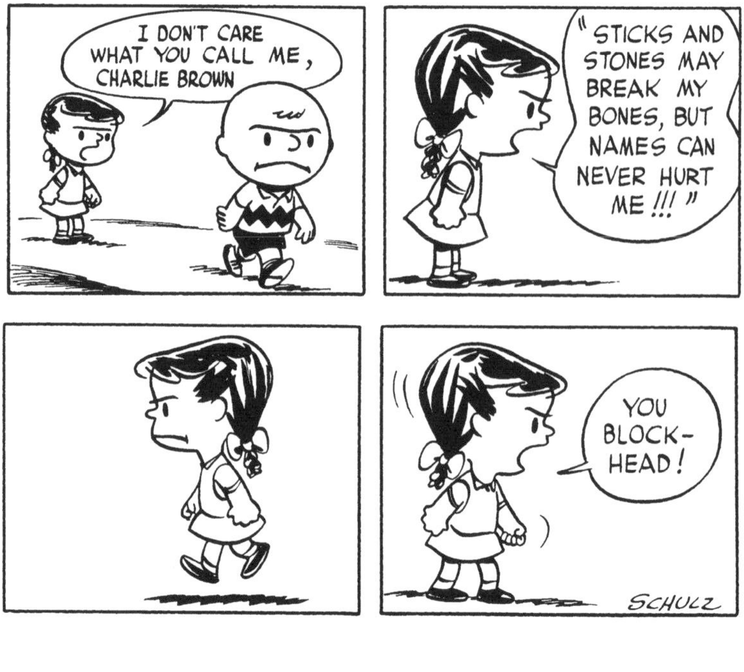
I DON'T CARE WHAT YOU CALL ME, CHARLIE BROWN
"STICKS AND STONES MAY BREAK MY BONES, BUT NAMES CAN NEVER HURT ME!!!"
YOU BLOCK-HEAD!
SCHULZ

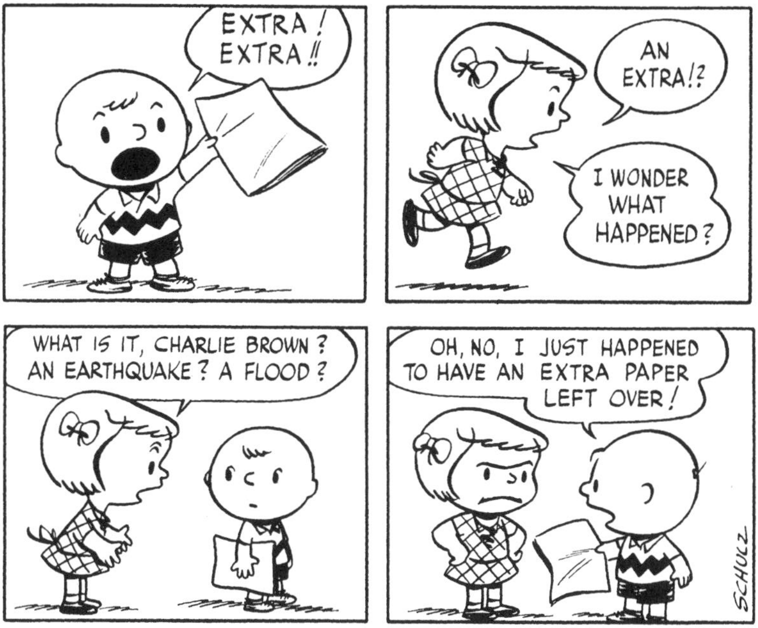
EXTRA! EXTRA!!
AN EXTRA!?
I WONDER WHAT HAPPENED?
WHAT IS IT, CHARLIE BROWN? AN EARTHQUAKE? A FLOOD?
OH, NO, I JUST HAPPENED TO HAVE AN EXTRA PAPER LEFT OVER!
SCHULZ

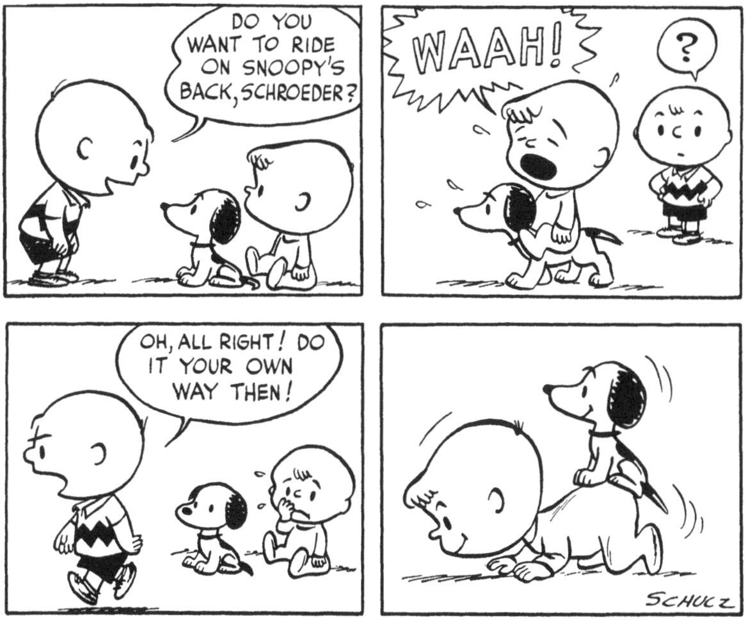
DO YOU WANT TO RIDE ON SNOOPY'S BACK, SCHROEDER?
WAAH!
?
OH, ALL RIGHT! DO IT YOUR OWN WAY THEN!
SCHULZ

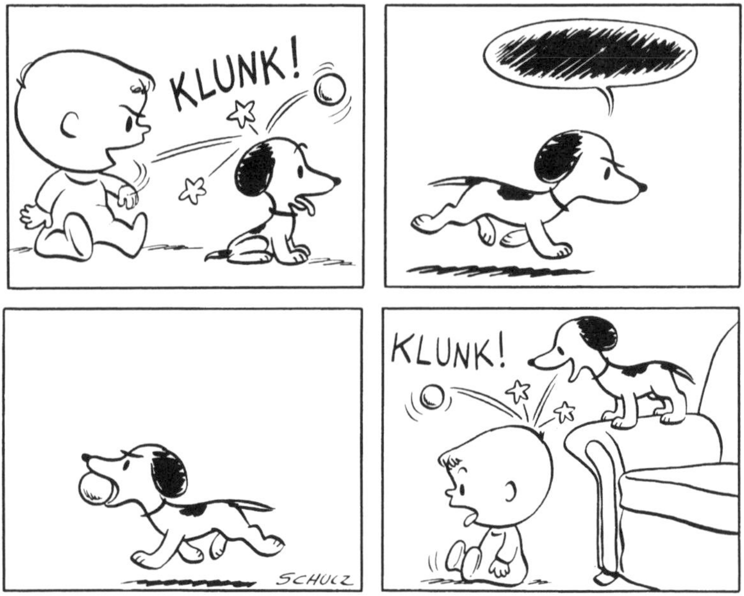
KLUNK!
KLUNK!
SCHULZ

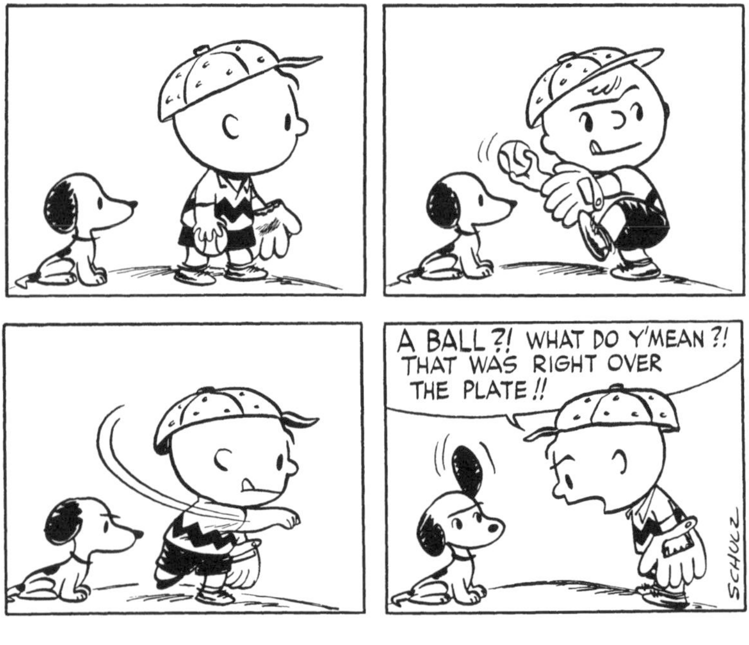
A BALL ?! WHAT DO Y'MEAN ?! THAT WAS RIGHT OVER THE PLATE !!
SCHULZ

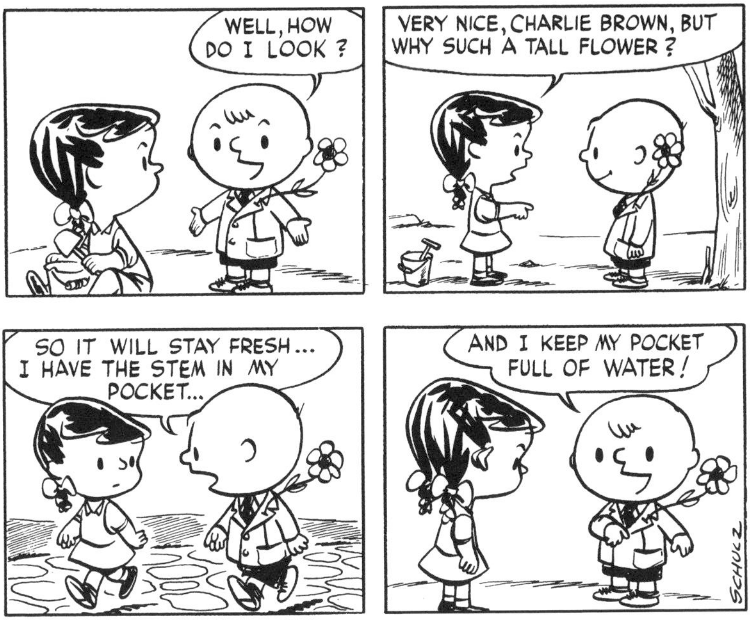
WELL, HOW DO I LOOK ?
VERY NICE, CHARLIE BROWN, BUT WHY SUCH A TALL FLOWER ?
SO IT WILL STAY FRESH... I HAVE THE STEM IN MY POCKET...
AND I KEEP MY POCKET FULL OF WATER !
SCHULZ

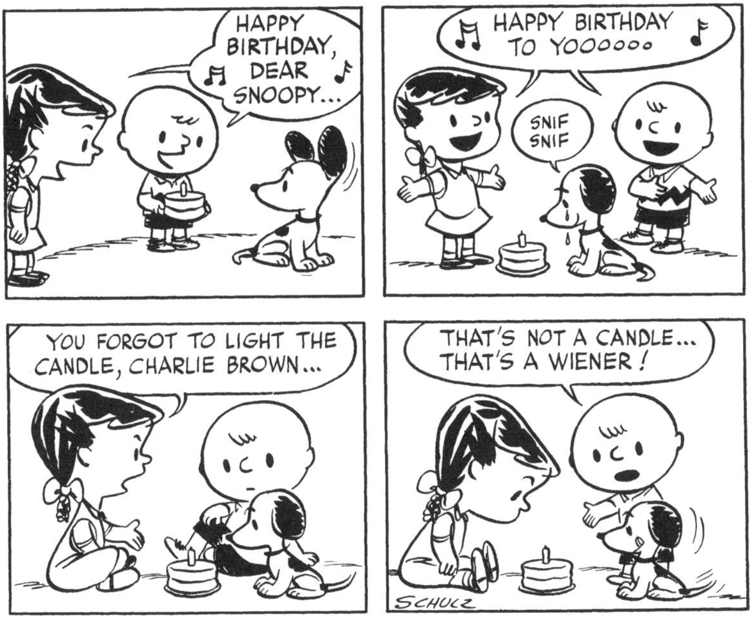
HAPPY BIRTHDAY, DEAR SNOOPY...
HAPPY BIRTHDAY TO YOOOOOO
SNIF SNIF
YOU FORGOT TO LIGHT THE CANDLE, CHARLIE BROWN...
THAT'S NOT A CANDLE... THAT'S A WIENER !
SCHULZ

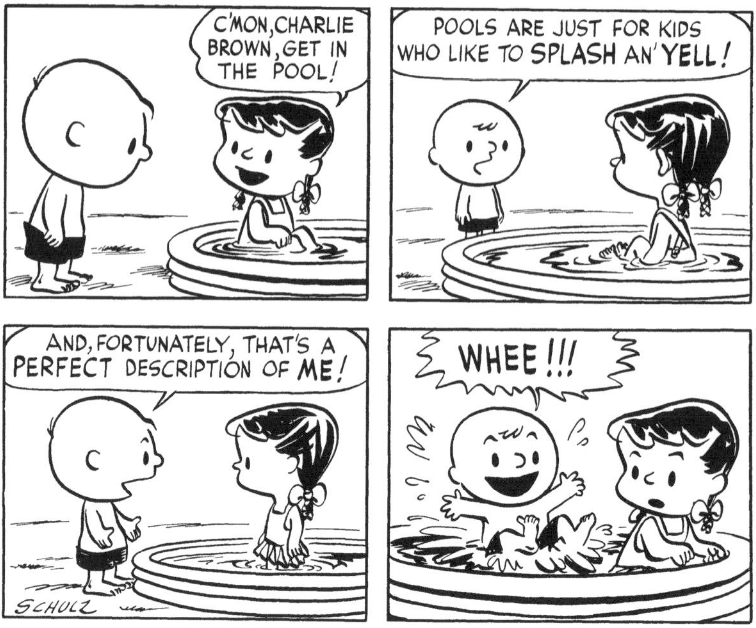
C'MON, CHARLIE BROWN, GET IN THE POOL!
POOLS ARE JUST FOR KIDS WHO LIKE TO SPLASH AN' YELL!
AND, FORTUNATELY, THAT'S A PERFECT DESCRIPTION OF ME!
SCHULZ
WHEE!!!

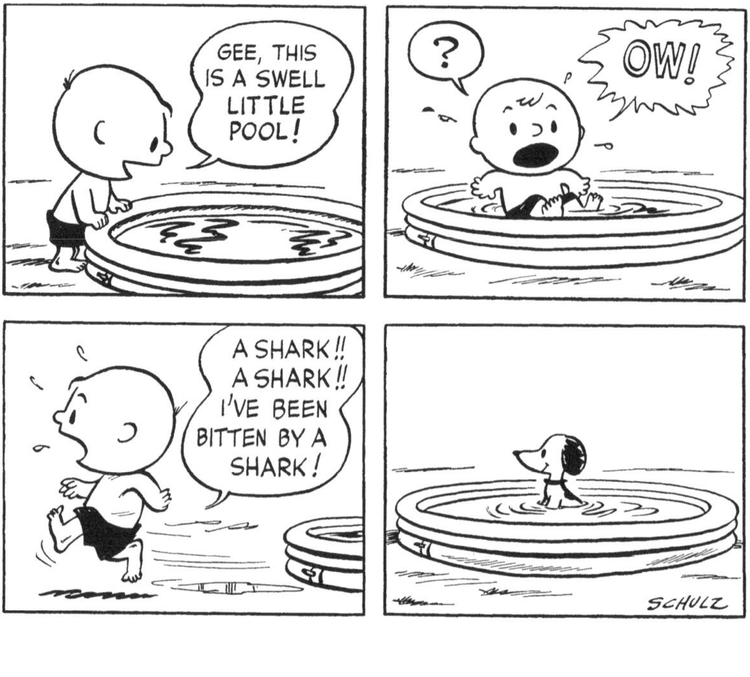
GEE, THIS IS A SWELL LITTLE POOL!
?
OW!
A SHARK!! A SHARK!! I'VE BEEN BITTEN BY A SHARK!
SCHULZ

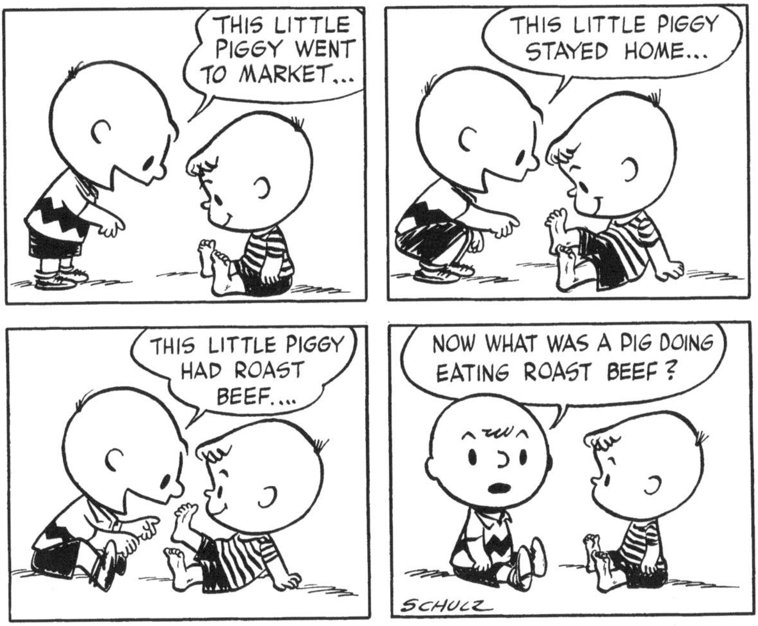
THIS LITTLE PIGGY WENT TO MARKET...
THIS LITTLE PIGGY STAYED HOME...
THIS LITTLE PIGGY HAD ROAST BEEF....
NOW WHAT WAS A PIG DOING EATING ROAST BEEF ?
SCHULZ

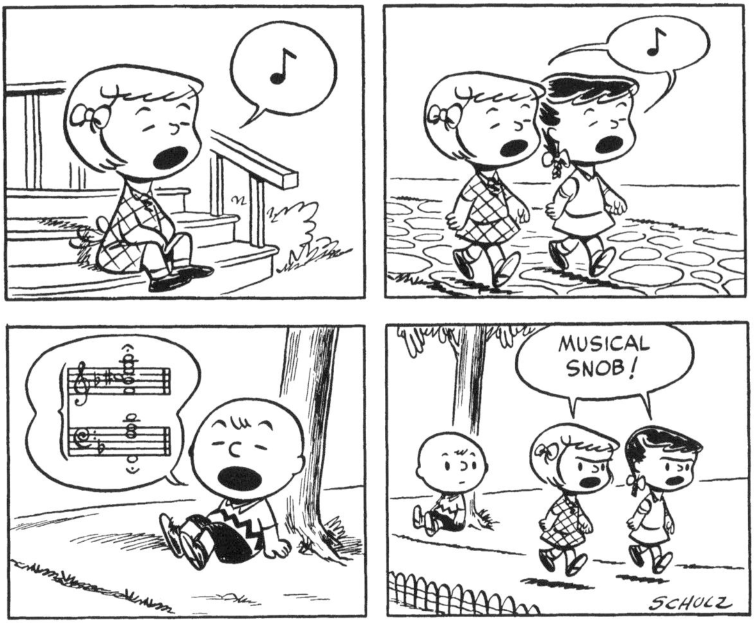
MUSICAL SNOB !
SCHULZ

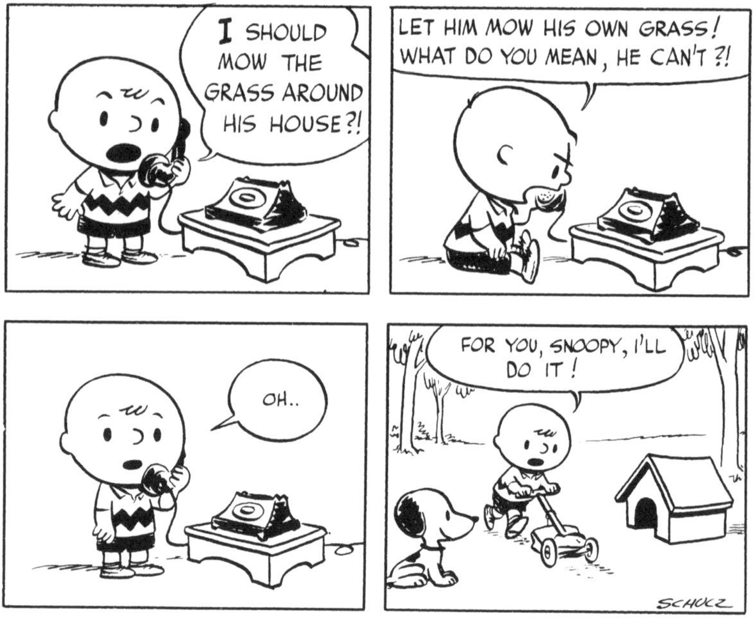
I SHOULD MOW THE GRASS AROUND HIS HOUSE?!
LET HIM MOW HIS OWN GRASS! WHAT DO YOU MEAN, HE CAN'T?!
OH..
FOR YOU, SNOOPY, I'LL DO IT!
SCHULZ

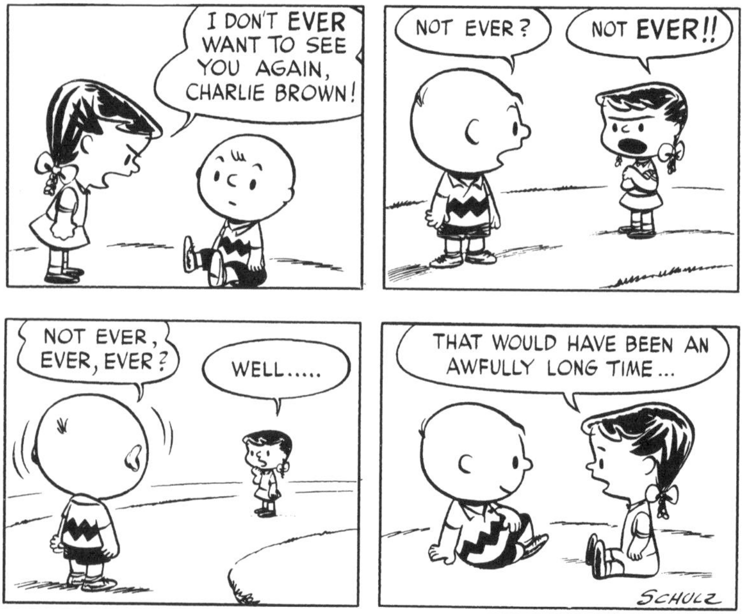
I DON'T EVER WANT TO SEE YOU AGAIN, CHARLIE BROWN!
NOT EVER?
NOT EVER!!
NOT EVER, EVER, EVER?
WELL.....
THAT WOULD HAVE BEEN AN AWFULLY LONG TIME...
SCHULZ

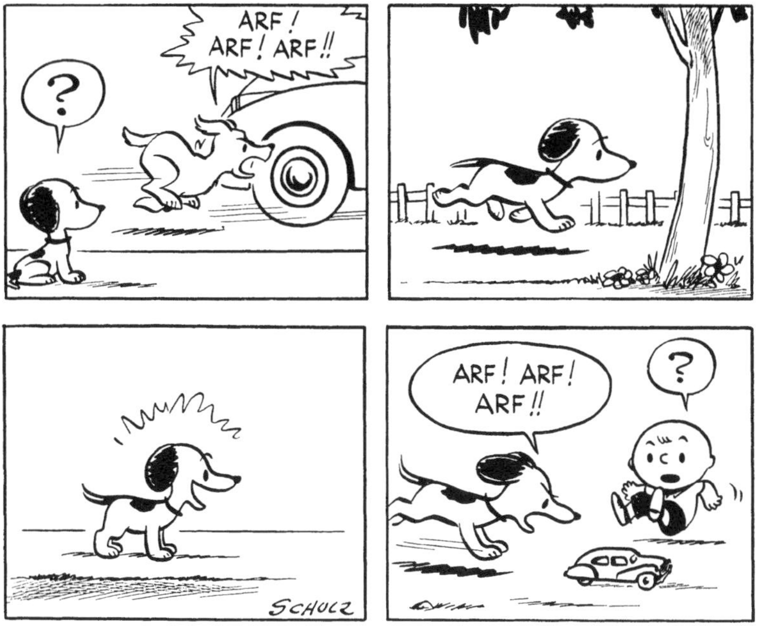
?
ARF! ARF! ARF!!
ARF! ARF! ARF!!
?
SCHULZ

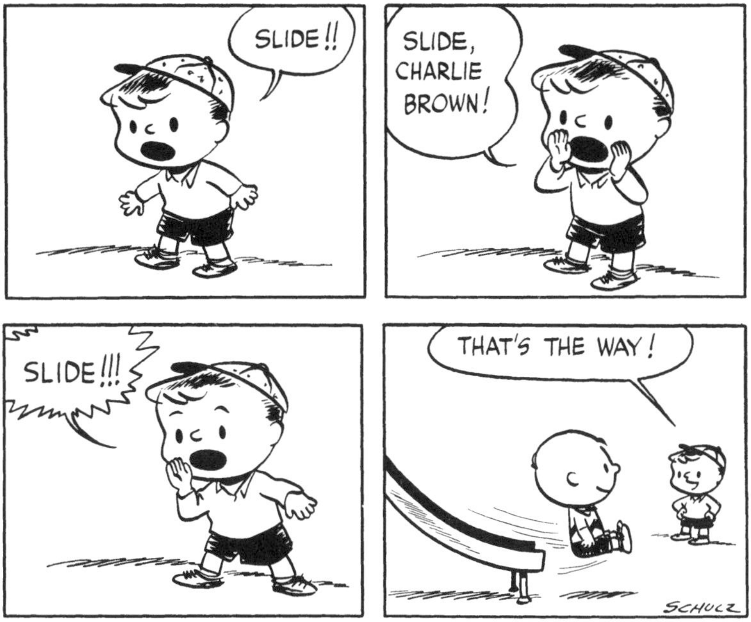
SLIDE!!
SLIDE, CHARLIE BROWN!
SLIDE!!!
THAT'S THE WAY!
SCHULZ

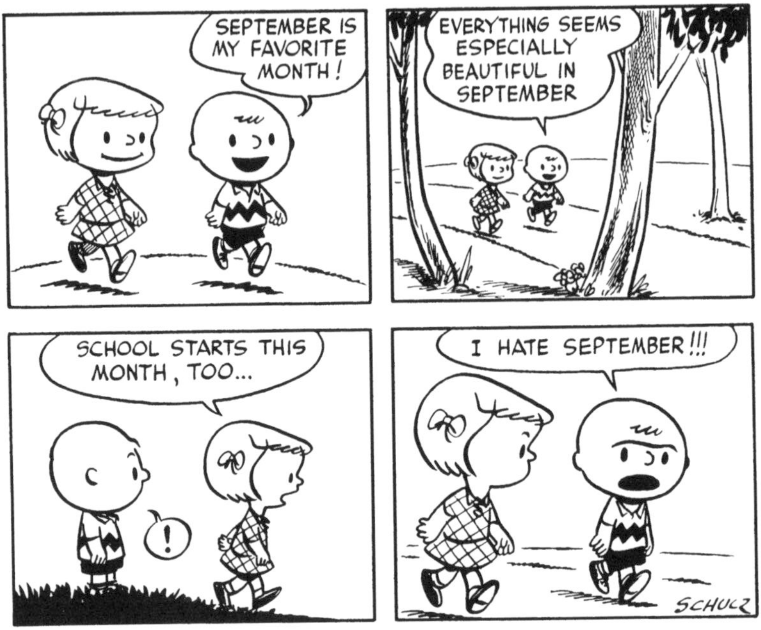
SEPTEMBER IS MY FAVORITE MONTH!
EVERYTHING SEEMS ESPECIALLY BEAUTIFUL IN SEPTEMBER
SCHOOL STARTS THIS MONTH, TOO...
!
I HATE SEPTEMBER!!!
SCHULZ

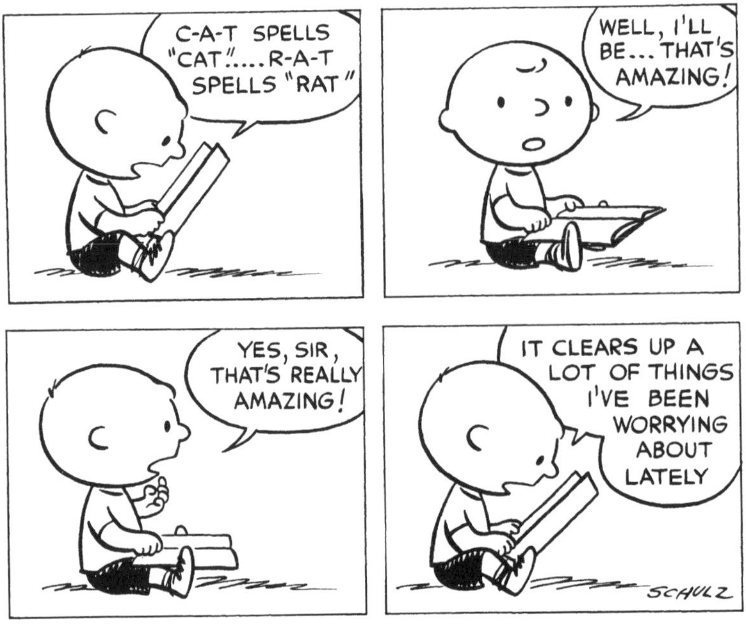
C-A-T SPELLS "CAT"!.... R-A-T SPELLS "RAT"
WELL, I'LL BE... THAT'S AMAZING!
YES, SIR, THAT'S REALLY AMAZING!
IT CLEARS UP A LOT OF THINGS I'VE BEEN WORRYING ABOUT LATELY
SCHULZ

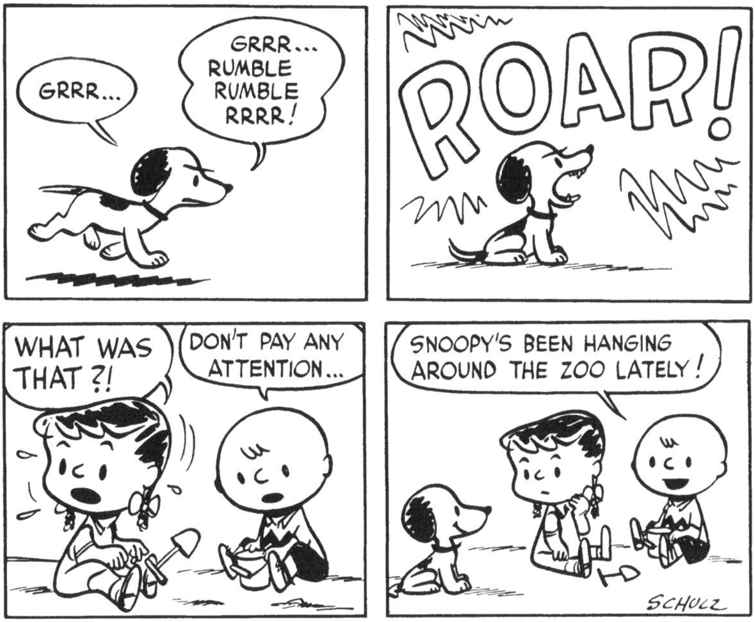
GRRR...
GRRR... RUMBLE RUMBLE RRRR!
ROAR!
WHAT WAS THAT ?!
DON'T PAY ANY ATTENTION...
SNOOPY'S BEEN HANGING AROUND THE ZOO LATELY!
SCHULZ

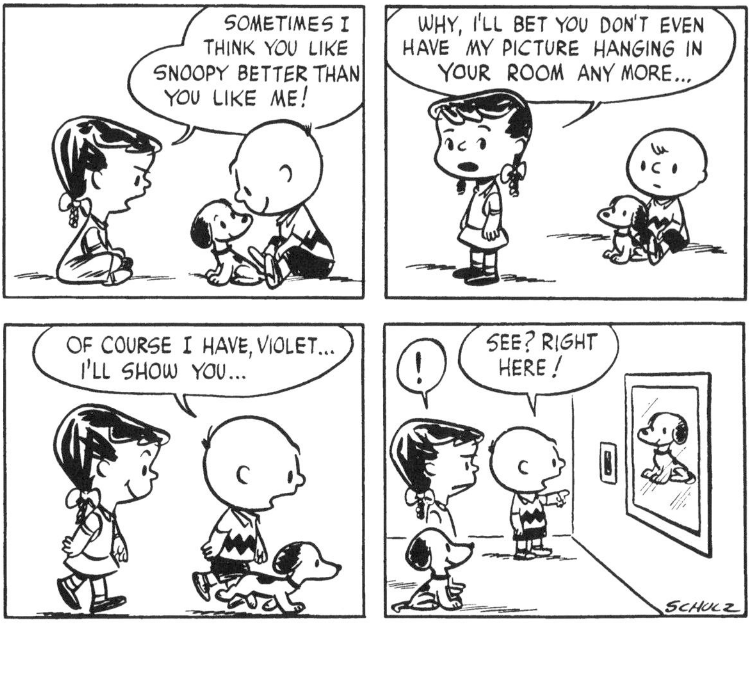
SOMETIMES I THINK YOU LIKE SNOOPY BETTER THAN YOU LIKE ME!
WHY, I'LL BET YOU DON'T EVEN HAVE MY PICTURE HANGING IN YOUR ROOM ANY MORE...
OF COURSE I HAVE, VIOLET... I'LL SHOW YOU...
!
SEE? RIGHT HERE!
SCHULZ

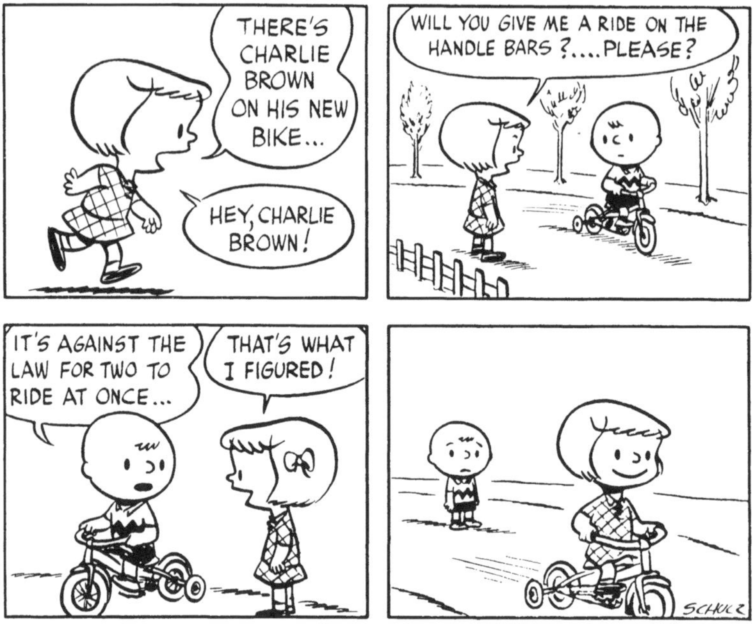
THERE'S CHARLIE BROWN ON HIS NEW BIKE...
HEY, CHARLIE BROWN!
WILL YOU GIVE ME A RIDE ON THE HANDLE BARS ?....PLEASE?
IT'S AGAINST THE LAW FOR TWO TO RIDE AT ONCE...
THAT'S WHAT I FIGURED!
SCHULZ

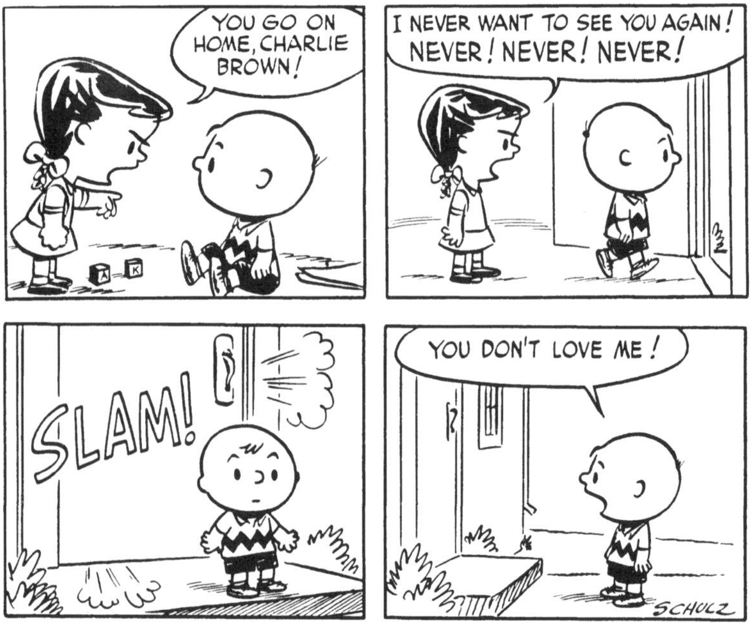
YOU GO ON HOME, CHARLIE BROWN!
I NEVER WANT TO SEE YOU AGAIN!
NEVER! NEVER! NEVER!
SLAM!
YOU DON'T LOVE ME!
SCHULZ

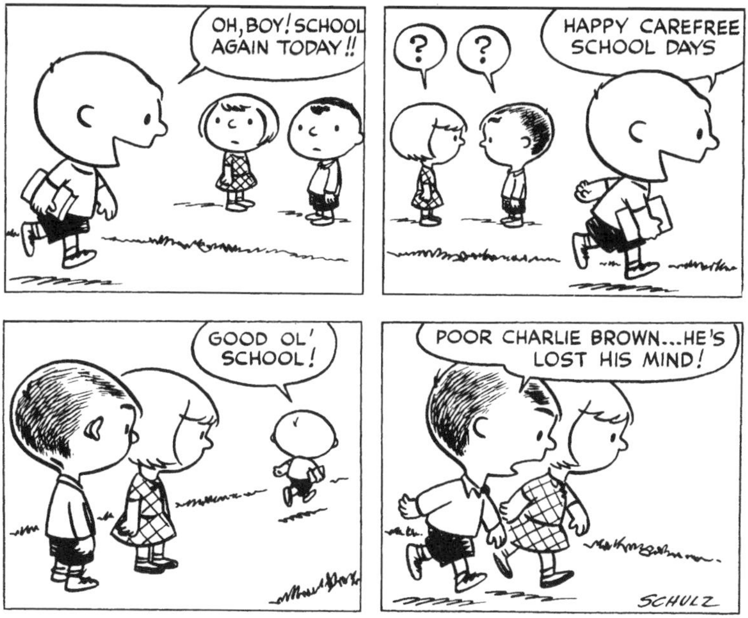
OH, BOY! SCHOOL AGAIN TODAY!!
?
?
HAPPY CAREFREE SCHOOL DAYS
GOOD OL' SCHOOL!
POOR CHARLIE BROWN...HE'S LOST HIS MIND!
SCHULZ

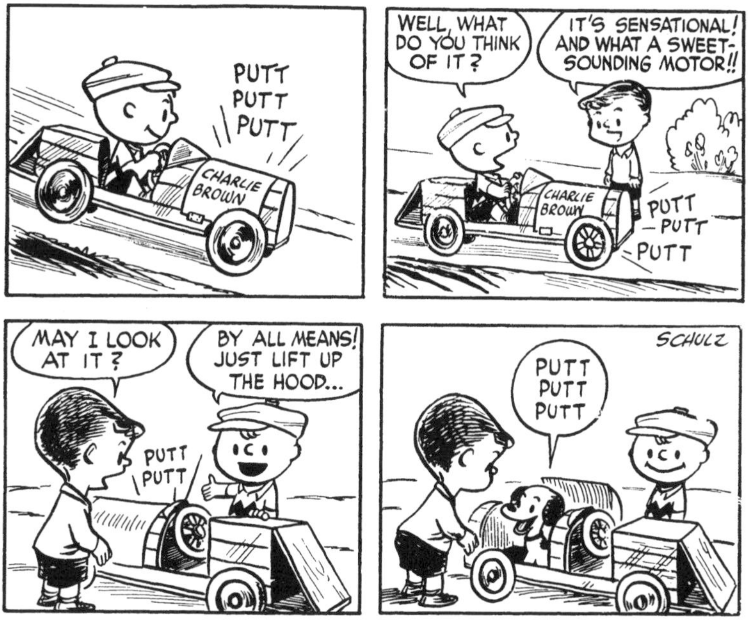
PUTT PUTT PUTT
CHARLIE BROWN
WELL, WHAT DO YOU THINK OF IT?
IT'S SENSATIONAL! AND WHAT A SWEET-SOUNDING MOTOR!!
CHARLIE BROWN
PUTT PUTT PUTT
MAY I LOOK AT IT?
BY ALL MEANS! JUST LIFT UP THE HOOD...
PUTT PUTT
SCHULZ
PUTT PUTT PUTT

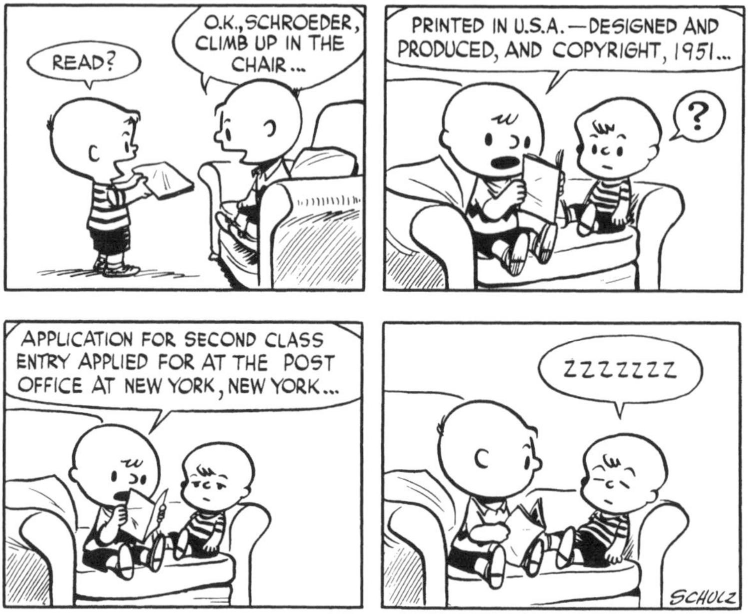
READ?
O.K., SCHROEDER, CLIMB UP IN THE CHAIR...
PRINTED IN U.S.A.—DESIGNED AND PRODUCED, AND COPYRIGHT, 1951...
?
APPLICATION FOR SECOND CLASS ENTRY APPLIED FOR AT THE POST OFFICE AT NEW YORK, NEW YORK...
ZZZZZZZ
SCHULZ

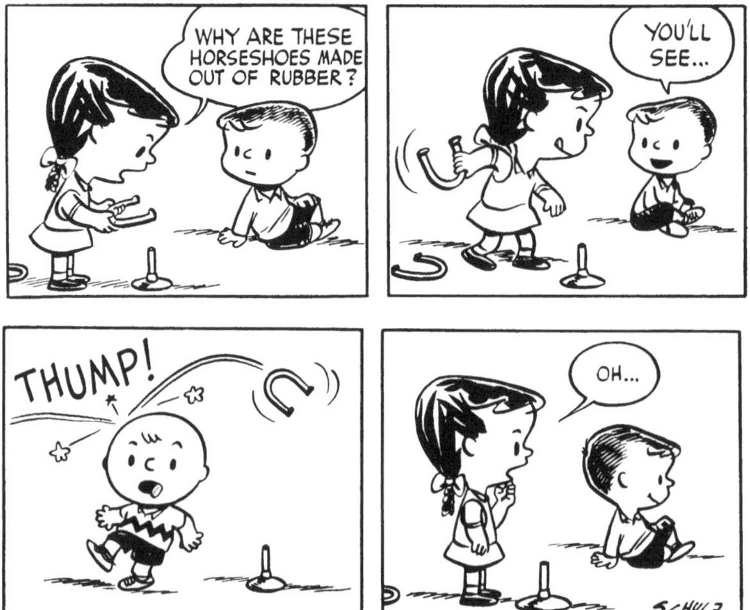
WHY ARE THESE HORSESHOES MADE OUT OF RUBBER?
YOU'LL SEE...
THUMP!
OH...
SCHULZ

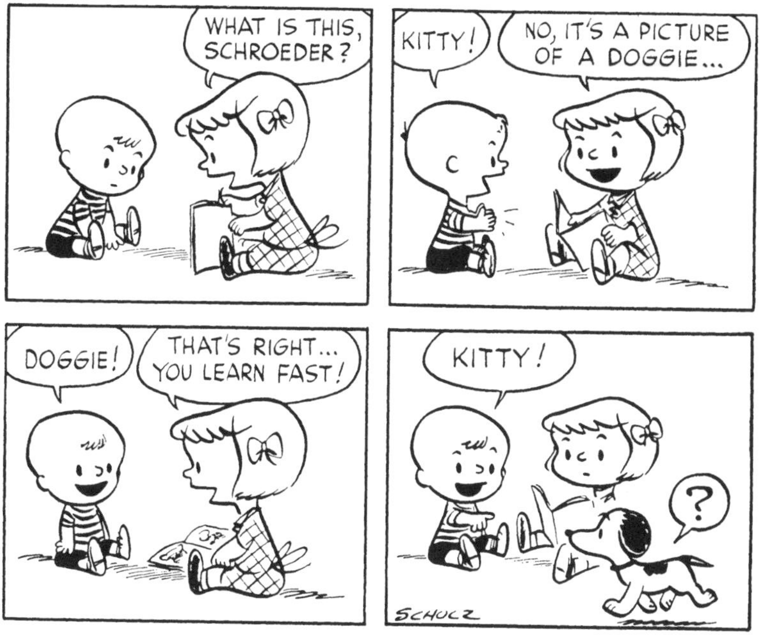
WHAT IS THIS, SCHROEDER?
KITTY!
NO, IT'S A PICTURE OF A DOGGIE...
DOGGIE!
THAT'S RIGHT... YOU LEARN FAST!
KITTY!
?
SCHULZ

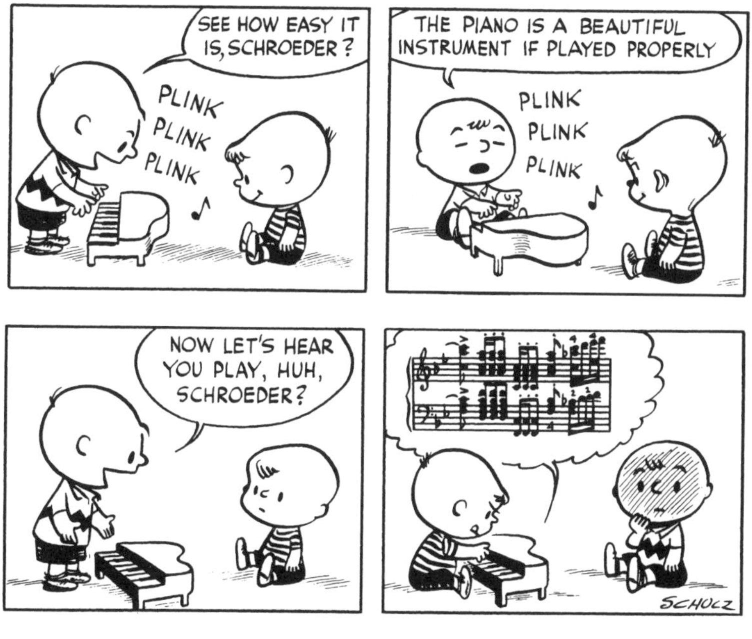
SEE HOW EASY IT IS, SCHROEDER?
PLINK
PLINK
PLINK
THE PIANO IS A BEAUTIFUL INSTRUMENT IF PLAYED PROPERLY
PLINK
PLINK
PLINK
NOW LET'S HEAR YOU PLAY, HUH, SCHROEDER?
SCHULZ

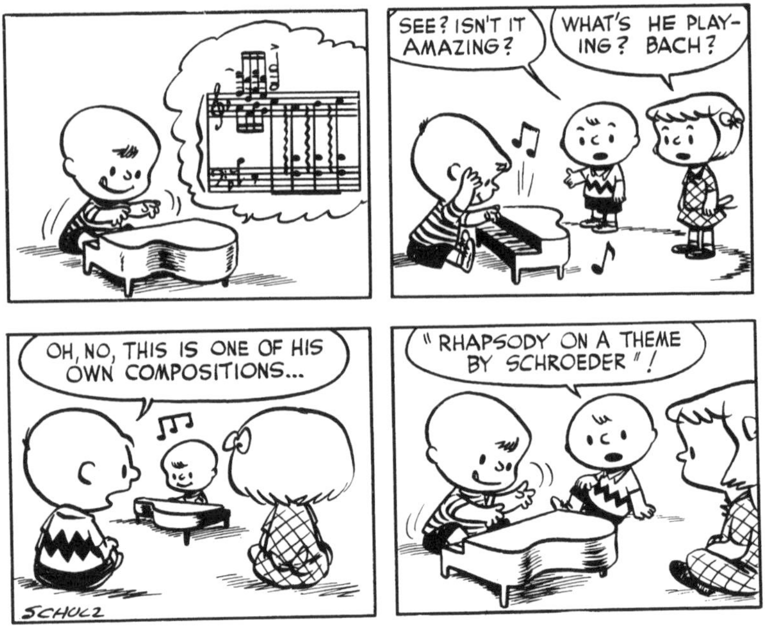
SEE? ISN'T IT AMAZING?
WHAT'S HE PLAY-ING? BACH?
OH, NO, THIS IS ONE OF HIS OWN COMPOSITIONS...
"RHAPSODY ON A THEME BY SCHROEDER"!
SCHULZ

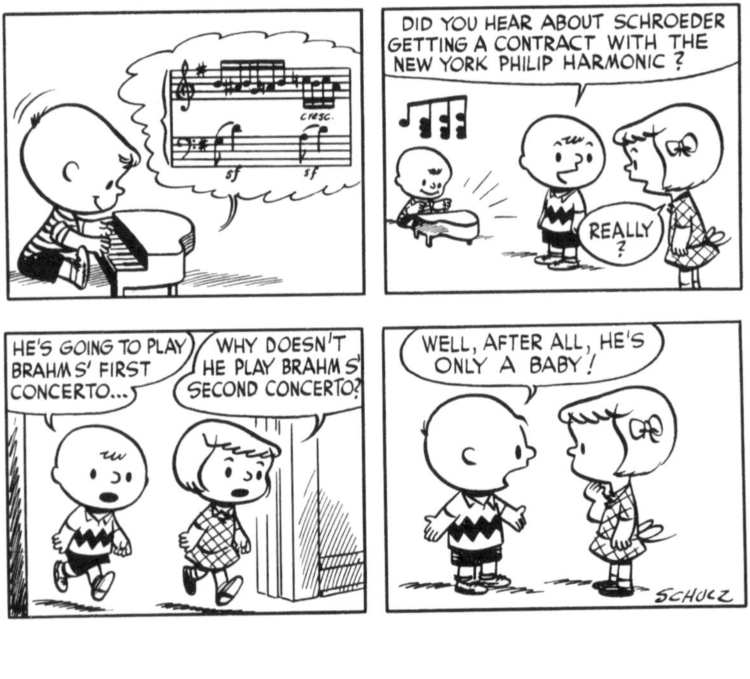
cresc.
sf
sf
DID YOU HEAR ABOUT SCHROEDER GETTING A CONTRACT WITH THE NEW YORK PHILIP HARMONIC?
REALLY?
HE'S GOING TO PLAY BRAHMS' FIRST CONCERTO...
WHY DOESN'T HE PLAY BRAHMS' SECOND CONCERTO?
WELL, AFTER ALL, HE'S ONLY A BABY!
SCHULZ

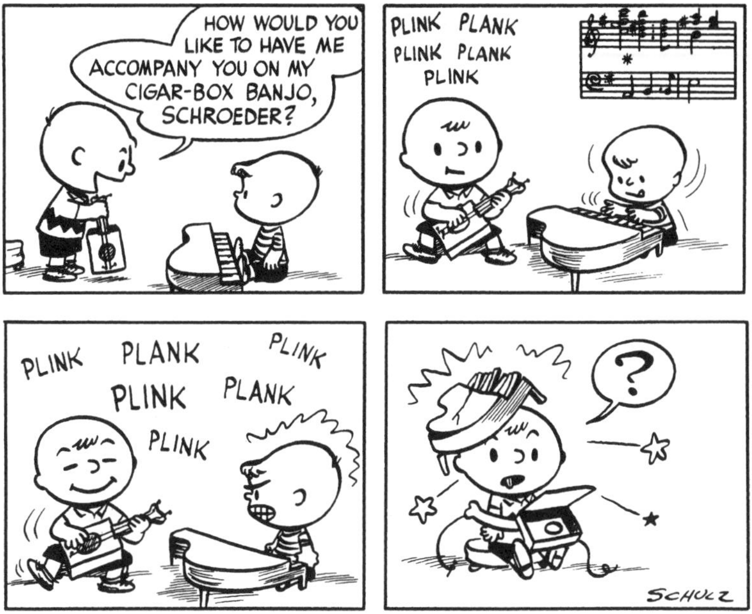
HOW WOULD YOU LIKE TO HAVE ME ACCOMPANY YOU ON MY CIGAR-BOX BANJO, SCHROEDER?
PLINK PLANK
PLINK PLANK
PLINK
PLINK
PLANK
PLINK
PLINK
PLANK
PLINK
?
SCHULZ

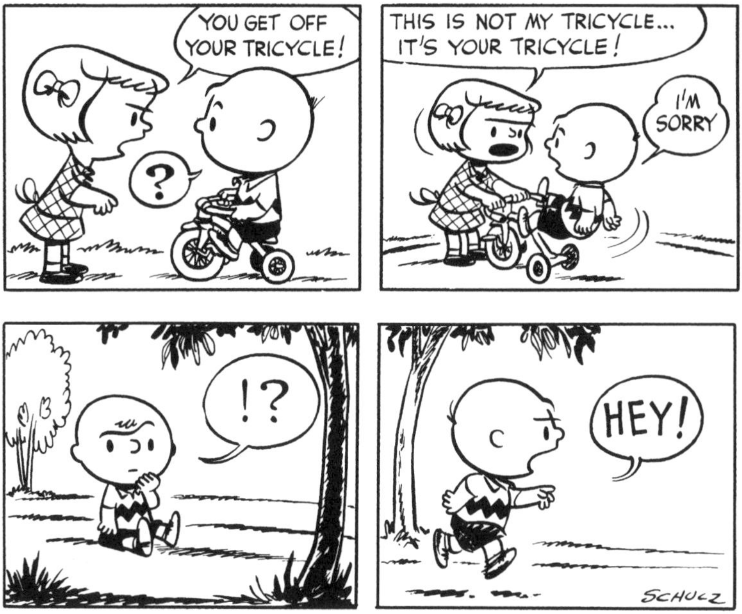
YOU GET OFF YOUR TRICYCLE!
?
THIS IS NOT MY TRICYCLE... IT'S YOUR TRICYCLE!
I'M SORRY
!?
HEY!
SCHULZ

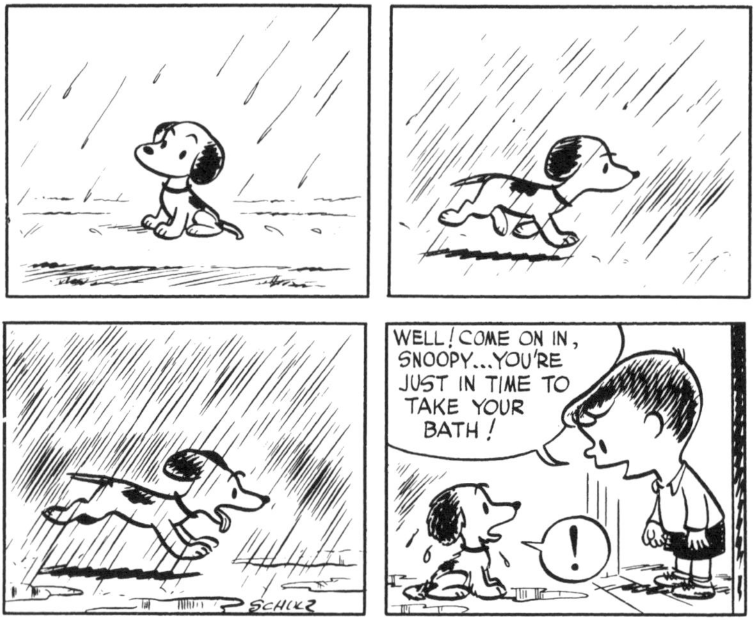
WELL! COME ON IN, SNOOPY...YOU'RE JUST IN TIME TO TAKE YOUR BATH!
!
SCHULZ

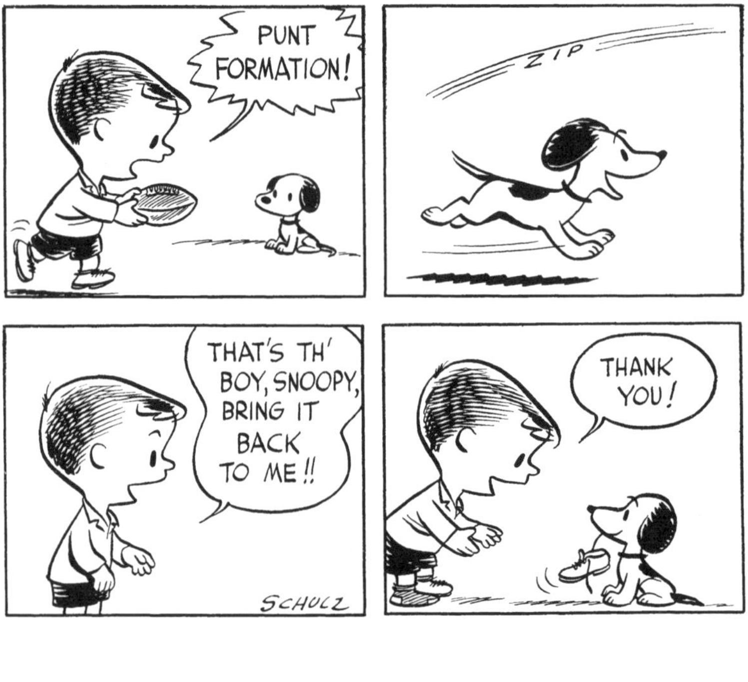
PUNT FORMATION!
ZIP
THAT'S TH' BOY, SNOOPY, BRING IT BACK TO ME!!
SCHULZ
THANK YOU!

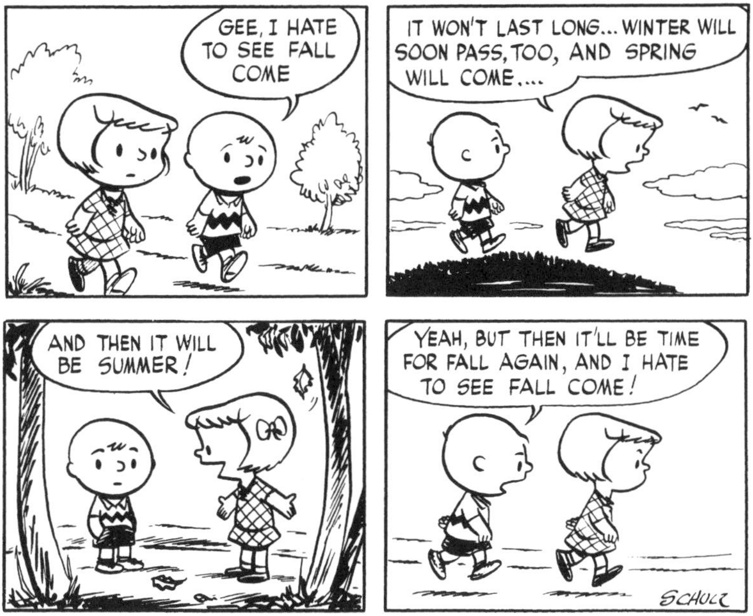
GEE, I HATE TO SEE FALL COME
IT WON'T LAST LONG... WINTER WILL SOON PASS, TOO, AND SPRING WILL COME....
AND THEN IT WILL BE SUMMER!
YEAH, BUT THEN IT'LL BE TIME FOR FALL AGAIN, AND I HATE TO SEE FALL COME!
SCHULZ

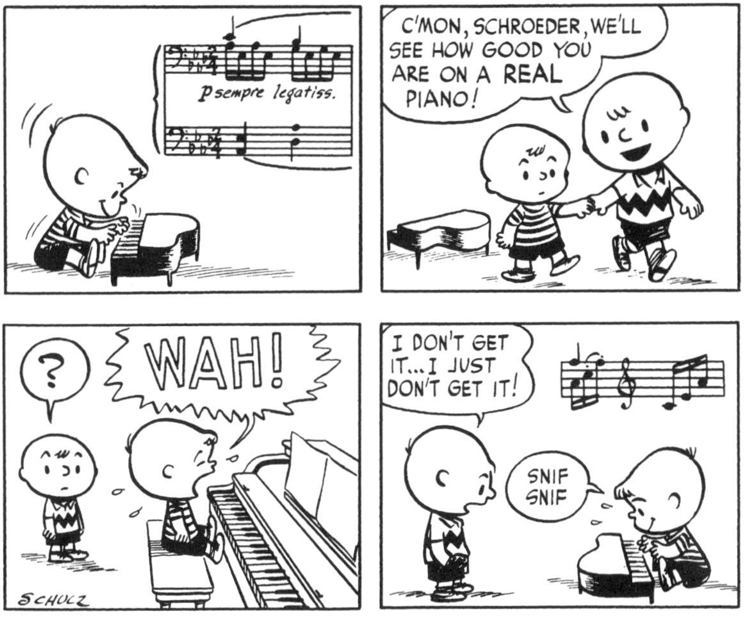
p sempre legatiss.
C'MON, SCHROEDER, WE'LL SEE HOW GOOD YOU ARE ON A REAL PIANO!
?
WAH!
SCHULZ
I DON'T GET IT... I JUST DON'T GET IT!
SNIF SNIF

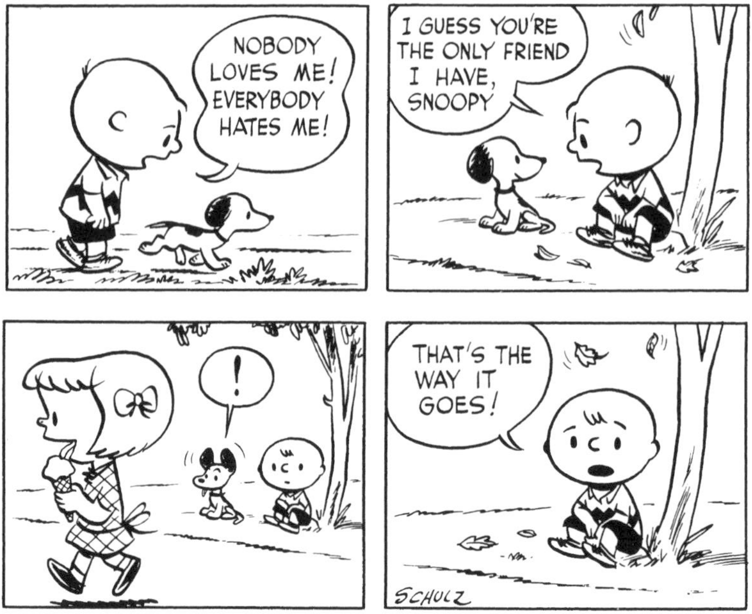
NOBODY LOVES ME! EVERYBODY HATES ME!
I GUESS YOU'RE THE ONLY FRIEND I HAVE, SNOOPY
!
THAT'S THE WAY IT GOES!
SCHULZ

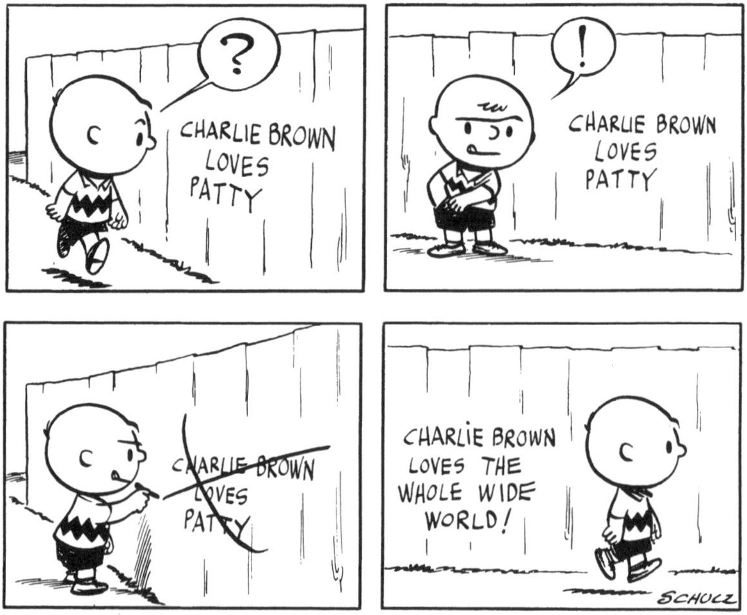
?
CHARLIE BROWN LOVES PATTY
!
CHARLIE BROWN LOVES PATTY
CHARLIE BROWN LOVES PATTY
CHARLIE BROWN LOVES THE WHOLE WIDE WORLD!
SCHULZ

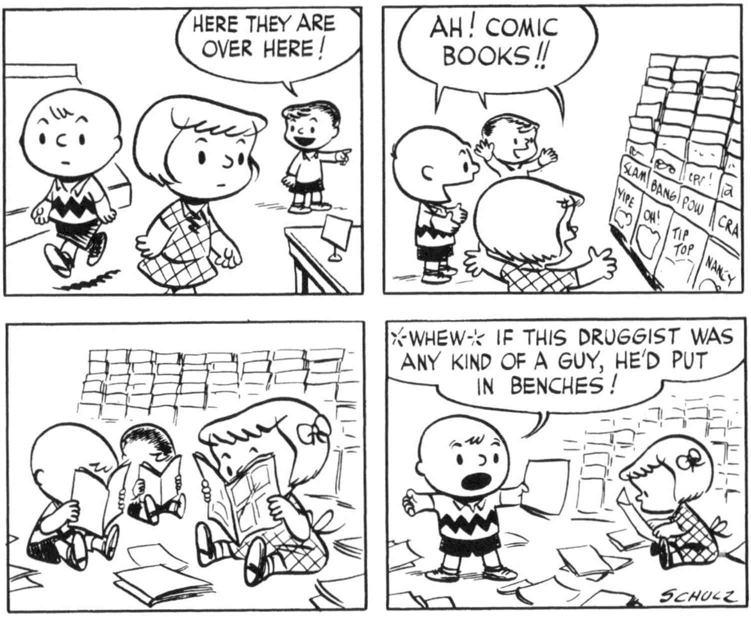
HERE THEY ARE OVER HERE!
AH! COMIC BOOKS!!
WHEW IF THIS DRUGGIST WAS ANY KIND OF A GUY, HE'D PUT IN BENCHES!
SCHULZ

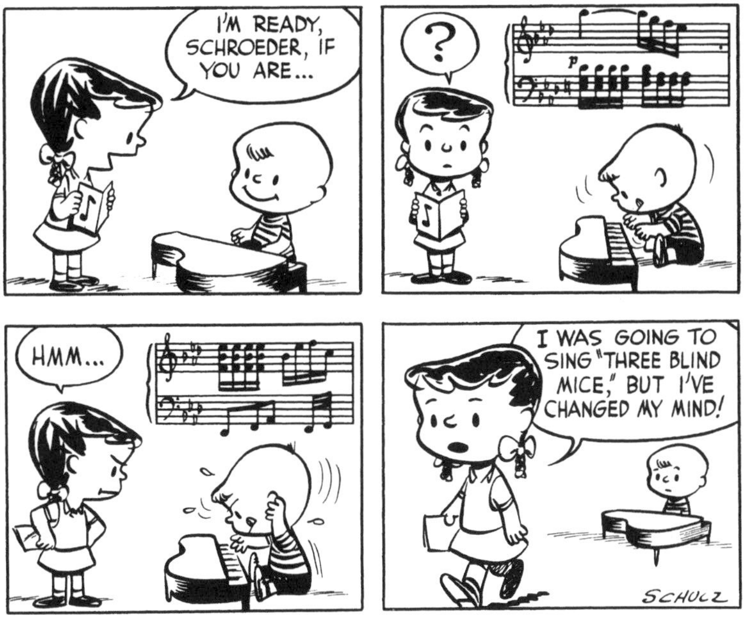
I'M READY, SCHROEDER, IF YOU ARE...
?
HMM...
I WAS GOING TO SING "THREE BLIND MICE," BUT I'VE CHANGED MY MIND!
SCHULZ

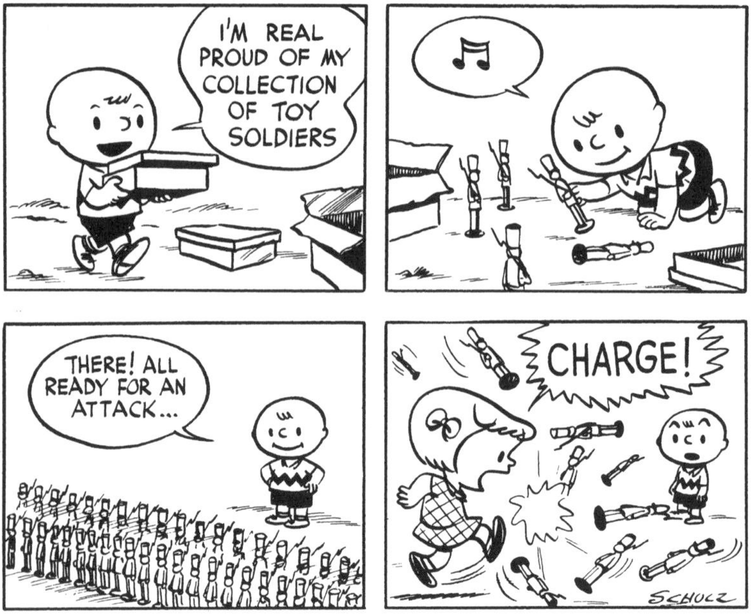
I'M REAL PROUD OF MY COLLECTION OF TOY SOLDIERS
THERE! ALL READY FOR AN ATTACK...
CHARGE!
SCHULZ

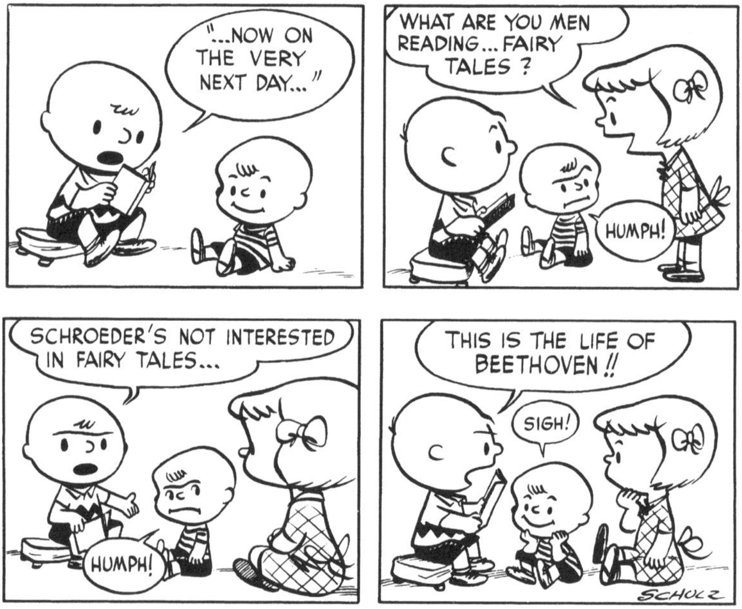
"...NOW ON THE VERY NEXT DAY..."
WHAT ARE YOU MEN READING... FAIRY TALES ?
HUMPH!
SCHROEDER'S NOT INTERESTED IN FAIRY TALES...
HUMPH!
THIS IS THE LIFE OF BEETHOVEN !!
SIGH!
SCHULZ

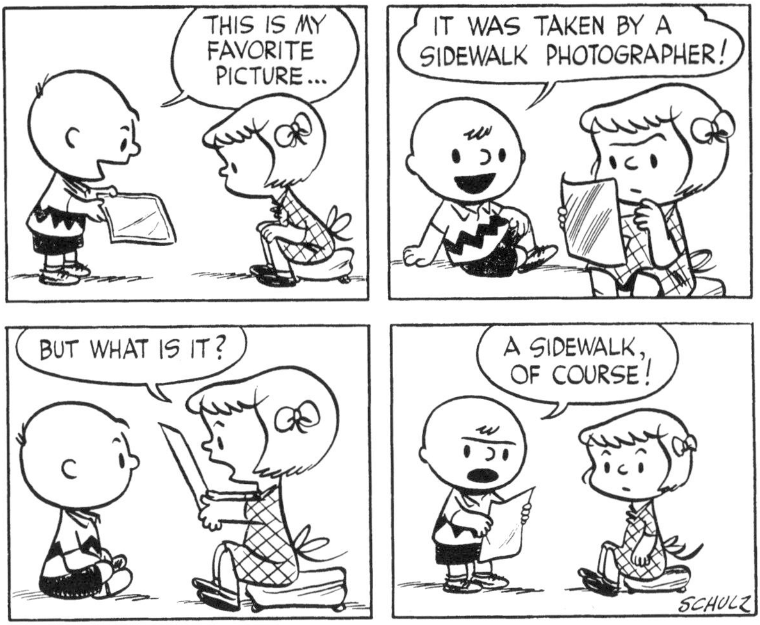
THIS IS MY FAVORITE PICTURE...
IT WAS TAKEN BY A SIDEWALK PHOTOGRAPHER!
BUT WHAT IS IT?
A SIDEWALK, OF COURSE!
SCHULZ

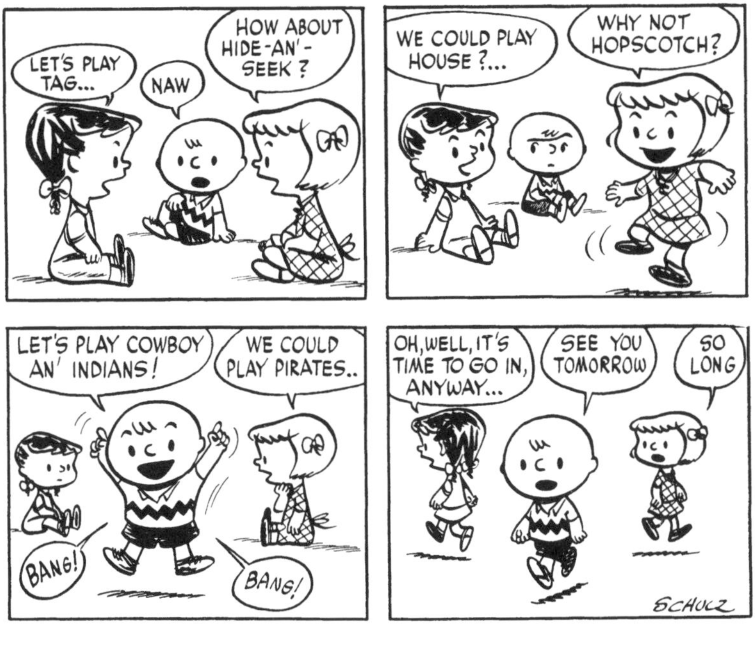
LET'S PLAY TAG...
NAW
HOW ABOUT HIDE-AN'-SEEK?
WE COULD PLAY HOUSE?...
WHY NOT HOPSCOTCH?
LET'S PLAY COWBOY AN' INDIANS!
WE COULD PLAY PIRATES..
BANG!
BANG!
OH, WELL, IT'S TIME TO GO IN, ANYWAY...
SEE YOU TOMORROW
SO LONG
SCHULZ

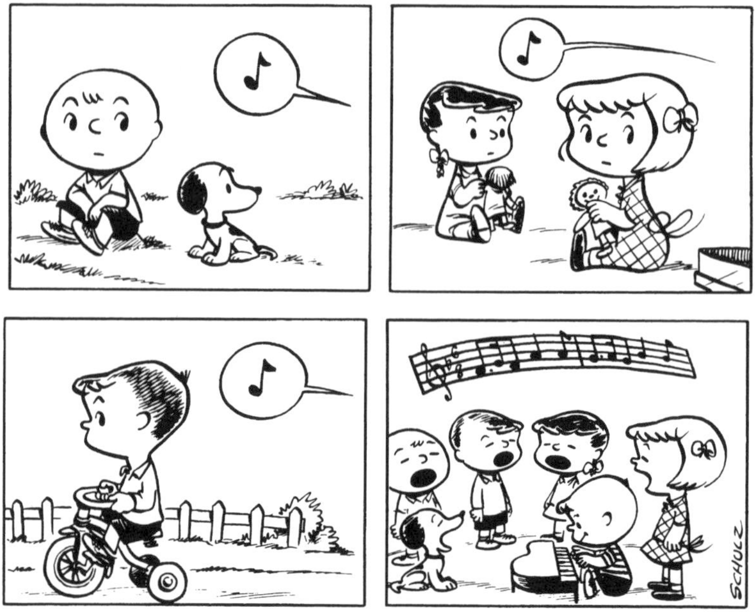
SCHULZ

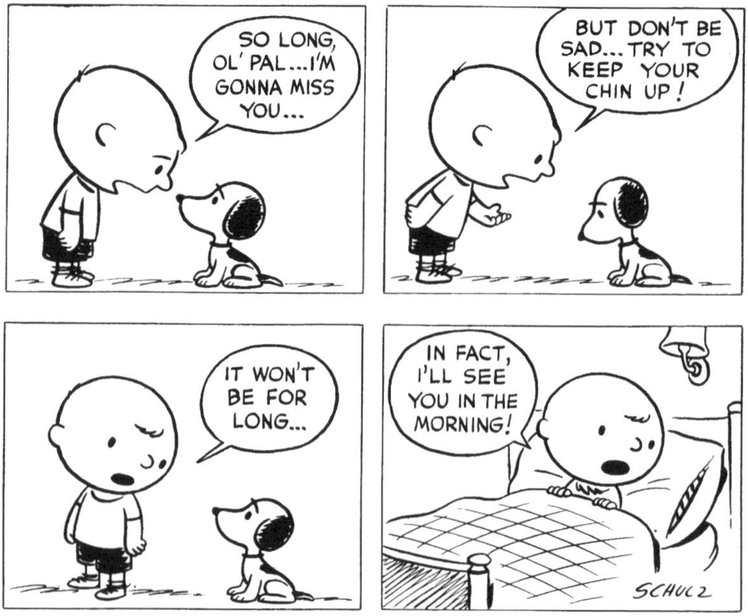
SO LONG, OL' PAL...I'M GONNA MISS YOU...
BUT DON'T BE SAD...TRY TO KEEP YOUR CHIN UP!
IT WON'T BE FOR LONG...
IN FACT, I'LL SEE YOU IN THE MORNING!
SCHULZ

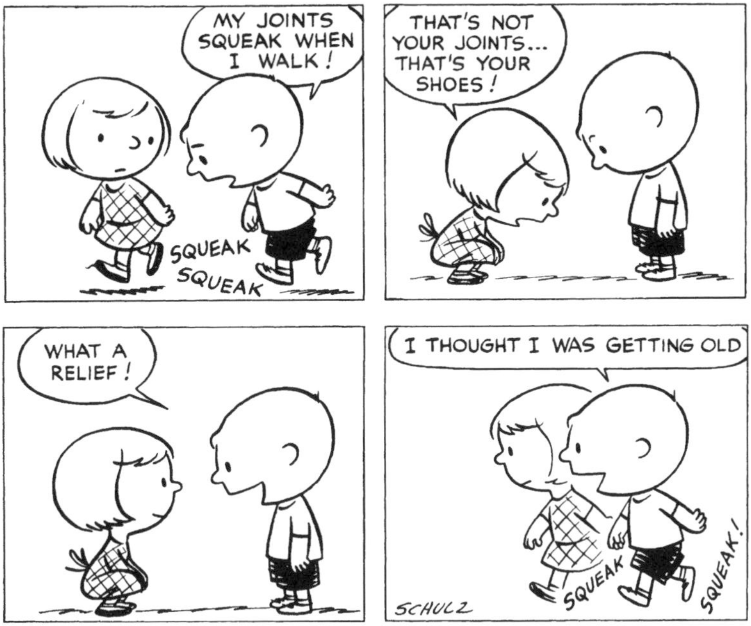
MY JOINTS SQUEAK WHEN I WALK!
SQUEAK
SQUEAK
THAT'S NOT YOUR JOINTS... THAT'S YOUR SHOES!
WHAT A RELIEF!
I THOUGHT I WAS GETTING OLD
SQUEAK
SQUEAK!
SCHULZ

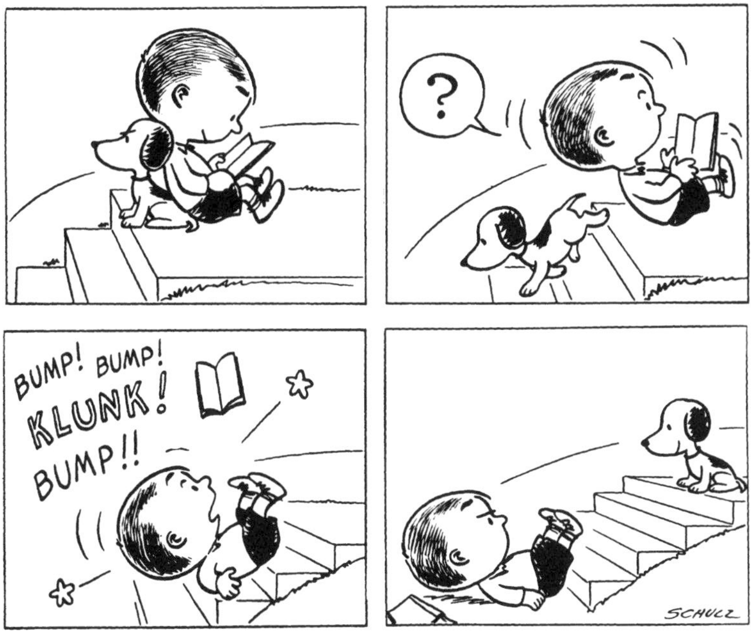
?
BUMP! BUMP!
KLUNK!
BUMP!!
SCHULZ

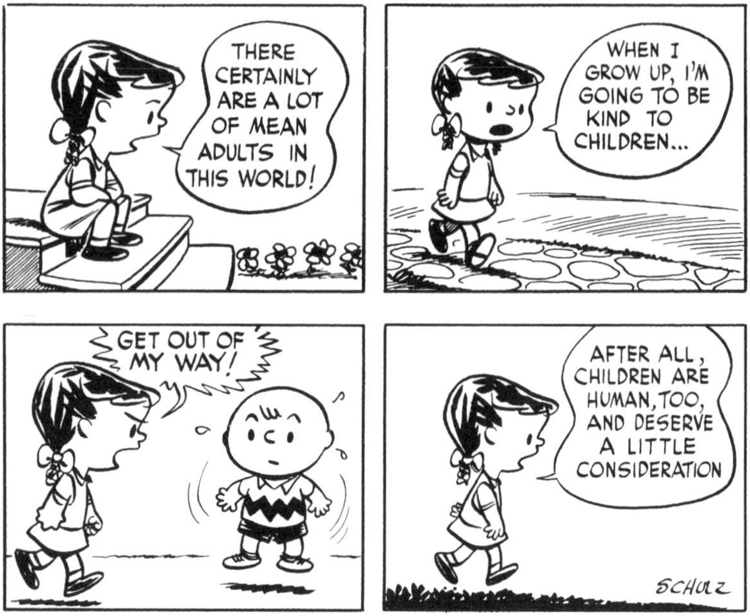
THERE CERTAINLY ARE A LOT OF MEAN ADULTS IN THIS WORLD!
WHEN I GROW UP, I'M GOING TO BE KIND TO CHILDREN...
GET OUT OF MY WAY!
AFTER ALL, CHILDREN ARE HUMAN, TOO, AND DESERVE A LITTLE CONSIDERATION
SCHULZ

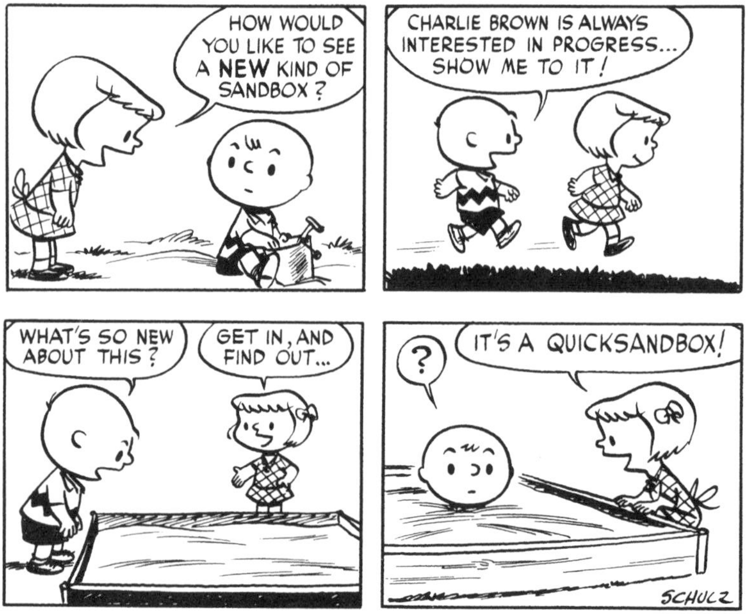
HOW WOULD YOU LIKE TO SEE A **NEW** KIND OF SANDBOX?
CHARLIE BROWN IS ALWAYS INTERESTED IN PROGRESS... SHOW ME TO IT!
WHAT'S SO NEW ABOUT THIS?
GET IN, AND FIND OUT...
?
IT'S A QUICKSANDBOX!
SCHULZ

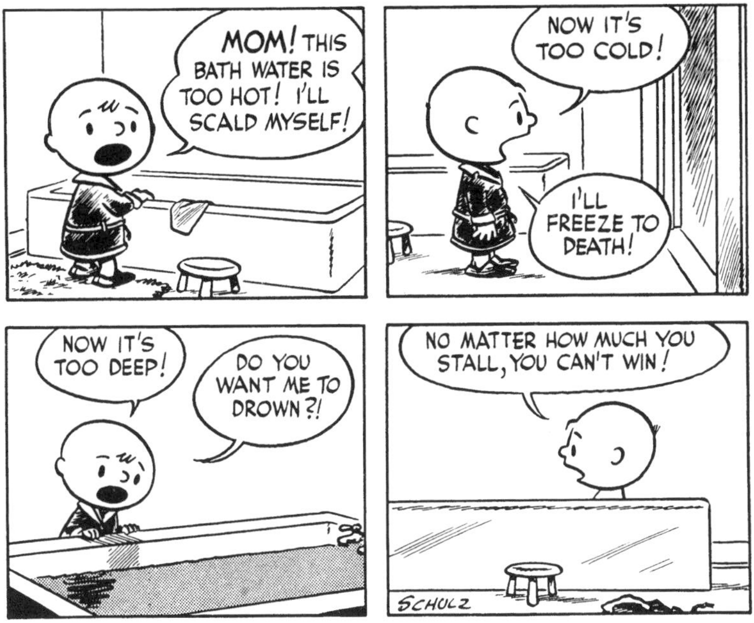
MOM! THIS BATH WATER IS TOO HOT! I'LL SCALD MYSELF!
NOW IT'S TOO COLD!
I'LL FREEZE TO DEATH!
NOW IT'S TOO DEEP!
DO YOU WANT ME TO DROWN?!
NO MATTER HOW MUCH YOU STALL, YOU CAN'T WIN!
SCHULZ

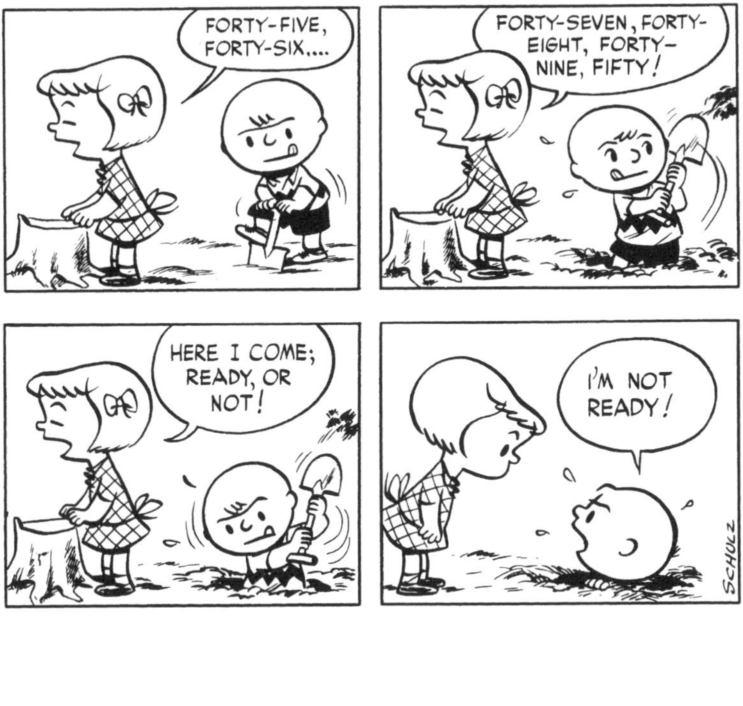
FORTY-FIVE, FORTY-SIX....
FORTY-SEVEN, FORTY-EIGHT, FORTY-NINE, FIFTY!
HERE I COME; READY, OR NOT!
I'M NOT READY!
SCHULZ

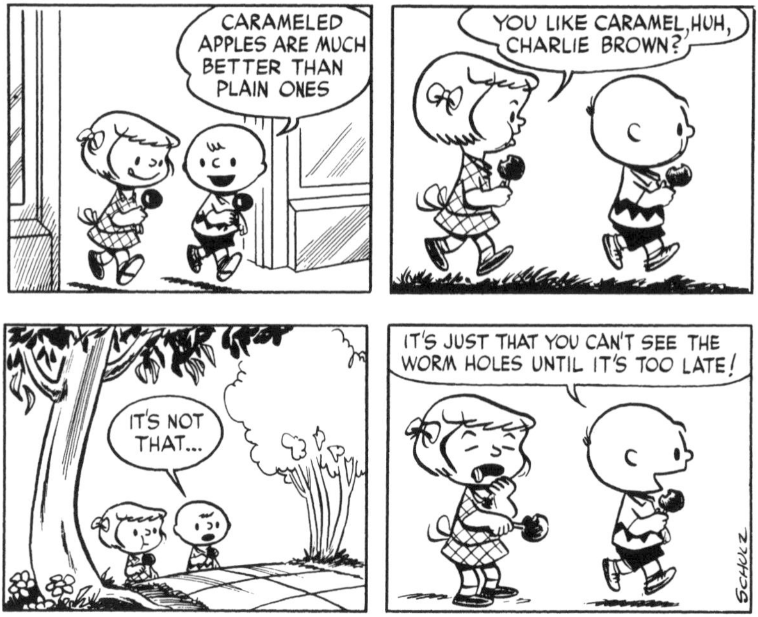
CARAMELED APPLES ARE MUCH BETTER THAN PLAIN ONES
YOU LIKE CARAMEL, HUH, CHARLIE BROWN?
IT'S NOT THAT...
IT'S JUST THAT YOU CAN'T SEE THE WORM HOLES UNTIL IT'S TOO LATE!
SCHULZ

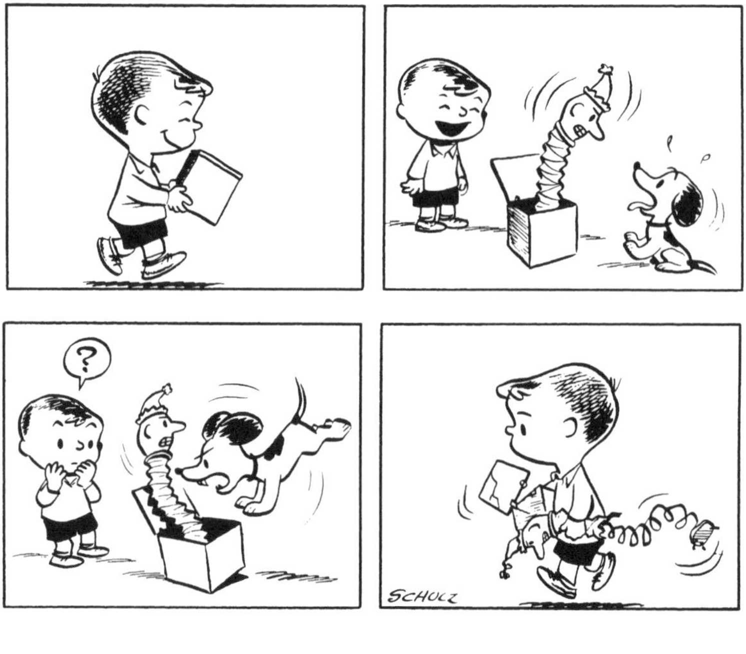
?
SCHULZ

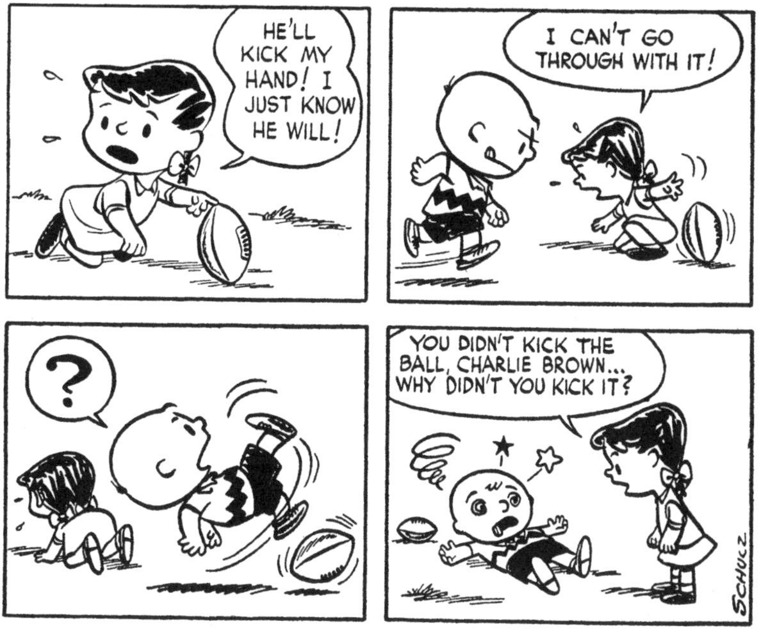
HE'LL KICK MY HAND! I JUST KNOW HE WILL!
I CAN'T GO THROUGH WITH IT!
?
YOU DIDN'T KICK THE BALL, CHARLIE BROWN... WHY DIDN'T YOU KICK IT?
SCHULZ

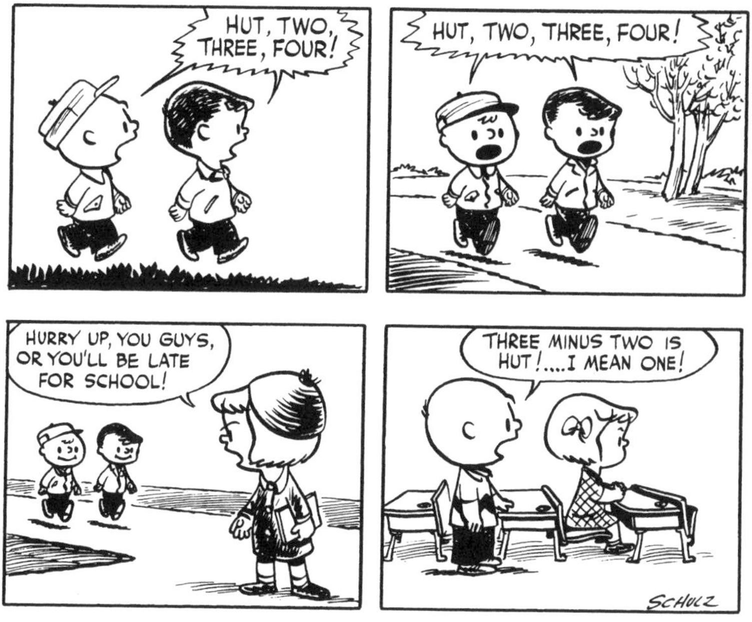
HUT, TWO, THREE, FOUR!
HUT, TWO, THREE, FOUR!
HURRY UP, YOU GUYS, OR YOU'LL BE LATE FOR SCHOOL!
THREE MINUS TWO IS HUT!....I MEAN ONE!
SCHULZ

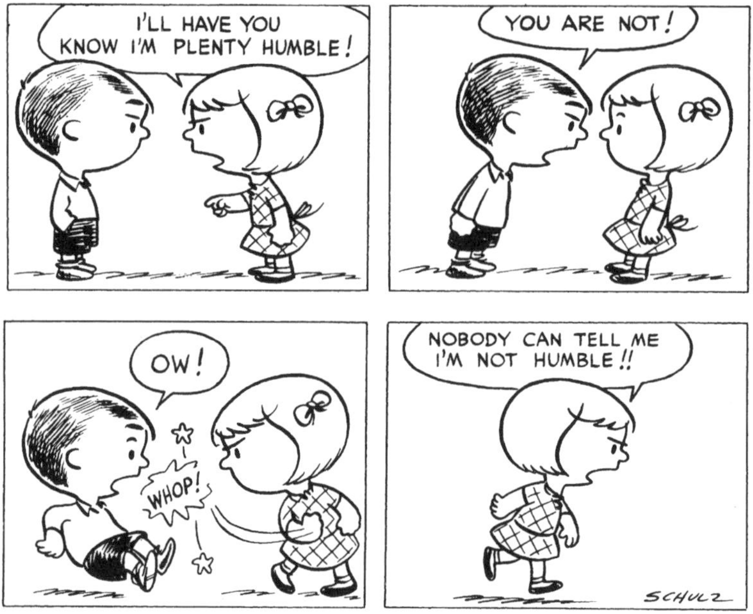
I'LL HAVE YOU KNOW I'M PLENTY HUMBLE!
YOU ARE NOT!
OW!
WHOP!
NOBODY CAN TELL ME I'M NOT HUMBLE!!
SCHULZ

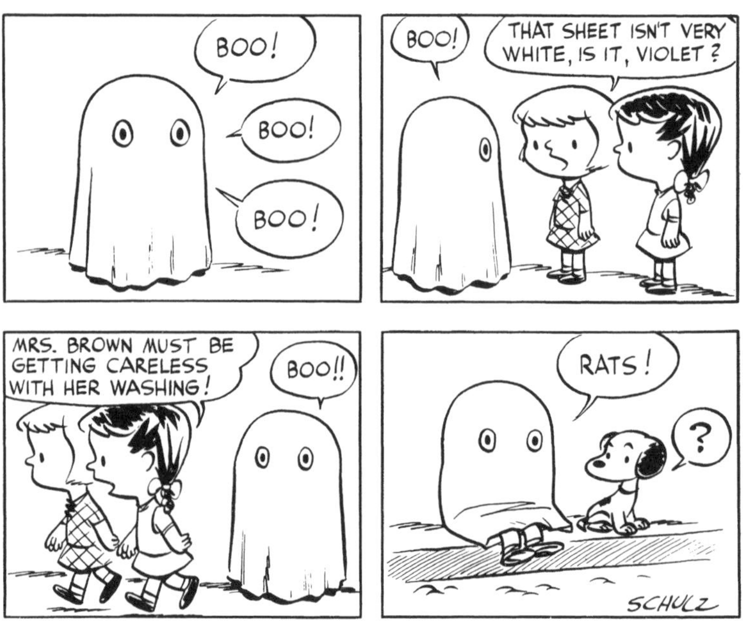
BOO!
BOO!
BOO!
BOO!
THAT SHEET ISN'T VERY WHITE, IS IT, VIOLET?
MRS. BROWN MUST BE GETTING CARELESS WITH HER WASHING!
BOO!!
RATS!
?
SCHULZ

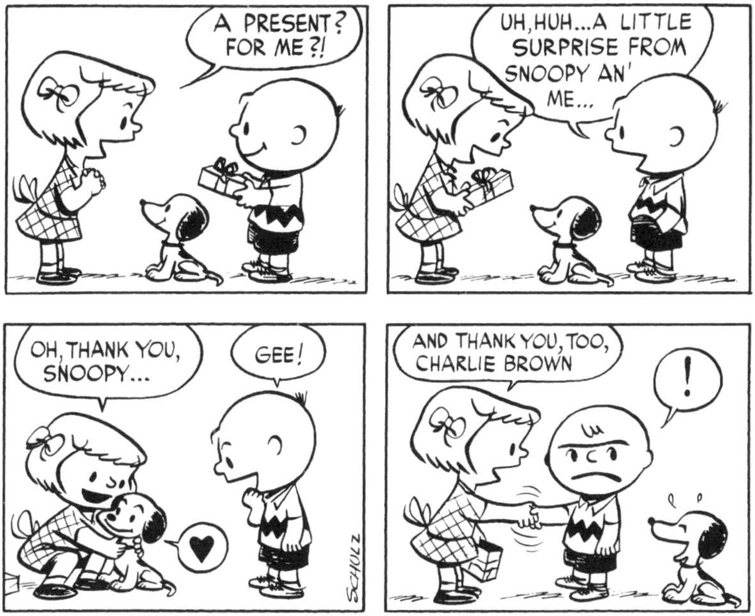
A PRESENT? FOR ME?!
UH, HUH...A LITTLE SURPRISE FROM SNOOPY AN' ME...
OH, THANK YOU, SNOOPY...
GEE!
AND THANK YOU, TOO, CHARLIE BROWN
!
SCHULZ

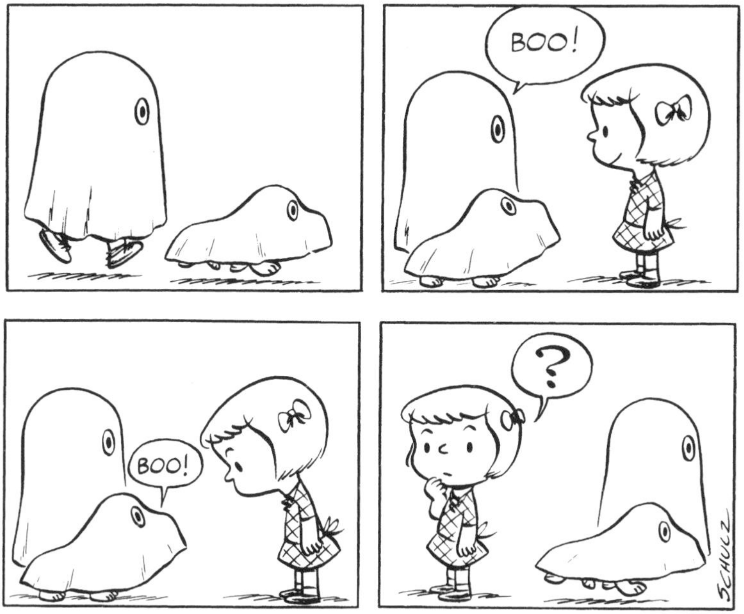
BOO!
BOO!
?
SCHULZ

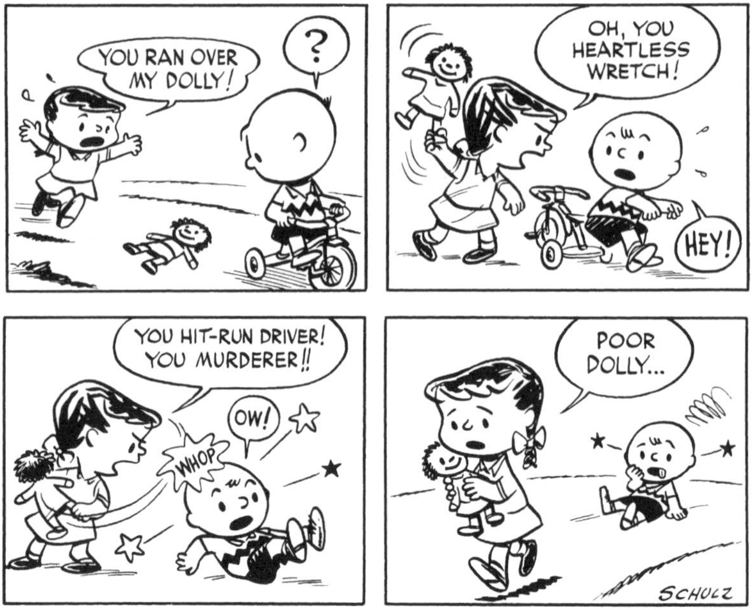

YOU RAN OVER MY DOLLY!
?
OH, YOU HEARTLESS WRETCH!
HEY!
YOU HIT-RUN DRIVER! YOU MURDERER!!
WHOP
OW!
POOR DOLLY...
SCHULZ

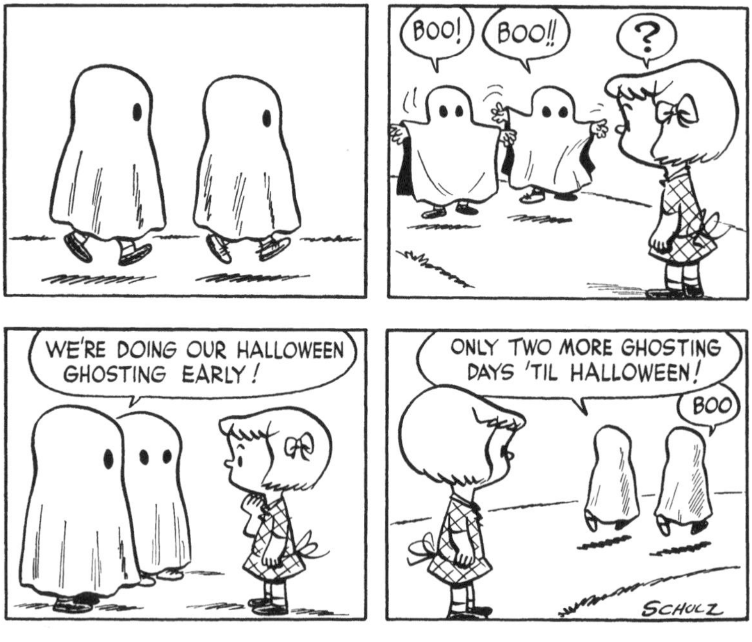

BOO!
BOO!!
?
WE'RE DOING OUR HALLOWEEN GHOSTING EARLY!
ONLY TWO MORE GHOSTING DAYS 'TIL HALLOWEEN!
BOO
SCHULZ

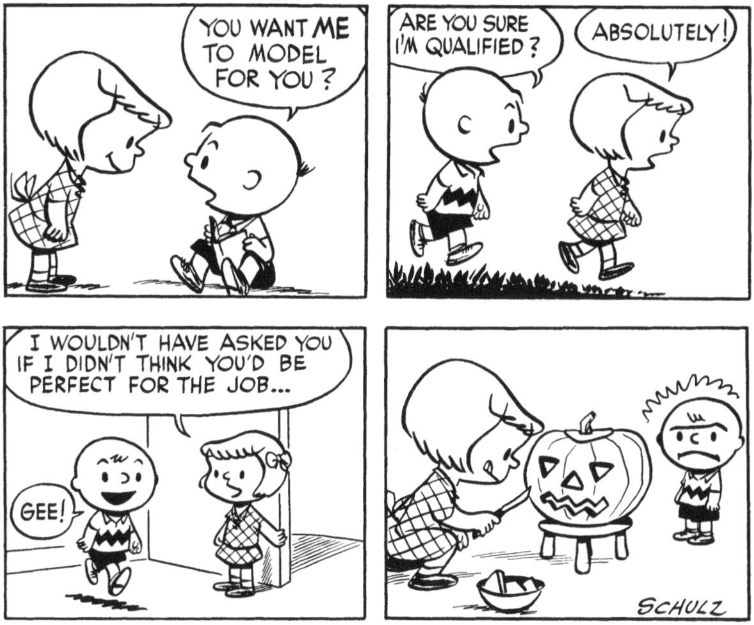
YOU WANT ME TO MODEL FOR YOU?
ARE YOU SURE I'M QUALIFIED?
ABSOLUTELY!
I WOULDN'T HAVE ASKED YOU IF I DIDN'T THINK YOU'D BE PERFECT FOR THE JOB...
GEE!
SCHULZ

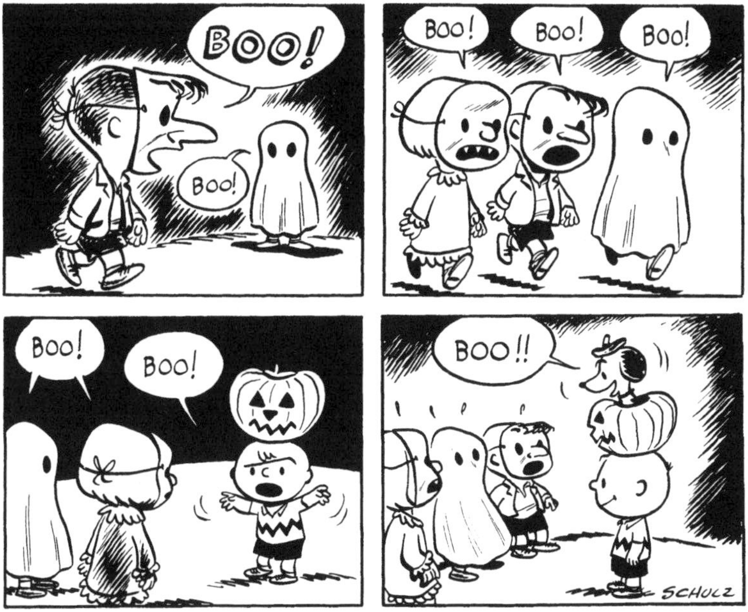
BOO!
BOO!
BOO!
BOO!
BOO!
BOO!
BOO!
BOO!!
SCHULZ

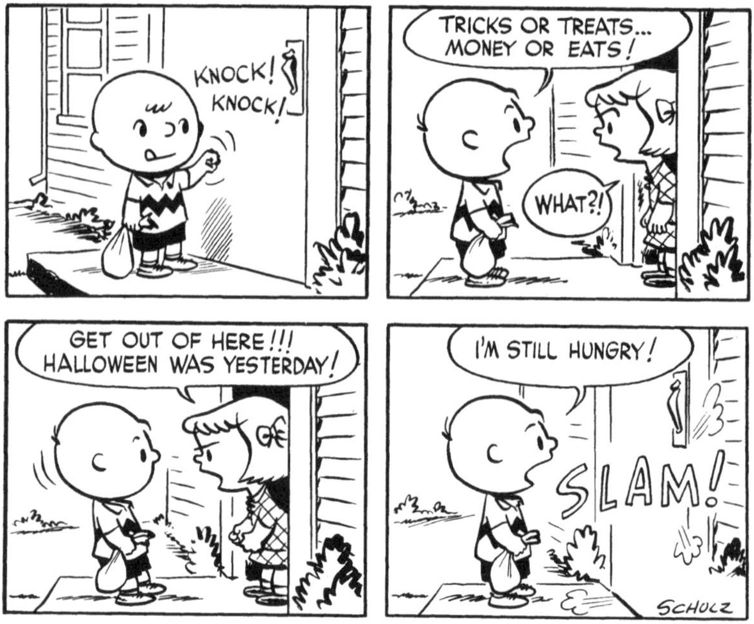
KNOCK! KNOCK!
TRICKS OR TREATS... MONEY OR EATS!
WHAT?!
GET OUT OF HERE!!! HALLOWEEN WAS YESTERDAY!
I'M STILL HUNGRY!
SLAM!
SCHULZ

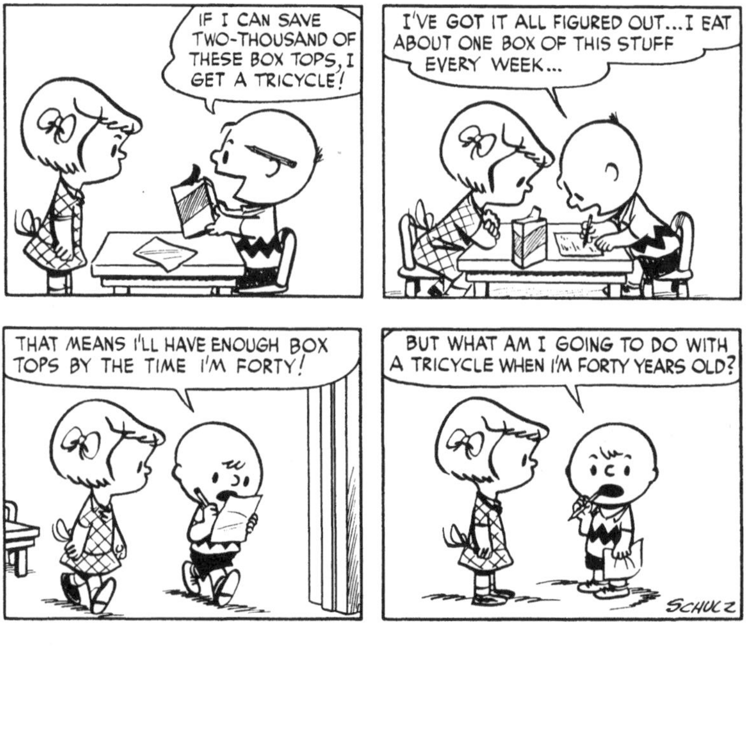
IF I CAN SAVE TWO-THOUSAND OF THESE BOX TOPS, I GET A TRICYCLE!
I'VE GOT IT ALL FIGURED OUT...I EAT ABOUT ONE BOX OF THIS STUFF EVERY WEEK...
THAT MEANS I'LL HAVE ENOUGH BOX TOPS BY THE TIME I'M FORTY!
BUT WHAT AM I GOING TO DO WITH A TRICYCLE WHEN I'M FORTY YEARS OLD?
SCHULZ

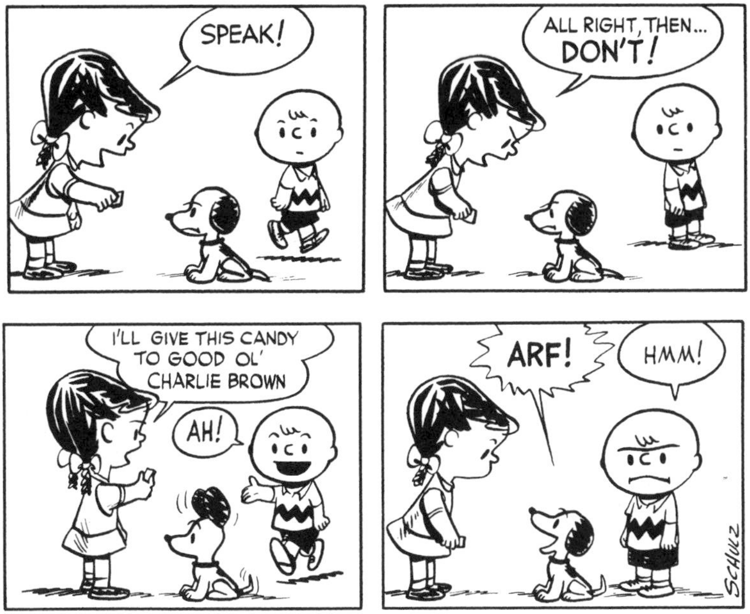
SPEAK!
ALL RIGHT, THEN... DON'T!
I'LL GIVE THIS CANDY TO GOOD OL' CHARLIE BROWN
AH!
ARF!
HMM!
SCHULZ

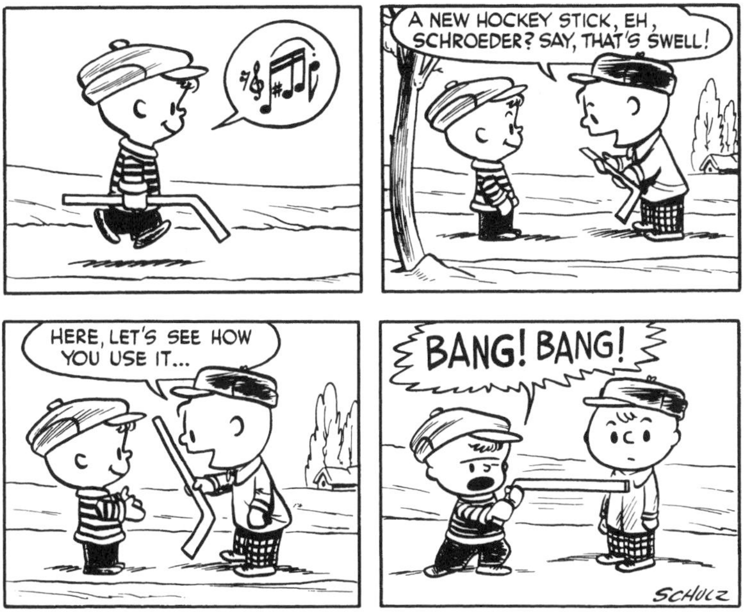
A NEW HOCKEY STICK, EH, SCHROEDER? SAY, THAT'S SWELL!
HERE, LET'S SEE HOW YOU USE IT...
BANG! BANG!
SCHULZ

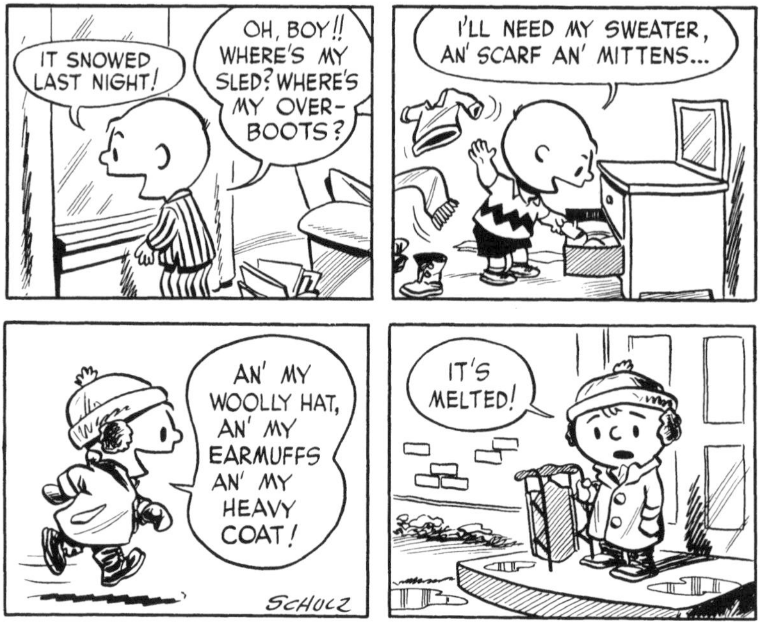
IT SNOWED LAST NIGHT!
OH, BOY!! WHERE'S MY SLED? WHERE'S MY OVER-BOOTS?
I'LL NEED MY SWEATER, AN' SCARF AN' MITTENS...
AN' MY WOOLLY HAT, AN' MY EARMUFFS AN' MY HEAVY COAT!
SCHULZ
IT'S MELTED!

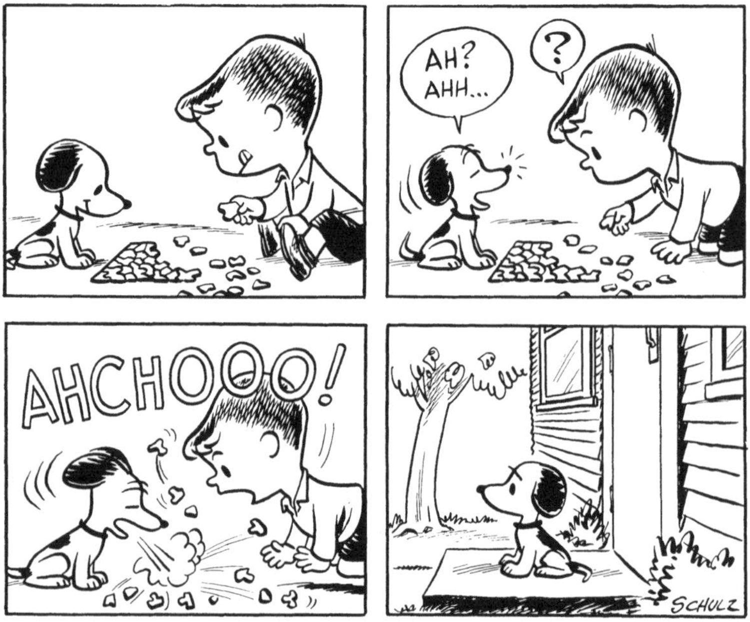
AH? AHH...
?
AHCHOOO!
SCHULZ

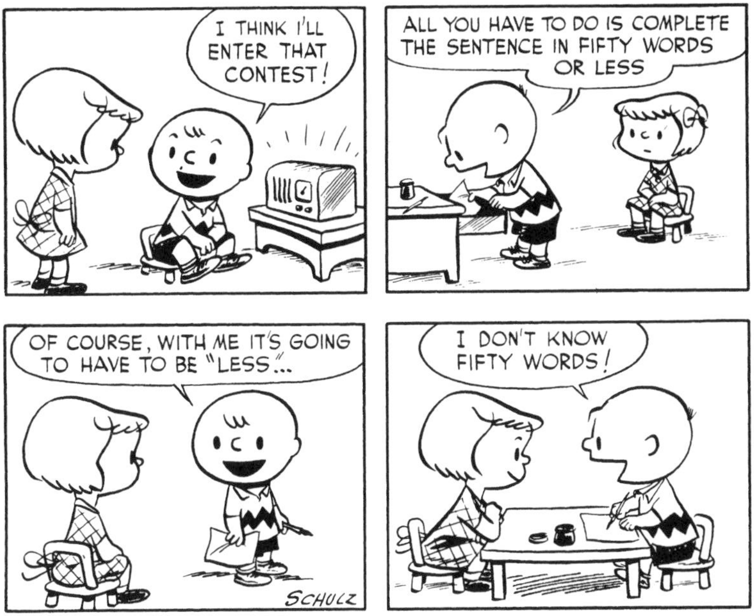
I THINK I'LL ENTER THAT CONTEST!
ALL YOU HAVE TO DO IS COMPLETE THE SENTENCE IN FIFTY WORDS OR LESS
OF COURSE, WITH ME IT'S GOING TO HAVE TO BE "LESS"...
I DON'T KNOW FIFTY WORDS!
SCHULZ

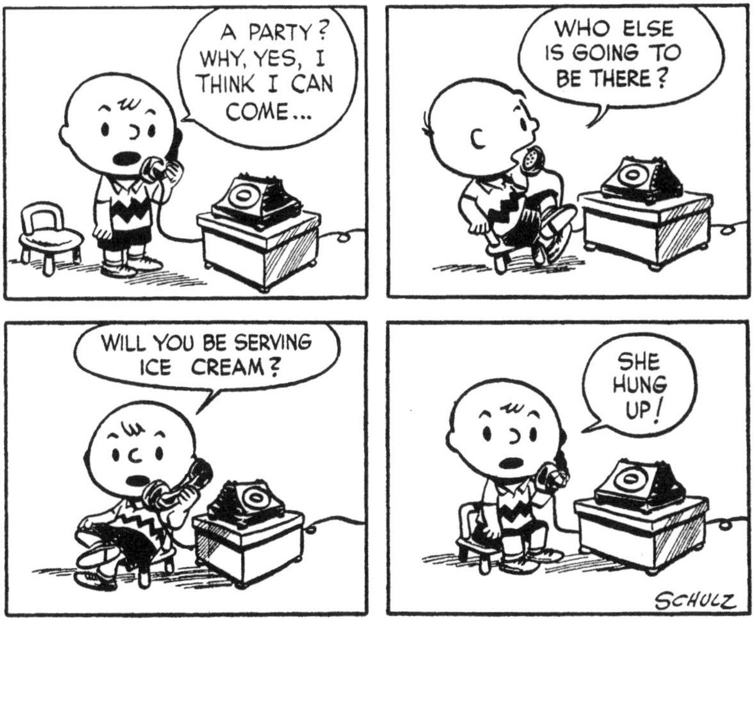
A PARTY? WHY, YES, I THINK I CAN COME...
WHO ELSE IS GOING TO BE THERE?
WILL YOU BE SERVING ICE CREAM?
SHE HUNG UP!
SCHULZ

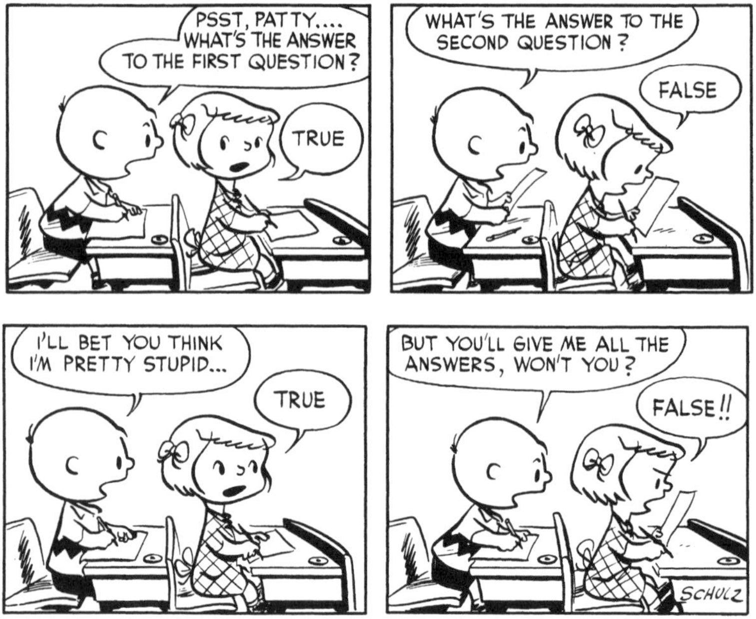
PSST, PATTY....
WHAT'S THE ANSWER
TO THE FIRST QUESTION?
TRUE
WHAT'S THE ANSWER TO THE
SECOND QUESTION?
FALSE
I'LL BET YOU THINK
I'M PRETTY STUPID...
TRUE
BUT YOU'LL GIVE ME ALL THE
ANSWERS, WON'T YOU?
FALSE!!
SCHULZ

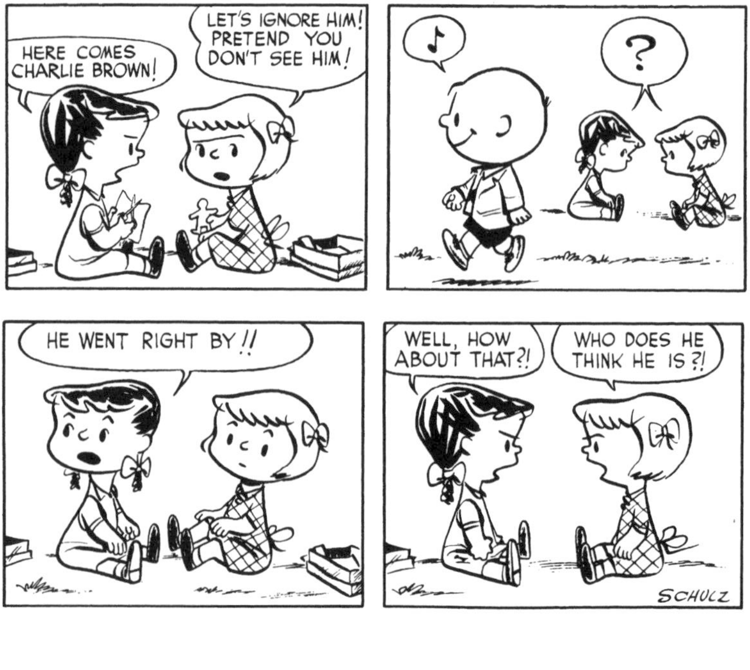
HERE COMES
CHARLIE BROWN!
LET'S IGNORE HIM!
PRETEND YOU
DON'T SEE HIM!
♪
?
HE WENT RIGHT BY!!
WELL, HOW
ABOUT THAT?!
WHO DOES HE
THINK HE IS?!
SCHULZ

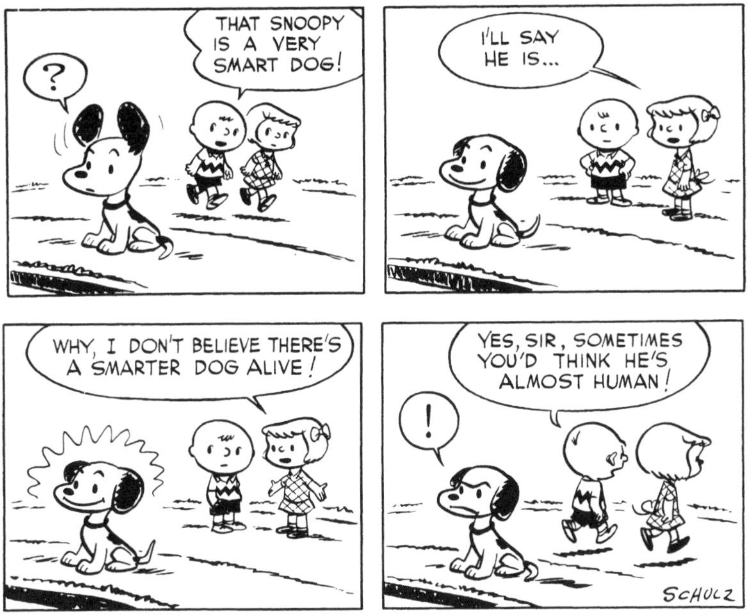
?
THAT SNOOPY IS A VERY SMART DOG!
I'LL SAY HE IS...
WHY, I DON'T BELIEVE THERE'S A SMARTER DOG ALIVE!
!
YES, SIR, SOMETIMES YOU'D THINK HE'S ALMOST HUMAN!
SCHULZ

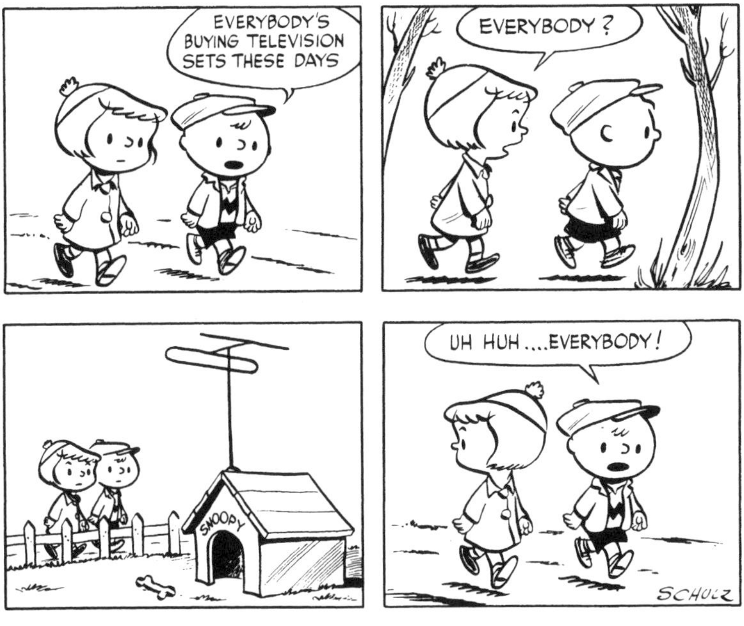
EVERYBODY'S BUYING TELEVISION SETS THESE DAYS
EVERYBODY?
SNOOPY
UH HUH....EVERYBODY!
SCHULZ

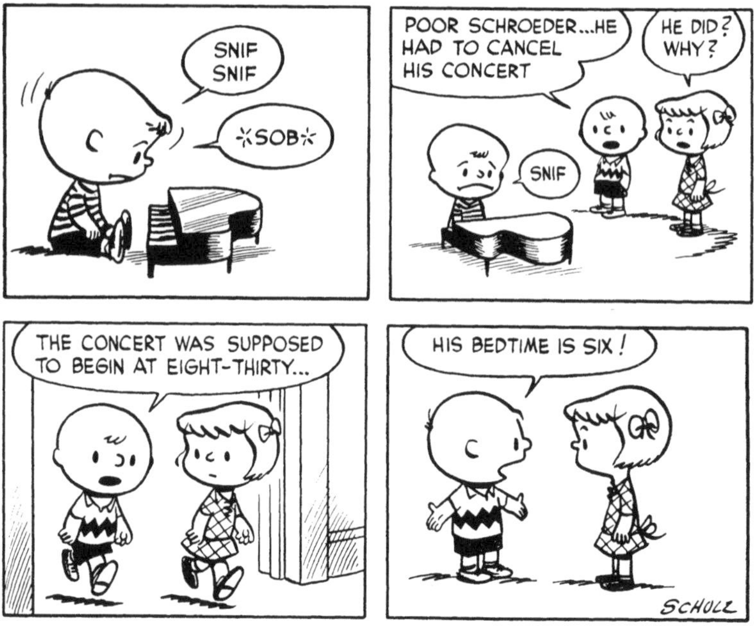
SNIF
SNIF
SOB
POOR SCHROEDER...HE HAD TO CANCEL HIS CONCERT
HE DID? WHY?
SNIF
THE CONCERT WAS SUPPOSED TO BEGIN AT EIGHT-THIRTY...
HIS BEDTIME IS SIX!
SCHULZ

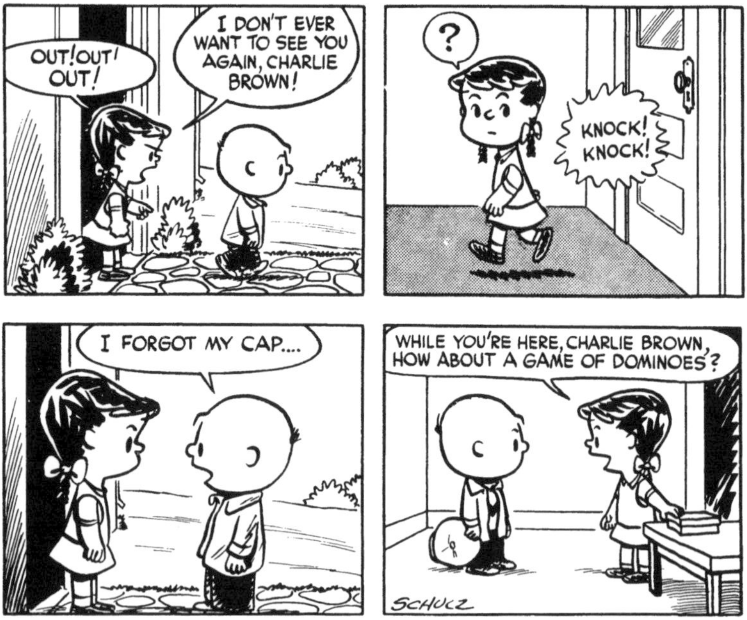
OUT! OUT! OUT!
I DON'T EVER WANT TO SEE YOU AGAIN, CHARLIE BROWN!
?
KNOCK! KNOCK!
I FORGOT MY CAP....
WHILE YOU'RE HERE, CHARLIE BROWN, HOW ABOUT A GAME OF DOMINOES?
SCHULZ

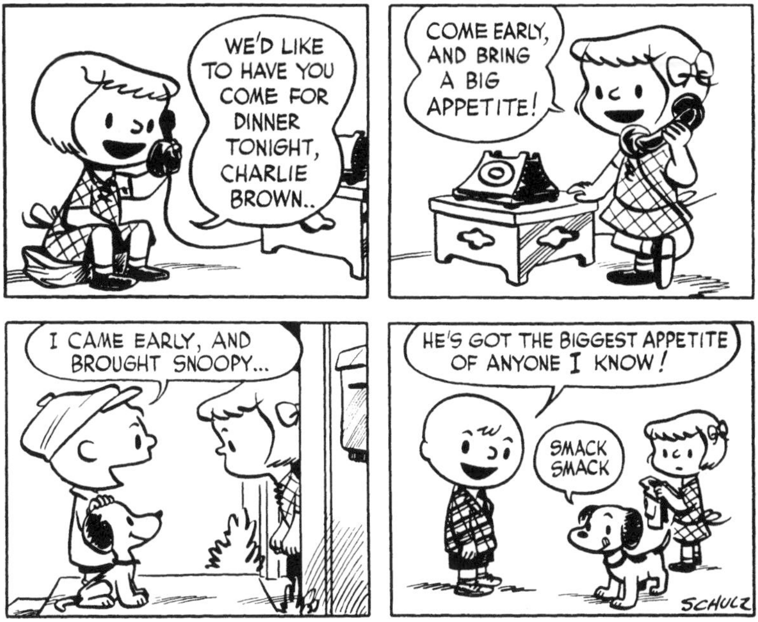
WE'D LIKE TO HAVE YOU COME FOR DINNER TONIGHT, CHARLIE BROWN..
COME EARLY, AND BRING A BIG APPETITE!
I CAME EARLY, AND BROUGHT SNOOPY...
HE'S GOT THE BIGGEST APPETITE OF ANYONE I KNOW!
SMACK SMACK
SCHULZ

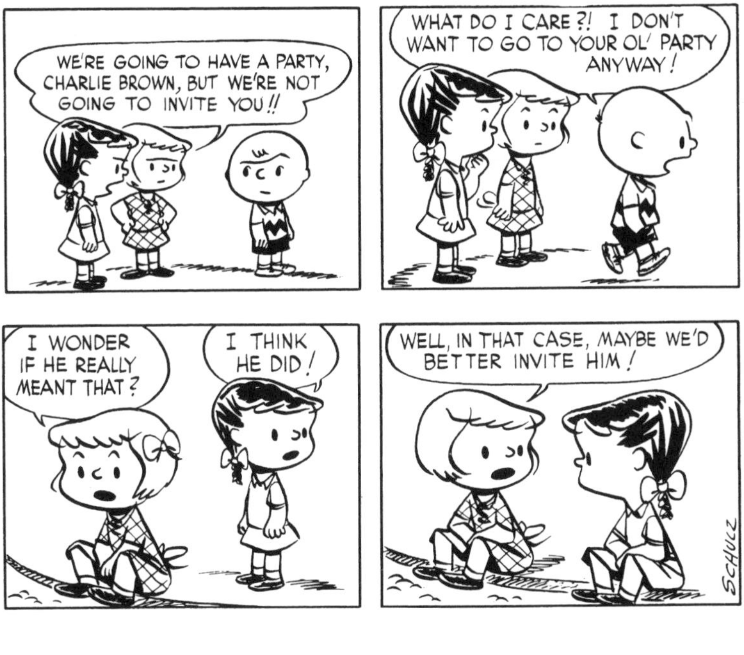
WE'RE GOING TO HAVE A PARTY, CHARLIE BROWN, BUT WE'RE NOT GOING TO INVITE YOU!!
WHAT DO I CARE?! I DON'T WANT TO GO TO YOUR OL' PARTY ANYWAY!
I WONDER IF HE REALLY MEANT THAT?
I THINK HE DID!
WELL, IN THAT CASE, MAYBE WE'D BETTER INVITE HIM!
SCHULZ

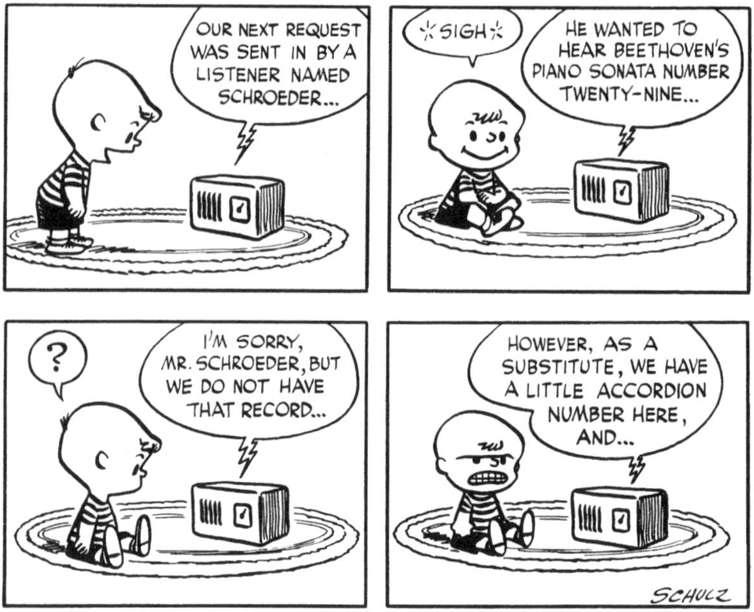
OUR NEXT REQUEST WAS SENT IN BY A LISTENER NAMED SCHROEDER...
SIGH
HE WANTED TO HEAR BEETHOVEN'S PIANO SONATA NUMBER TWENTY-NINE...
?
I'M SORRY, MR. SCHROEDER, BUT WE DO NOT HAVE THAT RECORD...
HOWEVER, AS A SUBSTITUTE, WE HAVE A LITTLE ACCORDION NUMBER HERE, AND...
SCHULZ

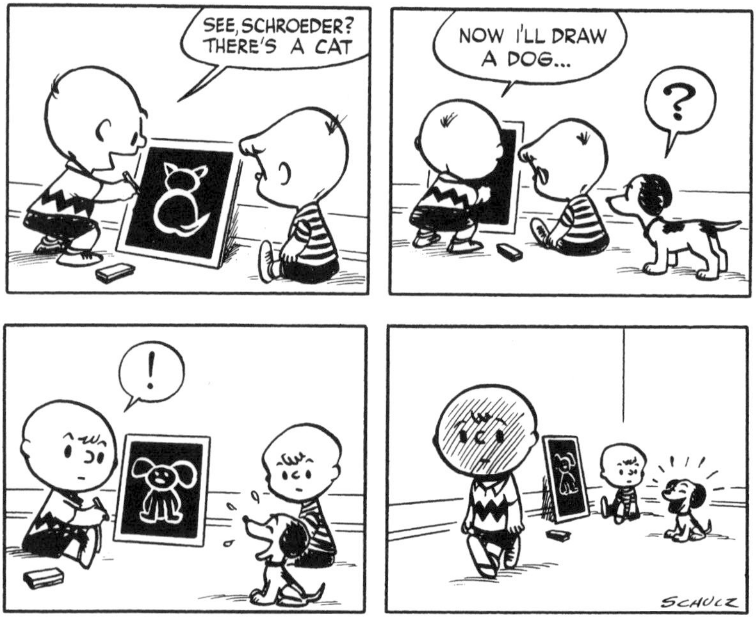
SEE, SCHROEDER? THERE'S A CAT
NOW I'LL DRAW A DOG...
?
!
SCHULZ

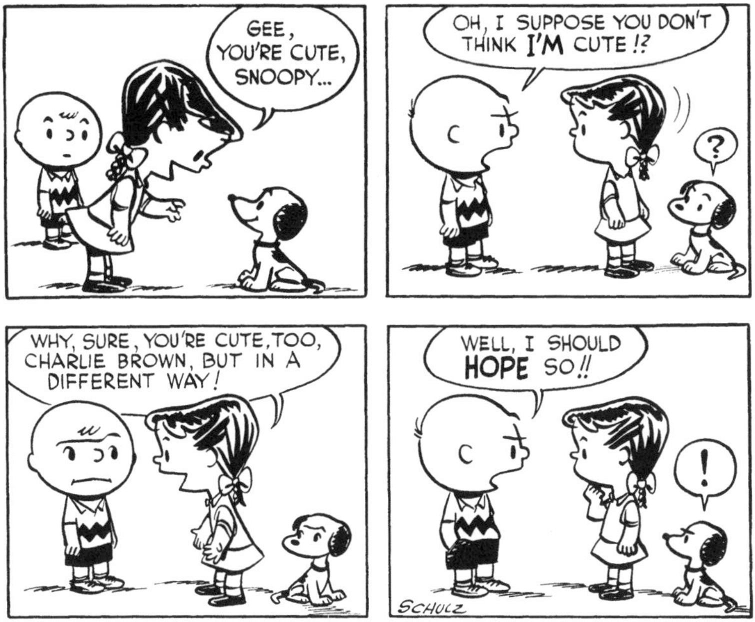
GEE, YOU'RE CUTE, SNOOPY...
OH, I SUPPOSE YOU DON'T THINK **I'M** CUTE!?
?
WHY, SURE, YOU'RE CUTE, TOO, CHARLIE BROWN, BUT IN A DIFFERENT WAY!
WELL, I SHOULD **HOPE** SO!!
!
SCHULZ

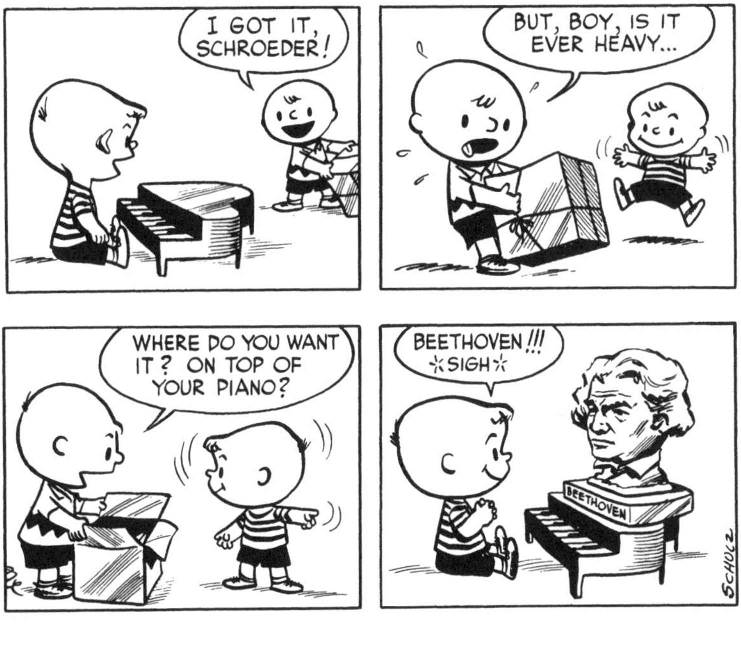
I GOT IT, SCHROEDER!
BUT, BOY, IS IT EVER HEAVY...
WHERE DO YOU WANT IT? ON TOP OF YOUR PIANO?
BEETHOVEN!!!
SIGH
BEETHOVEN
SCHULZ

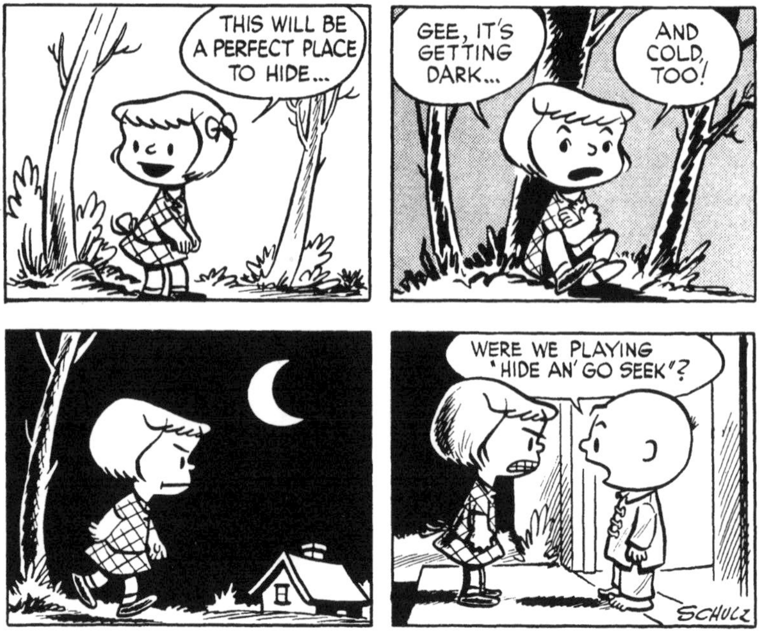
THIS WILL BE A PERFECT PLACE TO HIDE...
GEE, IT'S GETTING DARK...
AND COLD, TOO!
WERE WE PLAYING 'HIDE AN' GO SEEK'?
SCHULZ

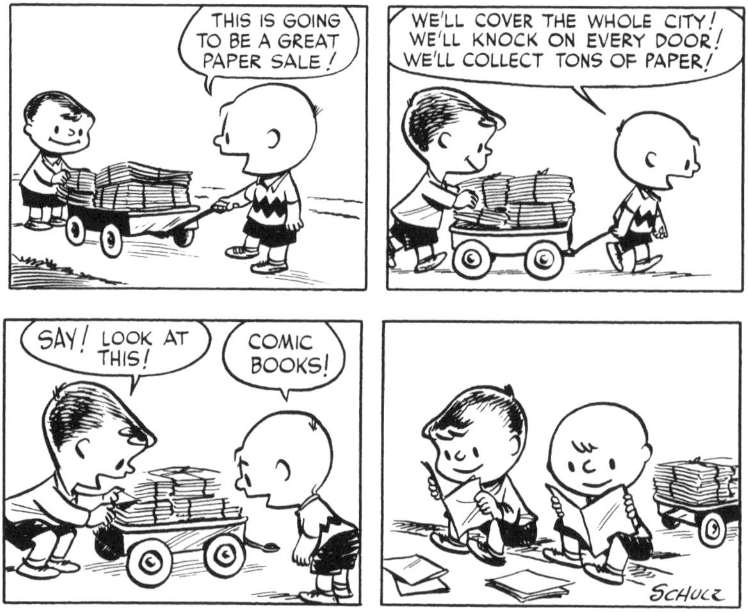
THIS IS GOING TO BE A GREAT PAPER SALE!
WE'LL COVER THE WHOLE CITY! WE'LL KNOCK ON EVERY DOOR! WE'LL COLLECT TONS OF PAPER!
SAY! LOOK AT THIS!
COMIC BOOKS!
SCHULZ

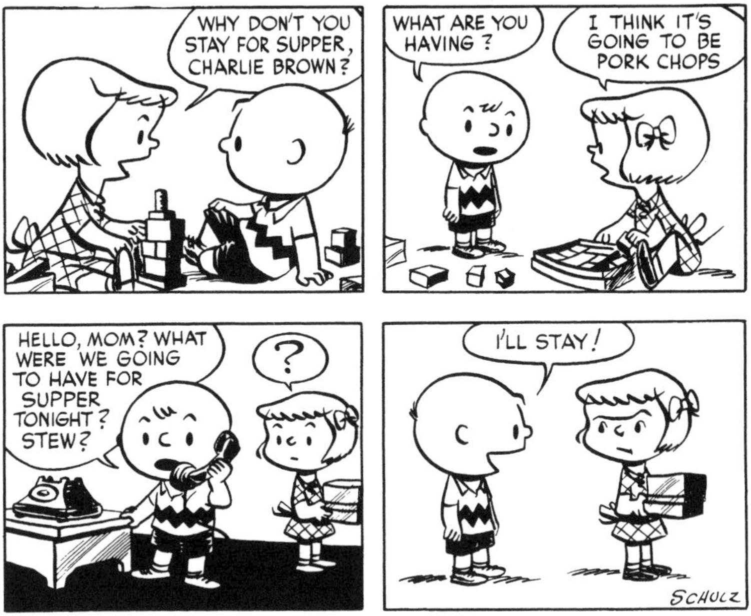
WHY DON'T YOU STAY FOR SUPPER, CHARLIE BROWN?
WHAT ARE YOU HAVING?
I THINK IT'S GOING TO BE PORK CHOPS
HELLO, MOM? WHAT WERE WE GOING TO HAVE FOR SUPPER TONIGHT? STEW?
?
I'LL STAY!
SCHULZ

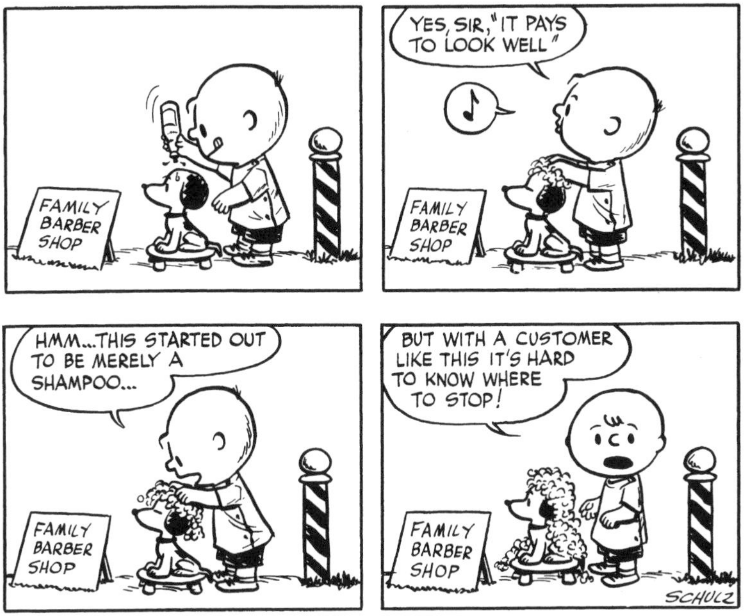
FAMILY BARBER SHOP
YES, SIR, "IT PAYS TO LOOK WELL"
FAMILY BARBER SHOP
HMM...THIS STARTED OUT TO BE MERELY A SHAMPOO...
FAMILY BARBER SHOP
BUT WITH A CUSTOMER LIKE THIS IT'S HARD TO KNOW WHERE TO STOP!
FAMILY BARBER SHOP
SCHULZ

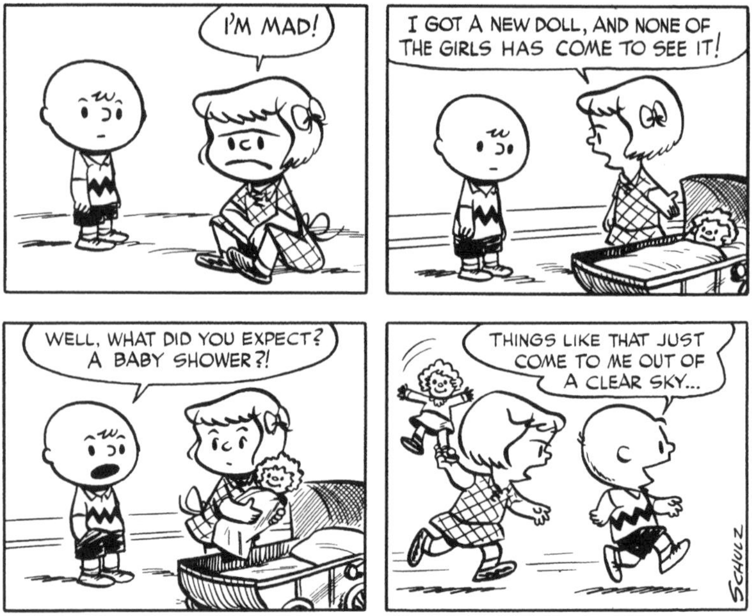
I'M MAD!
I GOT A NEW DOLL, AND NONE OF THE GIRLS HAS COME TO SEE IT!
WELL, WHAT DID YOU EXPECT? A BABY SHOWER?!
THINGS LIKE THAT JUST COME TO ME OUT OF A CLEAR SKY...
SCHULZ

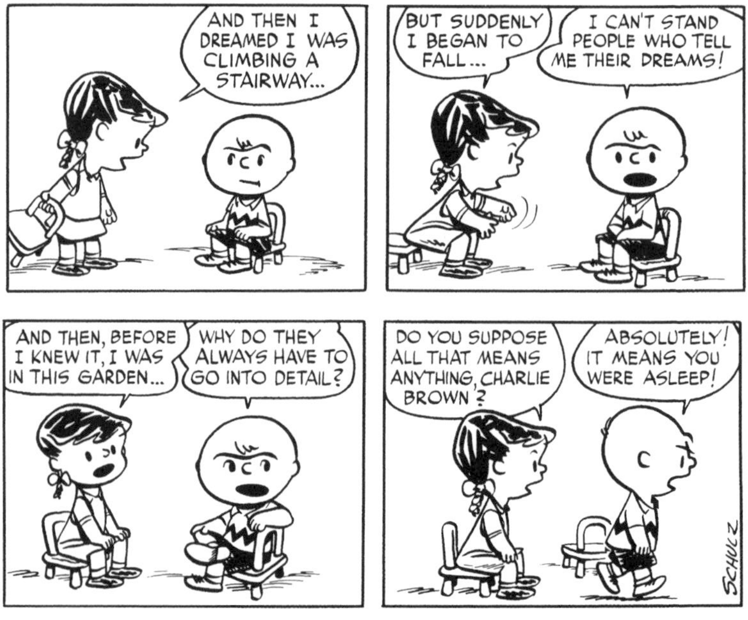
AND THEN I DREAMED I WAS CLIMBING A STAIRWAY...
BUT SUDDENLY I BEGAN TO FALL...
I CAN'T STAND PEOPLE WHO TELL ME THEIR DREAMS!
AND THEN, BEFORE I KNEW IT, I WAS IN THIS GARDEN...
WHY DO THEY ALWAYS HAVE TO GO INTO DETAIL?
DO YOU SUPPOSE ALL THAT MEANS ANYTHING, CHARLIE BROWN?
ABSOLUTELY! IT MEANS YOU WERE ASLEEP!
SCHULZ

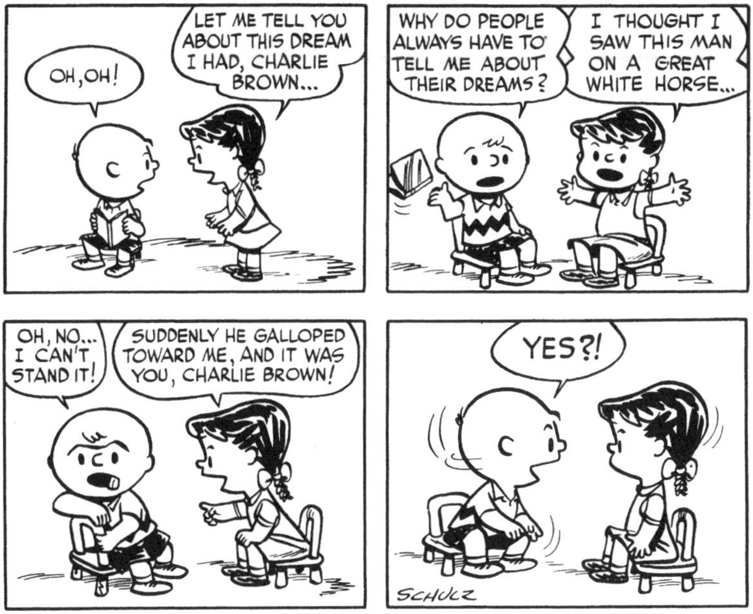
OH, OH!
LET ME TELL YOU ABOUT THIS DREAM I HAD, CHARLIE BROWN...
WHY DO PEOPLE ALWAYS HAVE TO TELL ME ABOUT THEIR DREAMS?
I THOUGHT I SAW THIS MAN ON A GREAT WHITE HORSE...
OH, NO... I CAN'T STAND IT!
SUDDENLY HE GALLOPED TOWARD ME, AND IT WAS YOU, CHARLIE BROWN!
YES?!
SCHULZ

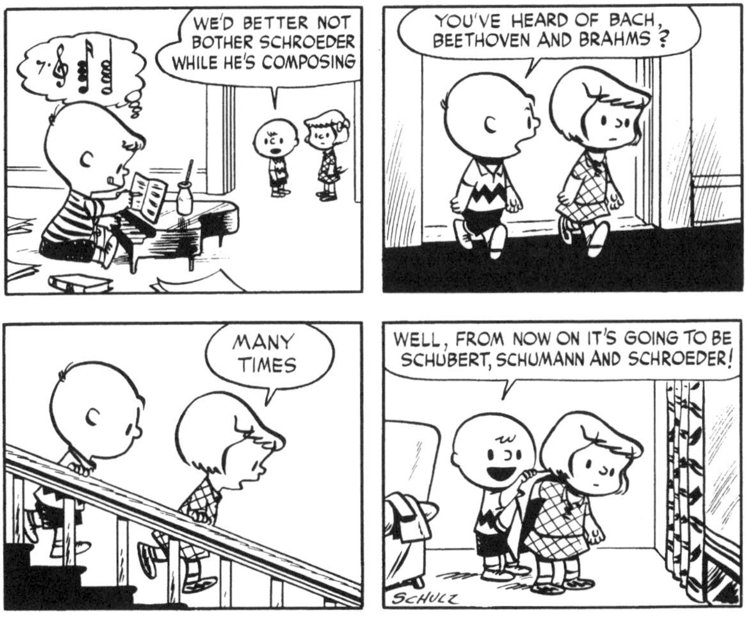
WE'D BETTER NOT BOTHER SCHROEDER WHILE HE'S COMPOSING
YOU'VE HEARD OF BACH, BEETHOVEN AND BRAHMS?
MANY TIMES
WELL, FROM NOW ON IT'S GOING TO BE SCHUBERT, SCHUMANN AND SCHROEDER!
SCHULZ

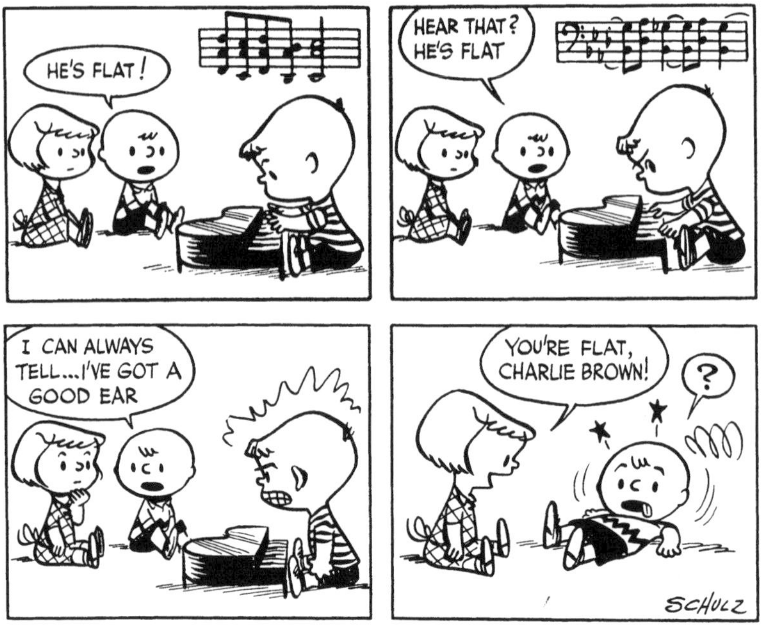
HE'S FLAT!
HEAR THAT? HE'S FLAT
I CAN ALWAYS TELL...I'VE GOT A GOOD EAR
YOU'RE FLAT, CHARLIE BROWN!
?
SCHULZ

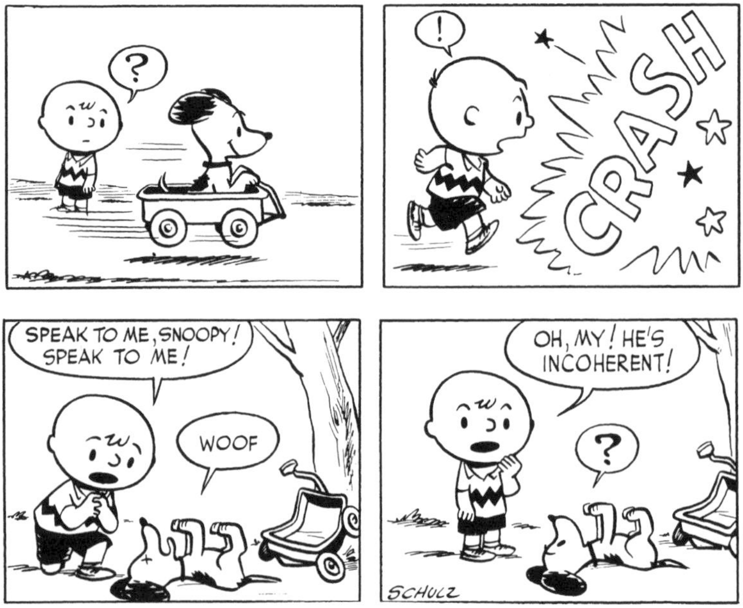
?
!
CRASH
SPEAK TO ME, SNOOPY! SPEAK TO ME!
WOOF
OH, MY! HE'S INCOHERENT!
?
SCHULZ

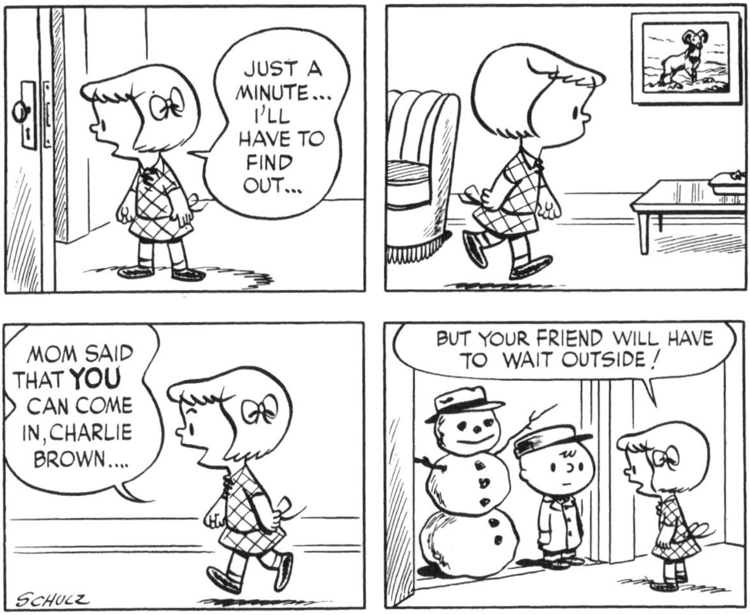
JUST A MINUTE... I'LL HAVE TO FIND OUT...
MOM SAID THAT **YOU** CAN COME IN, CHARLIE BROWN....
SCHULZ
BUT YOUR FRIEND WILL HAVE TO WAIT OUTSIDE!

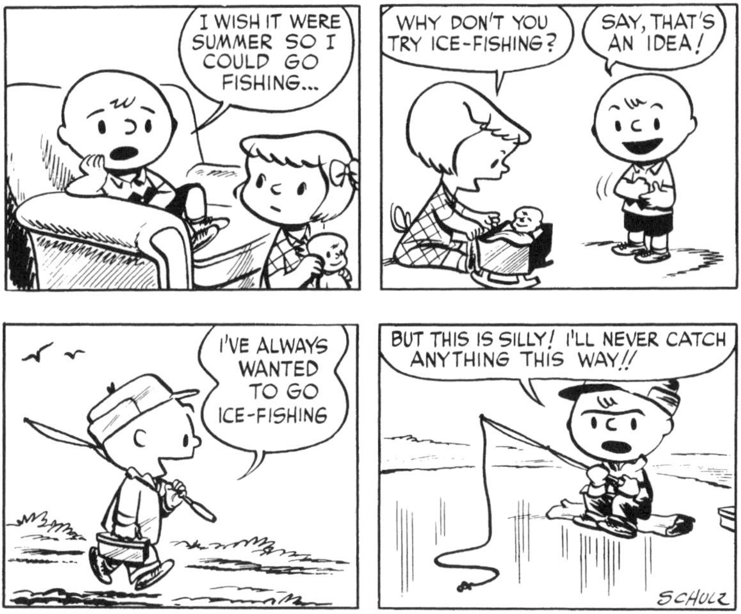
I WISH IT WERE SUMMER SO I COULD GO FISHING...
WHY DON'T YOU TRY ICE-FISHING?
SAY, THAT'S AN IDEA!
I'VE ALWAYS WANTED TO GO ICE-FISHING
BUT THIS IS SILLY! I'LL NEVER CATCH ANYTHING THIS WAY!!
SCHULZ

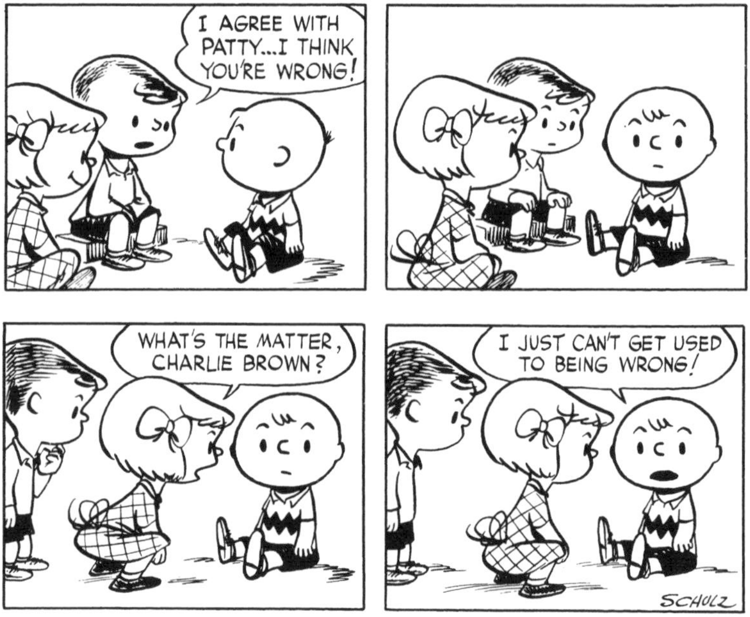
I AGREE WITH PATTY...I THINK YOU'RE WRONG!
WHAT'S THE MATTER, CHARLIE BROWN?
I JUST CAN'T GET USED TO BEING WRONG!
SCHULZ

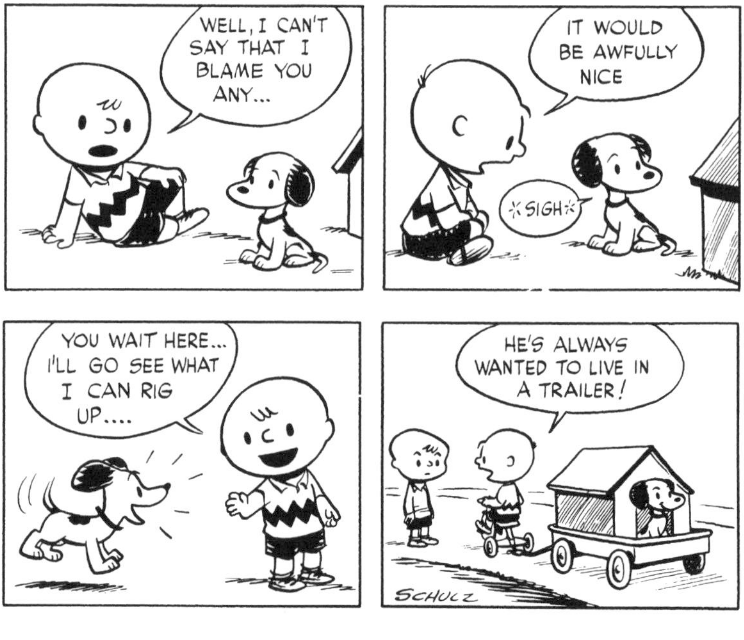
WELL, I CAN'T SAY THAT I BLAME YOU ANY...
IT WOULD BE AWFULLY NICE
SIGH
YOU WAIT HERE... I'LL GO SEE WHAT I CAN RIG UP....
HE'S ALWAYS WANTED TO LIVE IN A TRAILER!
SCHULZ

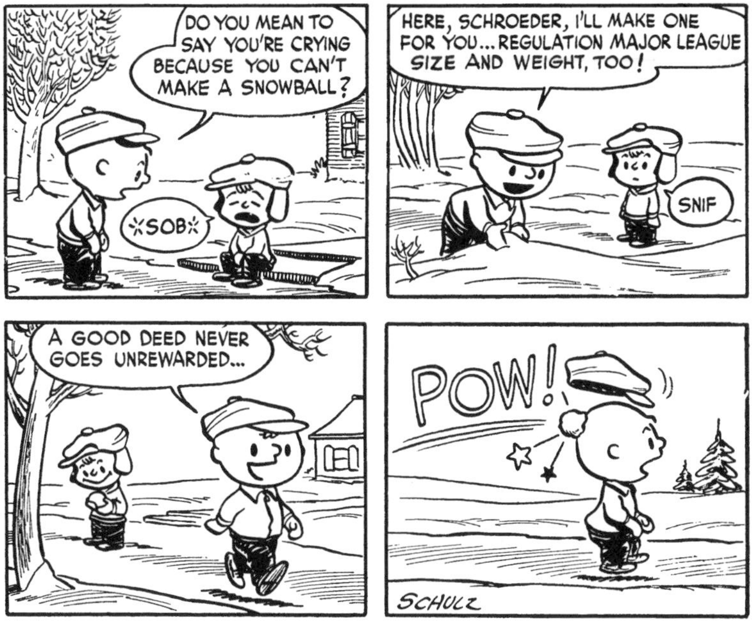
DO YOU MEAN TO SAY YOU'RE CRYING BECAUSE YOU CAN'T MAKE A SNOWBALL?
SOB
HERE, SCHROEDER, I'LL MAKE ONE FOR YOU... REGULATION MAJOR LEAGUE SIZE AND WEIGHT, TOO!
SNIF
A GOOD DEED NEVER GOES UNREWARDED...
POW!
SCHULZ

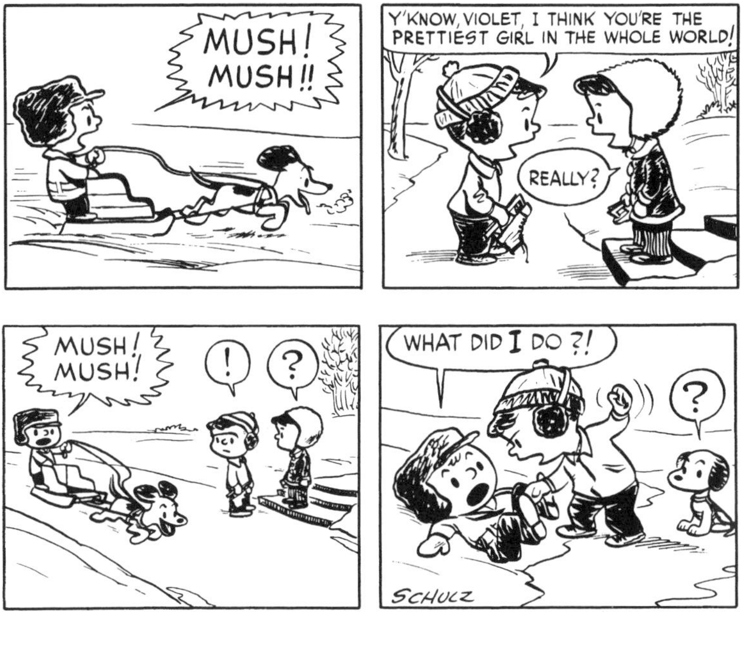
MUSH! MUSH!!
Y'KNOW, VIOLET, I THINK YOU'RE THE PRETTIEST GIRL IN THE WHOLE WORLD!
REALLY?
MUSH! MUSH!
!
?
WHAT DID I DO ?!
?
SCHULZ

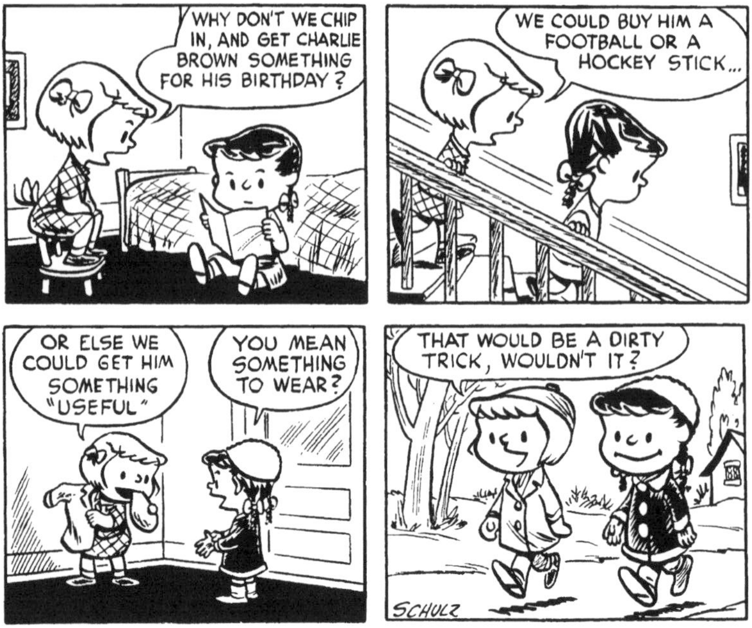
WHY DON'T WE CHIP IN, AND GET CHARLIE BROWN SOMETHING FOR HIS BIRTHDAY?
WE COULD BUY HIM A FOOTBALL OR A HOCKEY STICK...
OR ELSE WE COULD GET HIM SOMETHING "USEFUL"
YOU MEAN SOMETHING TO WEAR?
THAT WOULD BE A DIRTY TRICK, WOULDN'T IT?
SCHULZ

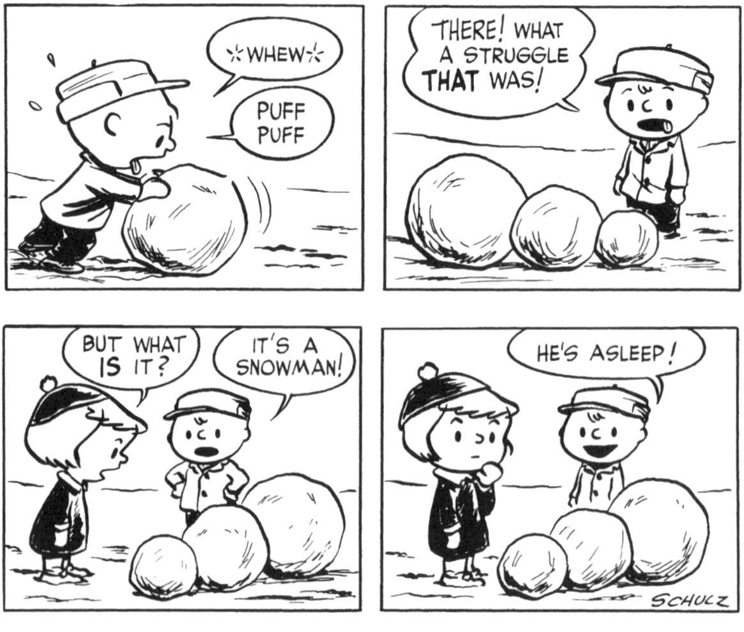
WHEW
PUFF PUFF
THERE! WHAT A STRUGGLE THAT WAS!
BUT WHAT IS IT?
IT'S A SNOWMAN!
HE'S ASLEEP!
SCHULZ

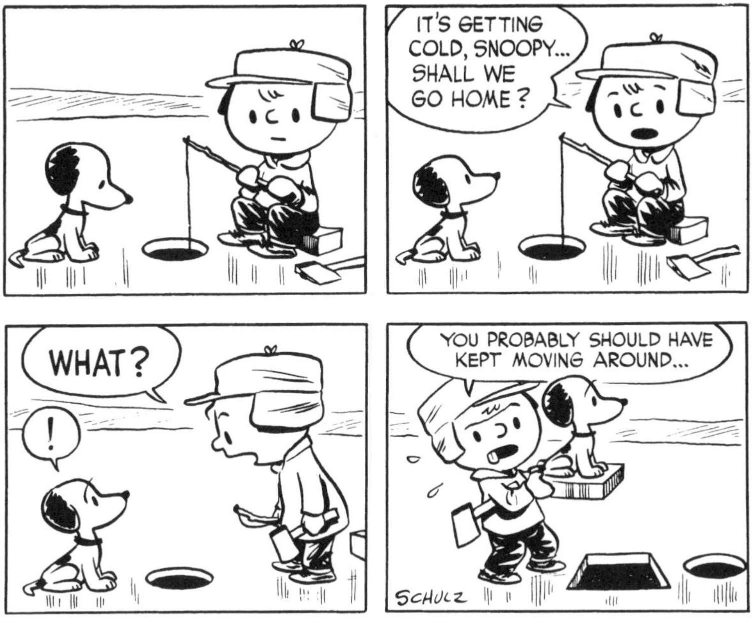
IT'S GETTING COLD, SNOOPY... SHALL WE GO HOME?
WHAT?
!
YOU PROBABLY SHOULD HAVE KEPT MOVING AROUND...
SCHULZ

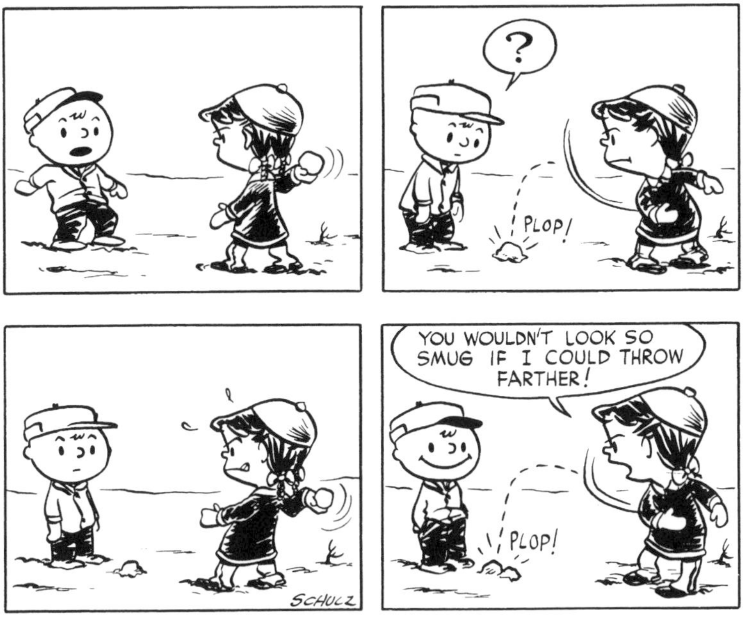
?
PLOP!
SCHULZ
YOU WOULDN'T LOOK SO SMUG IF I COULD THROW FARTHER!
PLOP!

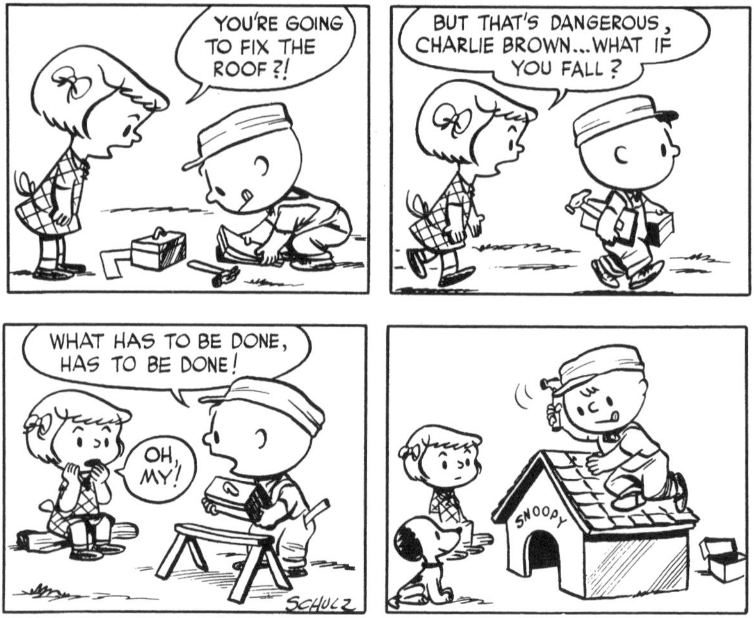
YOU'RE GOING TO FIX THE ROOF ?!
BUT THAT'S DANGEROUS, CHARLIE BROWN...WHAT IF YOU FALL ?
WHAT HAS TO BE DONE, HAS TO BE DONE!
OH, MY!
SNOOPY
SCHULZ

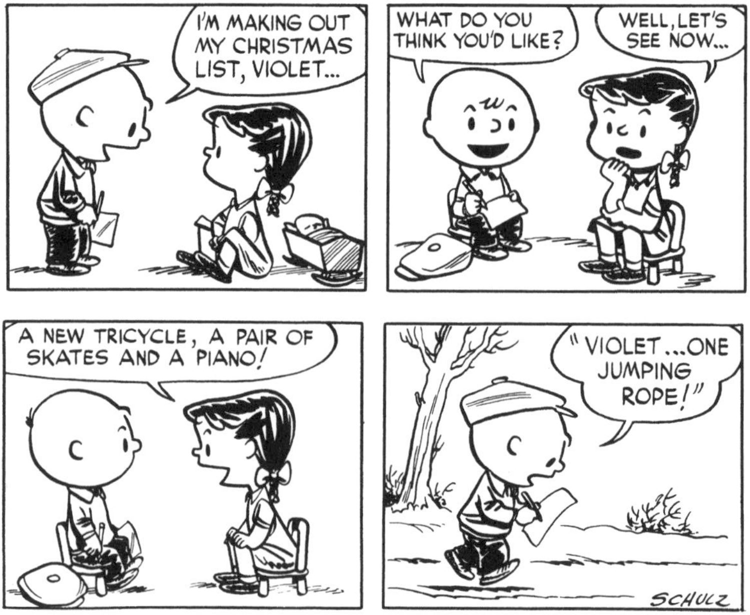
I'M MAKING OUT MY CHRISTMAS LIST, VIOLET...
WHAT DO YOU THINK YOU'D LIKE?
WELL, LET'S SEE NOW...
A NEW TRICYCLE, A PAIR OF SKATES AND A PIANO!
"VIOLET...ONE JUMPING ROPE!"
SCHULZ

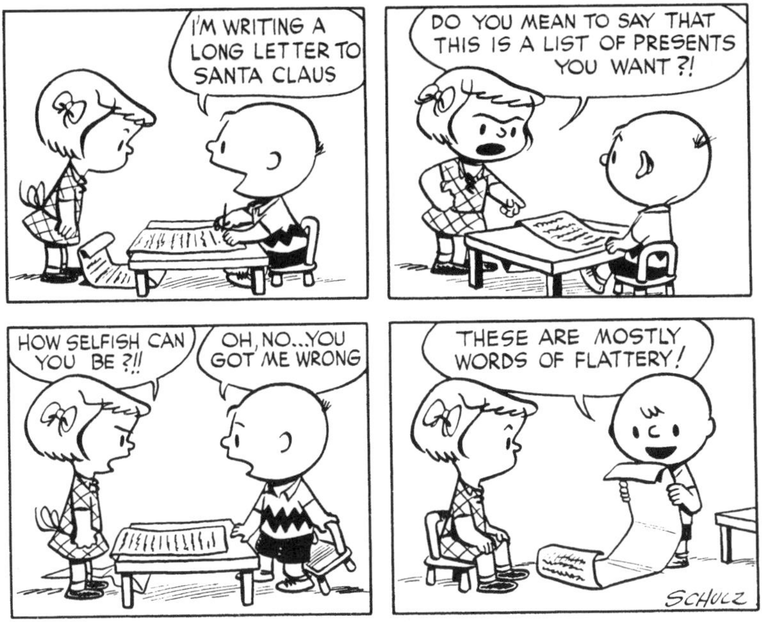
I'M WRITING A LONG LETTER TO SANTA CLAUS
DO YOU MEAN TO SAY THAT THIS IS A LIST OF PRESENTS YOU WANT ?!
HOW SELFISH CAN YOU BE ?!!
OH, NO...YOU GOT ME WRONG
THESE ARE MOSTLY WORDS OF FLATTERY!
SCHULZ

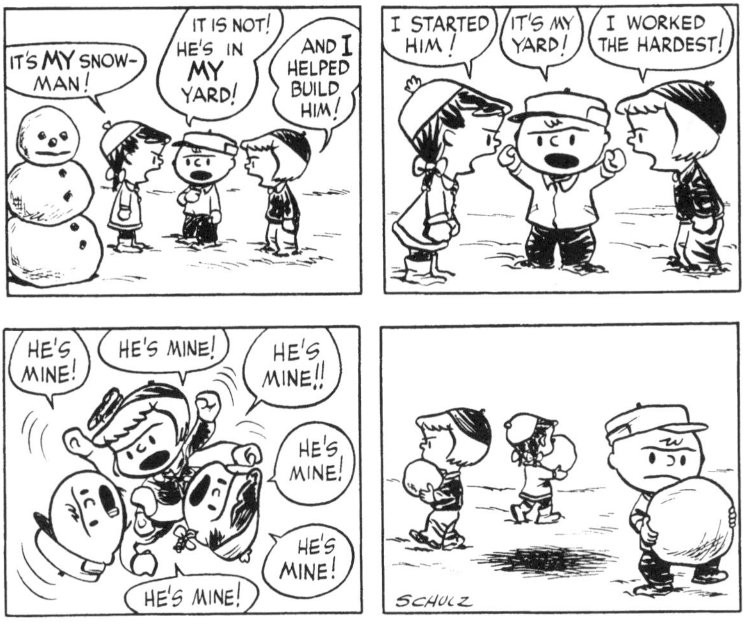
IT'S MY SNOW-MAN!
IT IS NOT! HE'S IN MY YARD!
AND I HELPED BUILD HIM!
I STARTED HIM!
IT'S MY YARD!
I WORKED THE HARDEST!
HE'S MINE!
HE'S MINE!
HE'S MINE!!
HE'S MINE!
HE'S MINE!
HE'S MINE!
SCHULZ

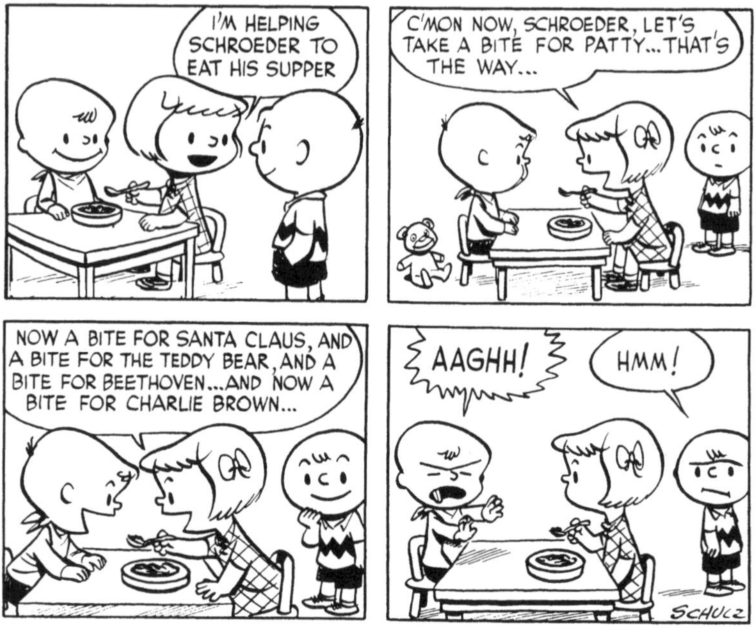
I'M HELPING SCHROEDER TO EAT HIS SUPPER
C'MON NOW, SCHROEDER, LET'S TAKE A BITE FOR PATTY...THAT'S THE WAY...
NOW A BITE FOR SANTA CLAUS, AND A BITE FOR THE TEDDY BEAR, AND A BITE FOR BEETHOVEN...AND NOW A BITE FOR CHARLIE BROWN...
AAGHH!
HMM!
SCHULZ

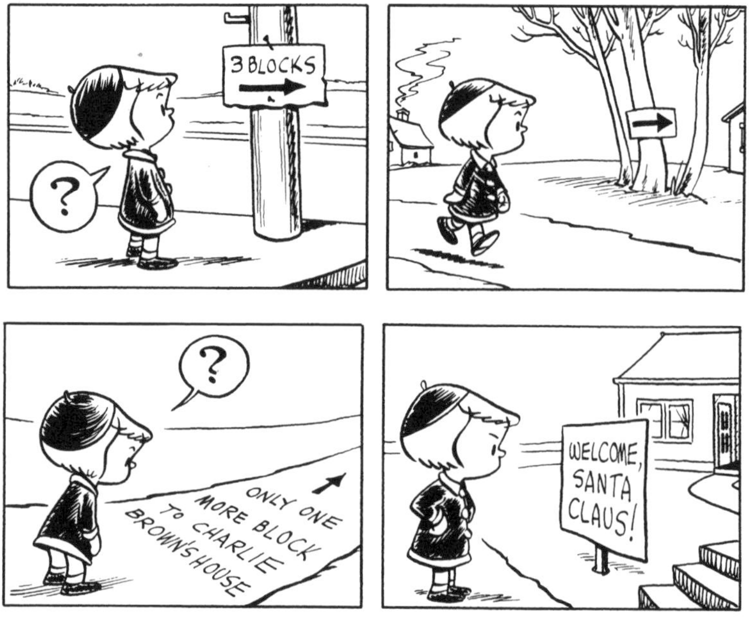
3 BLOCKS
?
?
ONLY ONE MORE BLOCK TO CHARLIE BROWN'S HOUSE
WELCOME, SANTA CLAUS!

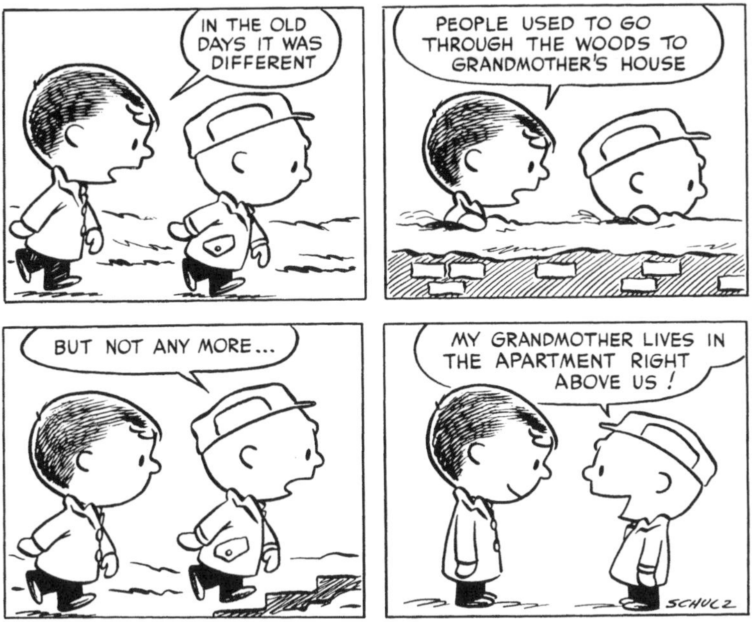
IN THE OLD DAYS IT WAS DIFFERENT
PEOPLE USED TO GO THROUGH THE WOODS TO GRANDMOTHER'S HOUSE
BUT NOT ANY MORE...
MY GRANDMOTHER LIVES IN THE APARTMENT RIGHT ABOVE US!
SCHULZ

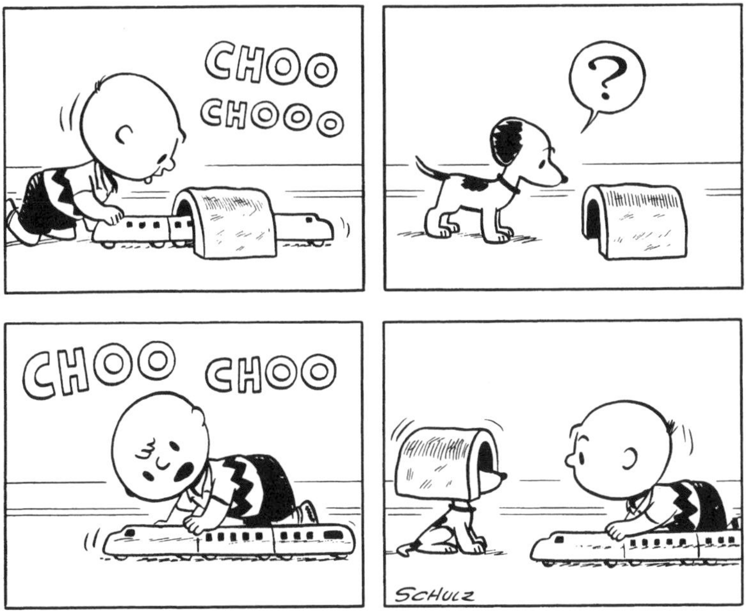
CHOO CHOOOO
?
CHOO CHOO
SCHULZ

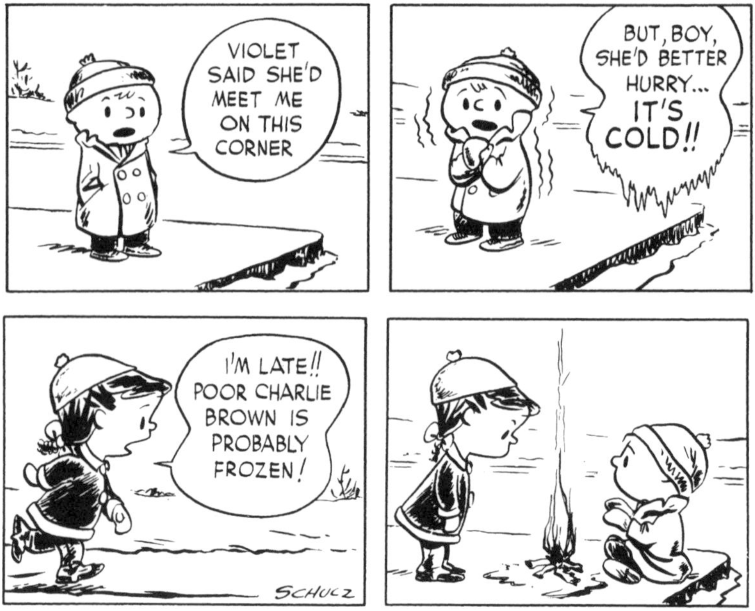
VIOLET SAID SHE'D MEET ME ON THIS CORNER
BUT, BOY, SHE'D BETTER HURRY... IT'S COLD!!
I'M LATE!! POOR CHARLIE BROWN IS PROBABLY FROZEN!
SCHULZ

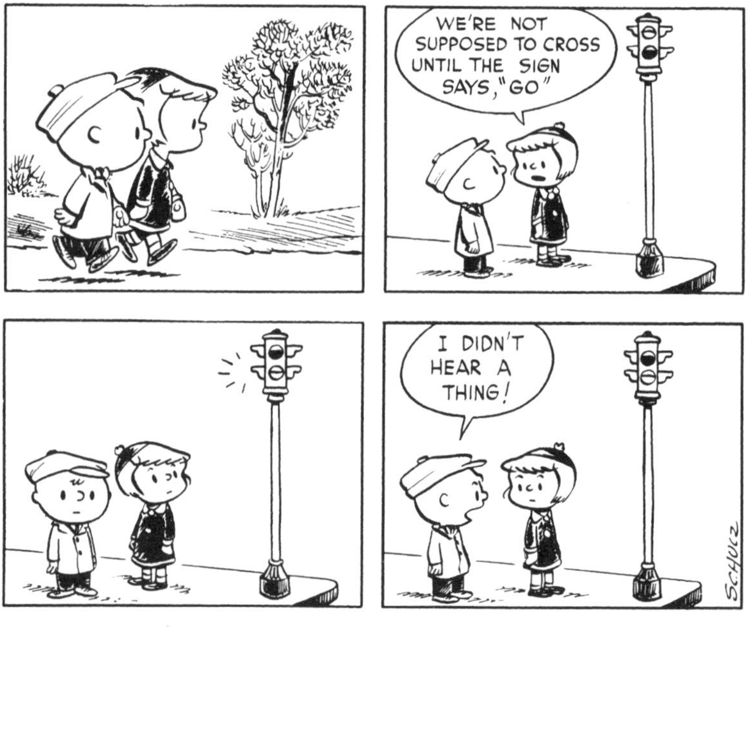
WE'RE NOT SUPPOSED TO CROSS UNTIL THE SIGN SAYS, "GO"
I DIDN'T HEAR A THING!
SCHULZ

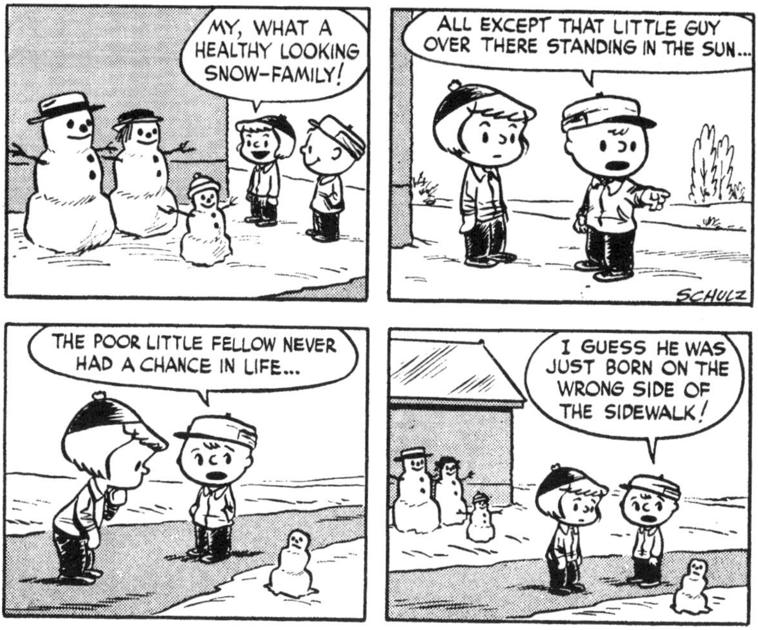
MY, WHAT A HEALTHY LOOKING SNOW-FAMILY!
ALL EXCEPT THAT LITTLE GUY OVER THERE STANDING IN THE SUN...
SCHULZ
THE POOR LITTLE FELLOW NEVER HAD A CHANCE IN LIFE...
I GUESS HE WAS JUST BORN ON THE WRONG SIDE OF THE SIDEWALK!

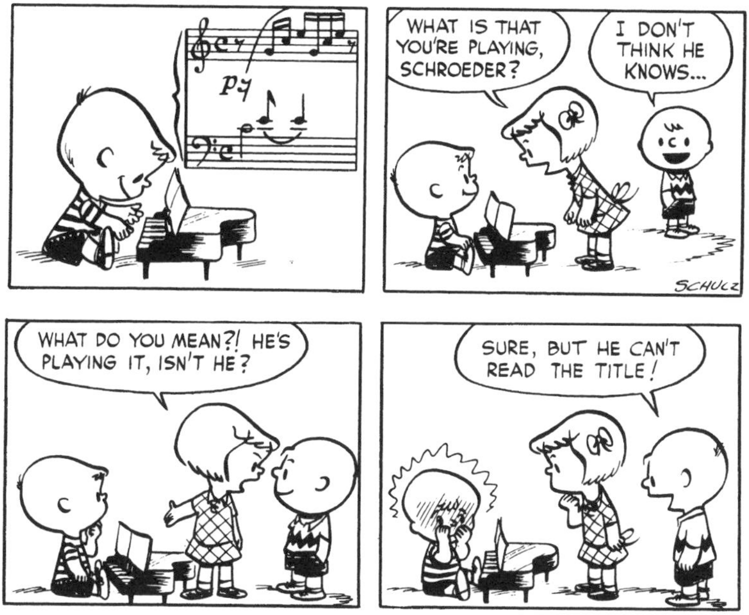
WHAT IS THAT YOU'RE PLAYING, SCHROEDER?
I DON'T THINK HE KNOWS...
SCHULZ
WHAT DO YOU MEAN?! HE'S PLAYING IT, ISN'T HE?
SURE, BUT HE CAN'T READ THE TITLE!

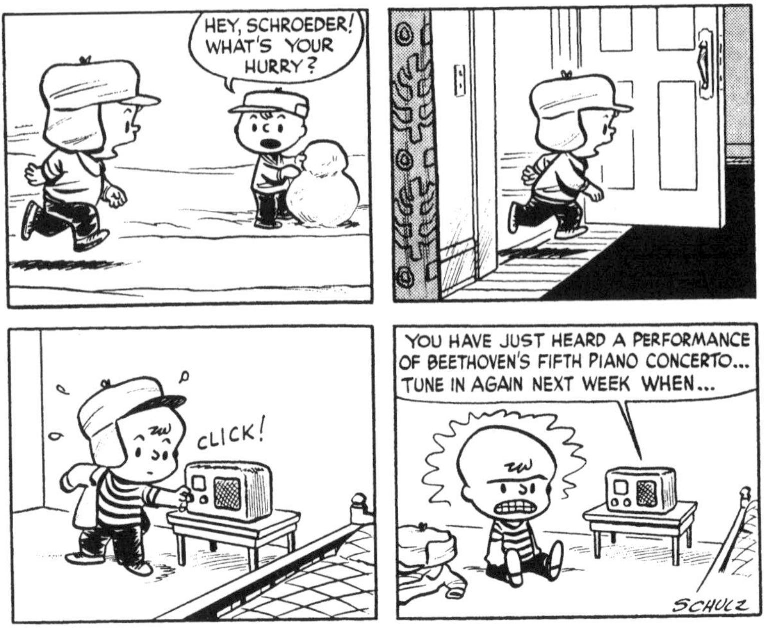
HEY, SCHROEDER! WHAT'S YOUR HURRY?
CLICK!
YOU HAVE JUST HEARD A PERFORMANCE OF BEETHOVEN'S FIFTH PIANO CONCERTO... TUNE IN AGAIN NEXT WEEK WHEN...
SCHULZ

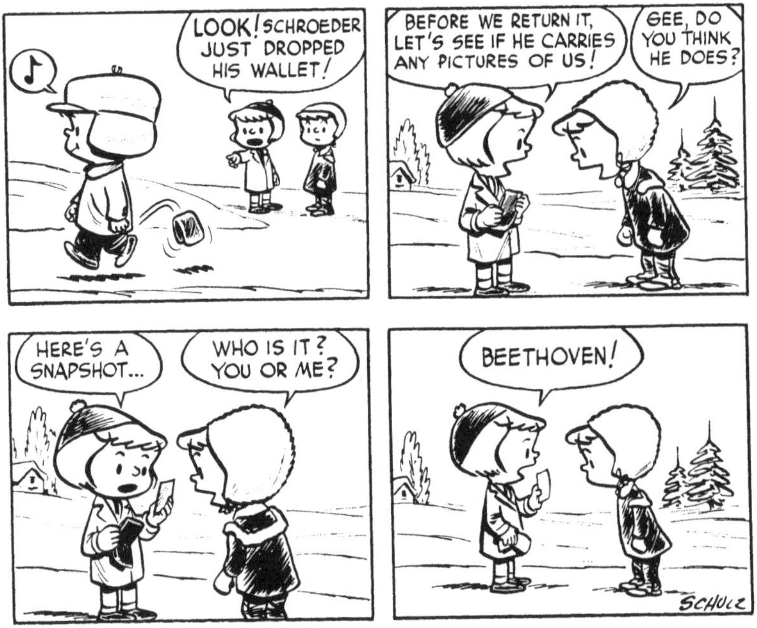
LOOK! SCHROEDER JUST DROPPED HIS WALLET!
BEFORE WE RETURN IT, LET'S SEE IF HE CARRIES ANY PICTURES OF US!
GEE, DO YOU THINK HE DOES?
HERE'S A SNAPSHOT...
WHO IS IT? YOU OR ME?
BEETHOVEN!
SCHULZ

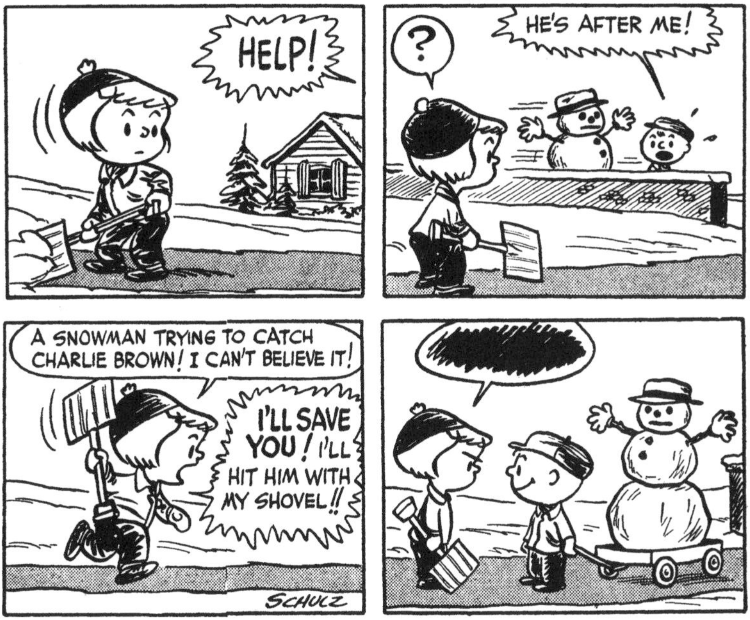
HELP!
?
HE'S AFTER ME!
A SNOWMAN TRYING TO CATCH CHARLIE BROWN! I CAN'T BELIEVE IT!
I'LL SAVE YOU! I'LL HIT HIM WITH MY SHOVEL!!
SCHULZ

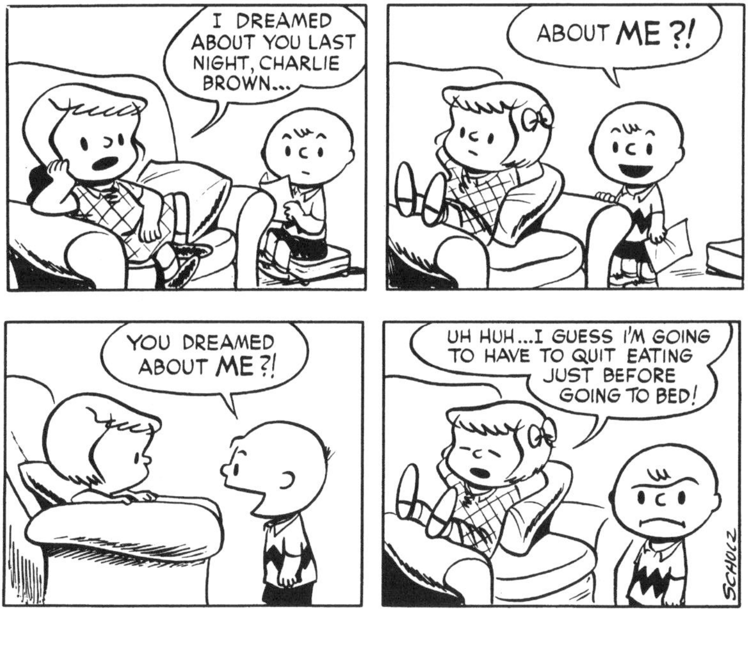
I DREAMED ABOUT YOU LAST NIGHT, CHARLIE BROWN...
ABOUT ME?!
YOU DREAMED ABOUT ME?!
UH HUH...I GUESS I'M GOING TO HAVE TO QUIT EATING JUST BEFORE GOING TO BED!
SCHULZ

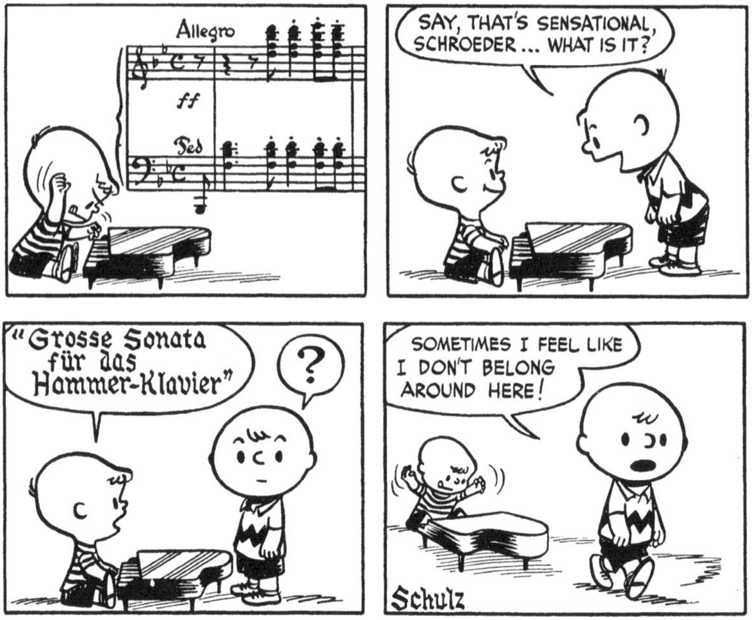
Allegro
ff
Ped
SAY, THAT'S SENSATIONAL, SCHROEDER... WHAT IS IT?
"Grosse Sonata für das Hammer-Klavier"
?
SOMETIMES I FEEL LIKE I DON'T BELONG AROUND HERE!
Schulz

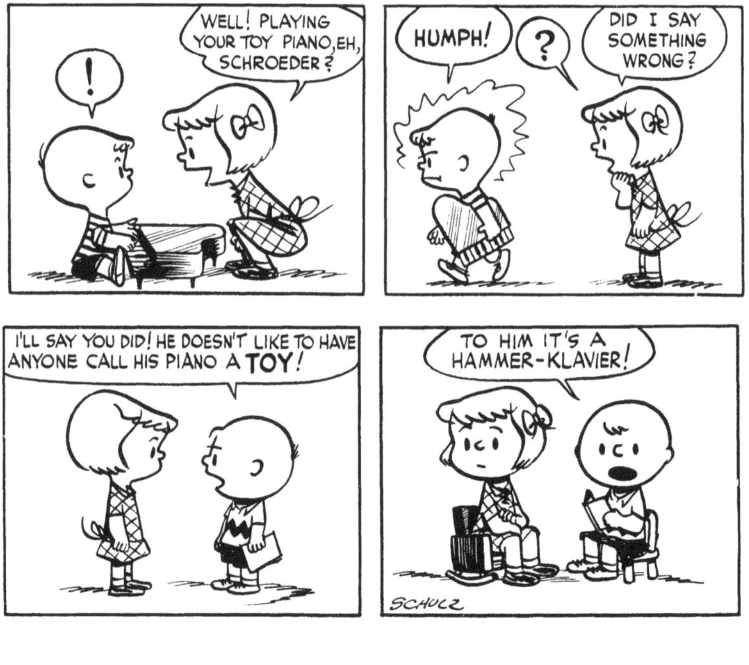
!
WELL! PLAYING YOUR TOY PIANO, EH, SCHROEDER?
HUMPH!
?
DID I SAY SOMETHING WRONG?
I'LL SAY YOU DID! HE DOESN'T LIKE TO HAVE ANYONE CALL HIS PIANO A TOY!
TO HIM IT'S A HAMMER-KLAVIER!
SCHULZ

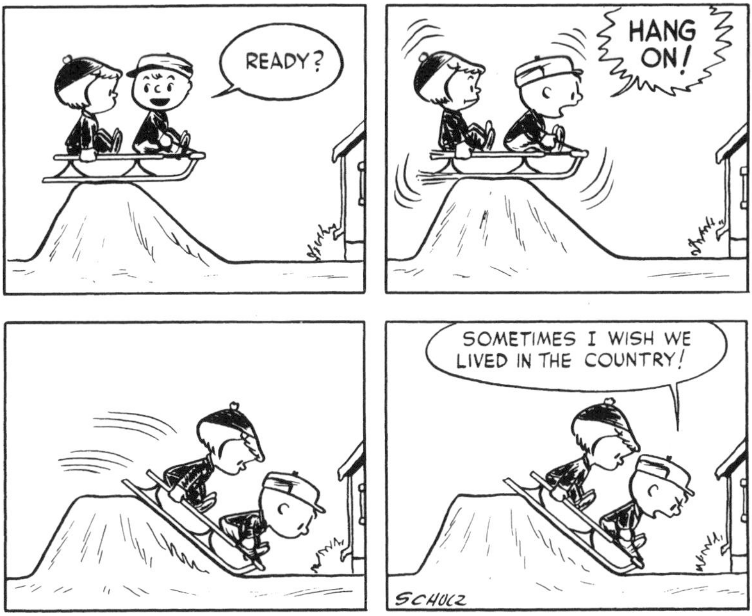
READY?
HANG ON!
SOMETIMES I WISH WE LIVED IN THE COUNTRY!
SCHULZ

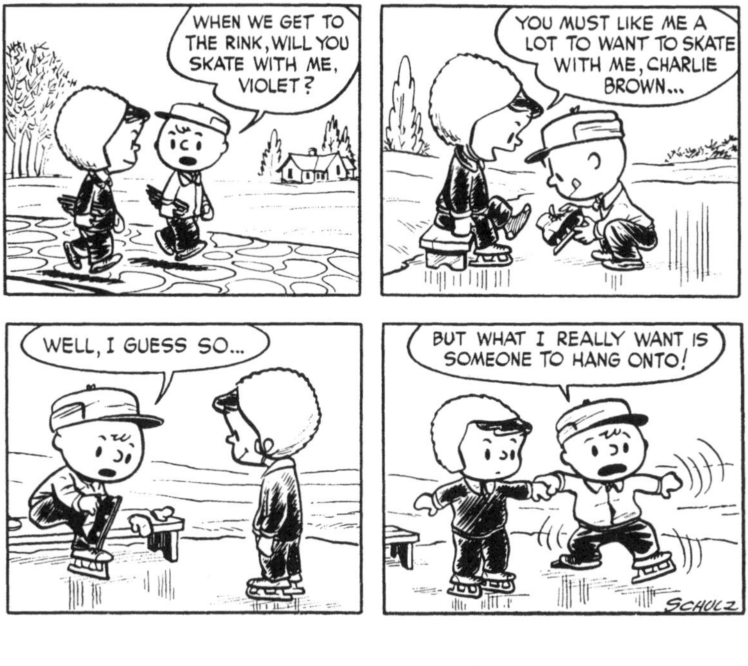
WHEN WE GET TO THE RINK, WILL YOU SKATE WITH ME, VIOLET?
YOU MUST LIKE ME A LOT TO WANT TO SKATE WITH ME, CHARLIE BROWN...
WELL, I GUESS SO...
BUT WHAT I REALLY WANT IS SOMEONE TO HANG ONTO!
SCHULZ

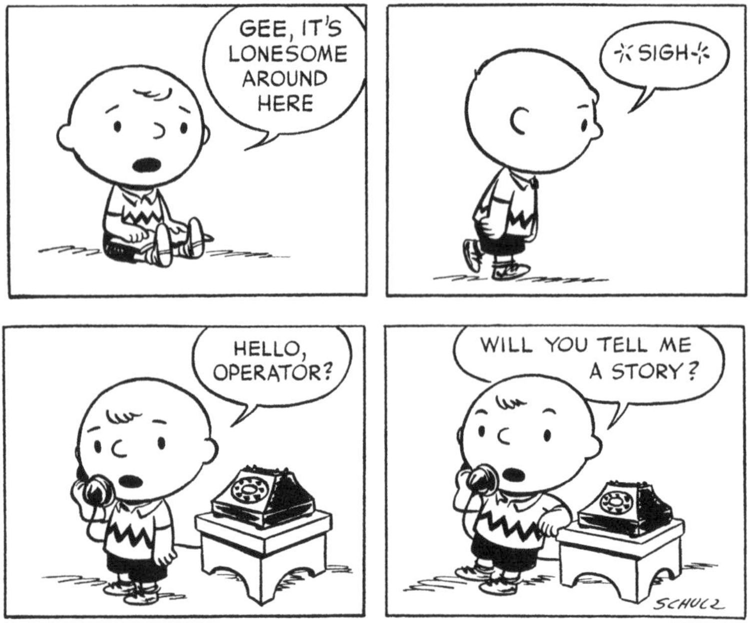
GEE, IT'S LONESOME AROUND HERE
SIGH
HELLO, OPERATOR?
WILL YOU TELL ME A STORY?
SCHULZ

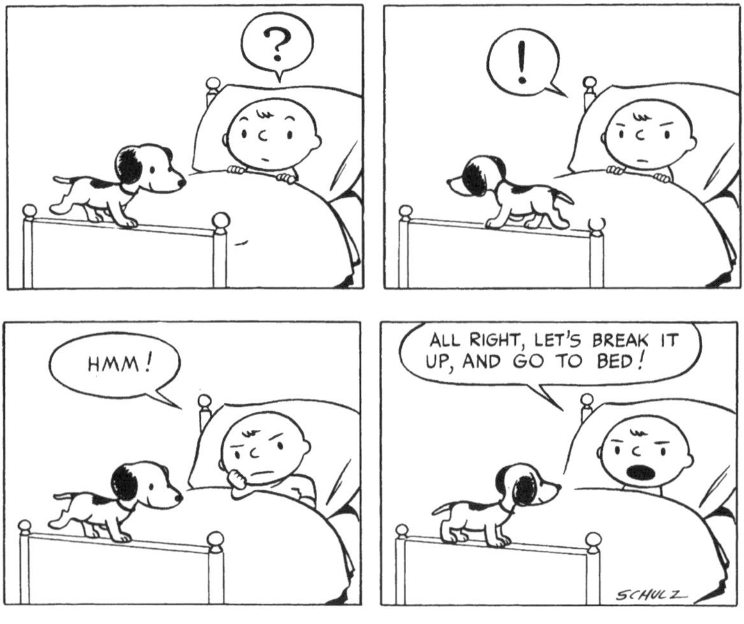
?
!
HMM!
ALL RIGHT, LET'S BREAK IT UP, AND GO TO BED!
SCHULZ